The American Presidency under Trump: The First Two Years

The American Presidency under Trump: The First Two Years

The First Two Years

Giuseppe Franco Ferrari (Ed.)

eleven
international publishing

Published, sold and distributed by Eleven International Publishing
P.O. Box 85576
2508 CG The Hague
The Netherlands
Tel.: +31 70 33 070 33
Fax: +31 70 33 070 30
email: sales@elevenpub.nl
www.elevenpub.com

Sold and distributed in USA and Canada
Independent Publishers Group
814 N. Franklin Street
Chicago, IL 60610, USA
Order Placement: +1 800 888 4741
Fax: +1 312 337 5985
orders@ipgbook.com
www.ipgbook.com

Eleven International Publishing is an imprint of Boom uitgevers Den Haag.

ISBN 978-94-6236-976-4
ISBN 978-94-6094-393-5 (e-book)

Table of Contents

Introduction

The conference held in Milan on 22 March 2019 was the logical follow-on to the workshop organized back in 2016 to examine the results of the Obama presidency.

Obviously, the time frame under analysis was much shorter than it was the previous time, and, of course, we were comparing two very different presidents.

It is common knowledge that, unlike his predecessor, President Trump has suffered bad press, but with this event our aim was to present an objective and non-partisan analysis of Trump's first two years in office.

A few words on the reasons why the group of Public Law at Bocconi University decided to organize a conference devoted to this theme. We can all agree that Donald Trump's victory in 2016 took many by surprise, although in hindsight maybe a more careful reading of what was happening in the United States at that time might have led many commentators to be more cautious in their predictions. The truth of the matter is that, although not probable, a win for Trump was always possible, especially bearing in mind the peculiar characteristics of the electoral system for the presidency.

Undoubtedly, Trump constitutes a clear break with past presidencies, and it is not by chance that on the domestic front his arch-enemies include not only Barack Obama, but also George W. Bush. As we saw during the course of the conference, there are many aspects of Trump's policies that are extremely difficult to nail down. Gallons of ink have been spilt on the controversial use that Trump makes of the social networks, in particular, Twitter. Often, important statements on both domestic and foreign policy seem to be dictated at the spur of the moment rather than after an attentive consideration of the pros and cons and the possible consequences for the United States and the world as a whole.

Let us now turn to the content of the conference and, consequentially, of the book. The conference was divided into two parts, with the second subdivided into three sessions. Thus, the first part of this book addresses recent trends in the US Government. In particular, there are chapters on the relationship between the presidency and Congress; the role of administrative agencies and the appointments made by President Trump. These are followed by chapters on Trump's political agenda vis-à-vis the Supreme Court and the President's approach towards States and Governors. The second part of the book first looks at the new trends in US policymaking. In particular, the first section comprises the proceedings of the session devoted to developments in the economic sphere, which was chaired by Attilio Geroni, Foreign Affairs Editor of Italy's leading financial newspaper, *Il Sole 24 Ore*. The second section of Part 2 contains chapters that focus on recent developments in the sphere of health, the topic of the second session chaired by the news director of RAI2 – Italy's second public TV channel – Gennaro Sangiuliano. Finally, in the chapters deriving from the session presided over by our colleague from Bocconi University Andrea Colli, we look at recent developments in the sphere of civil rights and international relations.

Finally, a few words of gratitude. The conference and book would not have been possible without the logistical support of the Bocconi Legal Studies Department and without financial support from the Baffi Carefin Centre for Applied Research on International Markets, Banking, Finance and Regulation, Bocconi School of Law and the *Centro di studi americani* in Rome. I would also like to underline that the conference took place under the auspices of the Fulbright programme and the Consulate General of the United States in Milan. I thank them all.

Giuseppe Franco Ferrari
Milan, 5 September, 2019

1 President Trump and the Congress

Giuseppe Franco Ferrari

1.1 The Political Structure of the Congress during the Trump Presidency

The relationship with Congress always defines the institutional environment where the presidency is due to operate and at the same time represents one of the most important yardsticks of the concrete evolution of the principle of separation of powers.[1]

In the first two years of his presidency, Donald Trump has enjoyed very favourable conditions, due to the presence of a Republican majority both in the Senate (51 to 47 plus two independents voting with the Democrats, Angus King, ME, and Bernie Sanders, VT) and in the House of Representatives (239 to 201, with five seats vacant at the end of the 115th Congress). A partial switch from unified government took place on 6 November 2018 with the mid-term elections, which confirmed, or rather strengthened, the Republican majority in the Senate (now 53 to 47) but delivered the House to the Democratic Party with a net gain of 39 seats and a majority of 234 to 201. The reasons for this change in the positioning of the electorate vary as usual between the possible overperforming of the presidential party in the former presidential elections, the abstention of the so-called 'weak partisans', the revenge motivations of the losers and the wish to balance presidential powers as they have been carried out in the last two years.[2] The fact remains that the scenario that President Trump is going to confront in the next two years is going to be quite different

1 This remark belongs both to the classical literature about the presidency (such as C.P. Patterson, *Presidential Government in the United Sates: The Unwritten Constitution*, University of North Carolina Press, North Carolina, 1947; C. Rossiter, *The American Presidency*, Harcourt, New York, 1956; E.S. Corwin, *The President, Office and Powers: History and Analysis of Practice and Opinion*, New York University Press, New York, 1941; G.C. Edwards III, *All the Margins: Presidential Leadership of Congress*, Yale University Press, New Haven, 1990, up to S.M. Milkis & M. Nelson, *The American Presidency. Origins and Development, 1776-2014*, 7th edn, Sage Publishing, Washington, DC, 2015) and to more recent writings (*see, e.g.*, H.J. Krent, *Presidential Powers*, New York University Press, New York, 2005; S. Prakash, 'Regulating Presidential Powers', *Cornell L. Rev.*, Vol. 91, No. 1, 2005, pp. 215-258; H.H. Bruff, 'The President and Congress: Separation of Powers in the United States of America', *Adel. L. Rev.*, Vol. 35, No. 1, 2014, pp. 205-224.

2 J.E. Campbell, 'Explaining Electoral Change in the 2018 US Midterm Elections: The Three Components of Electoral Mandates', *The Forum*, Vol. 16, No. 4, 2018, p. 513; J.L. Carson & A.A. Hitefield, 'Donald Trump, Nationalization, and the 2018 Midterm Elections', *The Forum*, Vol. 16, No. 4, 2018, p. 531; R.D. Williamson, 'Evaluating Candidate Positioning and Success in the 2018 Midterm Elections', *The Forum*, Vol. 16, No. 4, 2018, p. 653.

from the political framework of the first half of his term. The events at the beginning of 2019 are likely to be a representative sample of what the future is going to bring.

Political scientists and government scholars share the opinion that in recent years ideological polarization in Congress has been constantly growing.[3] It probably started in the 1970s and increased in the 1990s, following the same trend in the ensuing years. The Obama administration, by succeeding in winning approval of the healthcare reform, contributed to the embittering of the political climate. Yet the trend dates back much earlier and has concerned not only the ideological distance between the two parties, but even the quality of the debate inside each of them and their internal divisions,[4] although it is argued that the Republicans are more concerned by the polarization process, having developed a harsh hostility to compromise and a tough attitude towards their counterpart.[5] The causes, as well as the consequences, of this phenomenon are disputable: some authors mention the increased political and ideological alignment of the party constituencies, the stronger personality of the congressional leaders, which, however, is historically quite a frequent factor, and many others. Whatever the reasons for the polarization process, it is commonly noticed that it engenders a strong feeling of partisanship in the representative chambers, which yields congressional stalemate and/or gridlock in times of divided government but does not necessarily help the President even in periods of unified government. A majority party does not find it easier to legislate its programme when the polarization rate along party lines is high and the party itself is divided or is not solidly available to follow the President in the implementation of a programme that could disgruntle at least a part of its electorate, owing to strong ideological content or to divisive impact. In such cases, the difference between divided and unified government might be relatively modest. Furthermore, a higher degree of polarization between parties and in Congress makes it harder for a President, although theoretically advantaged by the availability of a congressional majority, to look for support at the minority. In such a context, in other words, the chances of bipartisan lawmaking are reduced, while a President will meet difficulties in having his

---

3 *See, e.g.*, S.M. Theriault, *Party Polarization in Congress*, Cambridge University Press, Cambridge, 2008; F.E. Lee, *Beyond Ideology: Politics, Principles, and Partisanship in the U.S. Senate*, The University of Chicago Press, Chicago, 2009; J.D. Ura & C.R. Ellis, 'Partisan Moods: Polarization and the Dynamics of Mass Party Preferences', *J. Pol.*, Vol. 74, No. 1, 2012, pp. 1-15; B.F. Schaffner, 'Party Polarization', *in* G.C. Edwards III, F.E. Lee & E. Schickler (Eds.), *The Oxford Handbook of the American Congress*, Oxford University Press, Oxford, 2011; G.C. Jacobson, 'Party Polarization in American Politics', *Pres. St. Q.*, Vol. 43, No. 4, 2013, pp. 688-708; B. Dan Wood & S. Jordan, *Party Polarization in America: The War over Two Social Contracts*, Cambridge University Press, Cambridge, 2017.

4 *See, e.g.*, G. Kabaservice, *Rule and Ruin: The Downfall of Moderation and the Destruction of the Republican Party, From Eisenhower to the Tea Party*, Oxford University Press, Oxford, 2012; B.F. Schaffner, M. Macwilliams & T. Nteta, 'Understanding White Polarization in the 2016 Vote for President: The Sobering Role of Racism and Sexism', *Pol. Sc. Q.*, Vol. 133, No. 1, 2018, pp. 9-34.

5 T.E. Mann & N.J. Ornstein, *It's even Worse than It Looks: How the American Constitutional System Collided with the Politics of Extremism*, Basic Books, New York, 2012.

legislative agenda enacted in Congress even by his majority, owing both to the conflict rate generated by the ideological distance between parties and to the divisiveness of his proposals.[6] Such difficulties may be overcome when a newly elected President can invoke a clear mandate from the people for the implementation of his agenda or at least of some well-defined measures. Some unsympathetic authors try to demonstrate that President Trump did not receive an evident and broad mandate, because of the percentage[7] and absolute number of popular votes[8] received in November 2016, of the polls, showing a low rate of agreement with some of his proposals after the presidential elections, or of the vagueness of his agenda, mentioning the need to make America great again, but straight-forward and not elusive only on a few topics.[9]

Political commentators emphasized since the beginning that President Trump definitely does not like "bringing lawmakers together, participating in logrolling and horse-trading, using his own expertise to find the right formulas".[10] It has been hard for him, therefore, to negotiate reform packages, because many congressmen of his party felt concrete possibilities of backlash in subscribing to some of his policies too willingly, while Paul D. Ryan, the Speaker of the House, and Mitch McConnell, the Republican leader of the Senate, have not been quite persuasive on occasions when it would have been necessary to stick to the presidential line but the 'survival instinct' was suggesting prudence. Sometimes they have been openly and harshly criticized by the President, such as in September 2017. It is also argued that the Republican Party itself is divided, if not fractured in segments[11] and that the President has not contributed to their cohesion. John McCain's personal hostility was so stunning as to impress many foreign observers.

With Nancy Pelosi, the House Democratic leader, and Chuck Schumer, Senate Minority Leader, he is said to have had very rare meetings in his first two years. Quite seldom have deals been agreed with the Democrats, even when they were reported to be available, such as about a low-priority infrastructure plan in 2017, and in those very few cases when they were reached, the manners used for the Republicans. All kinds of bipartisan cooperation have been refused by the President and consequently denied by the Democrats.

6 This and other dynamics are described by B. Sinclair, *Unorthodox Lawmaking: New Legislative Processes in the U.S. Congress*, 5th edn, CQ Press, Washington, DC, 2015.

7 46%.

8 About 3 million fewer than his competitor, Hillary Clinton.

9 *See, e.g.*, G.C. Edwards III, 'No Deal: Donald Trump's Leadership of Congress', *The Forum*, Vol. 15, No. 3, 2017, pp. 451-497. The presidential programme is analysed by areas in Holland & Knight, An Overview of What to Expect from the Trump Administration and the 115th Congress, Washington, DC, January 2017. Actually, the Remarks on the state of the Union issued on 28 February 2017 still focused only on themes such as deregulation, border security from the perspective of limiting drug crimes and Islamic terrorism, restarting the engine of the economy, replacing Obamacare and strengthening the military.

10 N. Ornstein, 'The Other Devil's Bargain', *Politics*, 21 August 2017.

11 T. Skopckol & V. Williamson, *The Tea Party and the Remaking of Republican Conservatism*, Oxford University Press, New York, 2012.

On several occasions, members of the presidential team have been at odds with each other, for example Treasury Secretary Mnuchin and OMB Director Mulvaney about the debt ceiling problem, again towards the end of 2017.

The political conditions described above have not prevented Congress from approving a good deal of statutes, and in July 2017 the President could proudly state to have signed more bills than any other President ever, although the unfriendly newspapers replied that many of them were low-profile or second-line bills.[12] However, in the greatest number of cases the Republicans have been compelled by the polarization context to resort to the procedures most suitable to bypass the Democrats, such as preparing and drafting bills outside of committees' hearings, in order to avoid criticism, or using the budget reconciliation process, which prevents filibustering. On the other hand, many White House initiatives have been completely ignored or have received little attention, never reaching the congressional agenda.

Another striking trend in the presidential style has been the tendency towards circumventing all congressional intervention both through the massive use of executive orders (EO), which is not new at all and was experimented on during the Obama years too, mainly during the years of the 'we can't wait' agenda,[13] and through strong pressure on the independent agencies in order to change the content of many regulations or to eliminate them altogether.[14] Furthermore, many important decisions have been made by the President alone, above all in the sphere of foreign policy, without any confrontations with the Congress: moves such as the exit from the Paris Agreement on climate change and the Trans-Pacific Partnership have been adopted unilaterally, exactly like the management of the tariff policy, the approach to the North Atlantic Treaty Organization (NATO) allies and the decision to get out of the anti-proliferation treaty with Russia.

---

12 *See, e.g.*, P. Bump, '60 Percent of the Bills Trump Has Signed into Law Have Been One Page Long', *Washington Post*, 5 July 2017; G. Kessler, 'No, President Trump. You Haven't Signed More Bills than Any Other President', *Washington Post*, 17 July 2017. In fact, the number of bills approved during the 115th Congress amounts to about 1000, but only 443 are reported to be relevant and/or implemented (321 of them proposed by Republicans, 122 by Democrats): comments on the activity of Congress vary from "most productive in a generation" (Paul D. Ryan, Speaker of the House) to "the laziest Congress" (Week). No result has been reached as far as the comprehensive insurance reform and the repeal of the Affordable Care Act are concerned, nor has any bill been approved with reference to infrastructure and education; however, some important bills have passed into law with bipartisan support, such as those regarding juvenile criminal justice, federal prisons reform, the adoption of sanctions on Russia, Iran and North Korea, the national flood insurance programme, the funding of the NASA in order to prepare for the exploration of Mars before 2033. In the 116th Congress, up to 3 March only 12 bills have been signed, 5 proposed by Republicans and 7 by Democrats. The activity of Congress is reported in details on the site www.govtrack.us.

13 *See* G.F. Ferrari, 'The Obama Presidency (2008-2016)', *in* G.F. Ferrari (Ed.), *The American Presidency after Barack Obama*, Eleven International Publishing, Leiden, 2011, p. 13. A summary of the Obama years, useful benchmark for comparisons with the Trump era, A. Rudalevige, 'Old Laws, New Meanings: Obama's Brand of Presidential Imperialism', *Syracuse L. Rev.*, Vol. 66, No. 1, 2016, p. 1.

14 *See infra*, para. 3.

Such a method may have greatly simplified the working of the American government, but it has also reduced Congress' oversight of US foreign policy and tariff practice. It has been observed[15] that the trend towards presidential unilateralism started at the beginning of the post-Cold War era. Yet such a concentration of individual protagonism runs the risk of minimizing Congress' constraints on the presidency and of altering the system of checks and balances between constitutional powers, which is the very essence of the American form of government. Meanwhile, it is reported that the number of hearings of some of the most important committees, such as the Senate Foreign Relations Committee and the Armed Services Committee, has decreased dramatically,[16] with a possible decline of congressional expertise in the pertinent areas. And obviously, the polarization degree is likely to increase.

1.2 Veto Power and the Use of Signing Statements

Ideological polarization has apparently concerned more the congressional environment and the relationship between parties in the light of the presidential approach than possible direct confrontations between the Congress as legislature and the President in his power to sign bills into laws or veto them straight away. Since the invalidation of the line item veto by the Supreme Court in *Clinton v. City of New York*,[17] Presidents have been prevented from severing provisions they do not share from the text submitted to them; they have no more constitutional devices to object to a bill other than vetoing it and developing their critical considerations in the accompanying statement when returning it to Congress.[18] Therefore, in times of strong ideological juxtaposition, even when the homogeneity between the Legislature and the Executive is total, as in the 115th Congress, but the alignment of President and Congress is imperfect, it should have been reasonable to expect at least some vetoes, and a somewhat larger number of them when one of two chambers has been lost by the President's party. To the contrary, no veto has ever been opposed during the Trump presidency up to the end of March 2019.

There are no easy interpretations of this phenomenon. All Presidents learn very soon that the interaction with Congress is never smooth, above all when the ideological divide is very deep. Donald Trump has virtually no previous political experience, his adjustment to the pace of the Congress has been neither plain nor quick and his approach has been combative if not aggressive. Therefore, while the Democrats have adopted a defensive

15 J.M. Goldgeier & E.N. Saunders, 'The Unconstitutional Presidency: Checks and Balances Eroded Long Before Trump', *Council on Foreign Relations*, 14 August 2018.

16 Id.

17 524 U.S. 417, (1998).

18 *Lear Sigler, Inc. v. Lehman*, 842 F.2d 1102-1124 (9th Circuit 1988).

stand, the Republicans have not been proactive either: not always being in line with some of his sharp positions, many of them have preferred not to expose themselves to his harsh critics, often avoiding attention or adopting a low-profile attitude.[19] As a consequence, minor pieces of legislation have often been easily approved, and important statutes have been deferred or agreed on after long and wearying negotiations. In both cases there were no political reasons to oppose the final text.[20] President Trump has thus added no vetoes to the 2,574 recorded in American constitutional history.

On the contrary, the use of signing statements has had a new impulse. The President has resorted to it seven times in 2017, 30 times in 2018 and five times in the first two months of 2019. Obama had pledged during the 2008 campaign to reduce their number to cases where constitutionally relevant questions might request his intervention, and had partially kept his promise,[21] reducing and almost completely eliminating those classified by some scholars as rhetoric or "press release" signing statements.[22] The sectors that President Trump has preferentially used to add statements on signing bills into law have been appropriations,[23] defence and foreign policy,[24] where the presidential competence sphere is more in need of preservation, environment.[25] These interest fields are more or less the same that triggered the attention of former Presidents:[26] there is substantial continuity between Presidents and between unified and divided Congresses, at least in terms

19 *See, e.g.*, S.W. Stathis, 'Enough Posturing: Congress Should Embrace Veto Override', *The Hill*, 1 January 2019.

20 Some general considerations about the legislative process in J. Bergner, 'The Congressional Apprentice. How Trump Is Approaching Capitol Hill', *Foreign Affairs*, September/October 2017, p. 99.

21 *See* Ferrari, 2011, p. 13.

22 *See* J. Neureuther, *The Quiet Revolution: What the Evolution of the Presidential Veto Power Can Tell Us about the Modern Use of Presidential Signing Statements*, VDM Verlag Dr. Müller, Saarbrücken, 2011; C.S. Kelley, 'Rhetoric and Reality? Unilateralism and the Obama Administration', *Soc. Sci. Q.*, Vol. 93, No. 5, 2012, pp. 1146-1160; C.S. Kelley, B.W. Marshall & D.J. Watts, 'Assessing the Rhetorical Side of Presidential Signing Statement's', *Pres. Stud. Q.*, Vol. 43, No. 2, 2013, pp. 274-298; E. Newland, 'Executive Orders in the Court', *Yale L. J.*, Vol. 124, No. 6, 2015, pp. 2026-2099, D.B. Rodriguez, E.H. Stiglitz & B.R. Weingast, 'Executive Opportunism, Presidential Signing Statements, and the Separation of Powers', *J. Legal Analysis*, Vol. 8, No. 1, 2016, pp. 95-119.

23 *E.g.* Consolidated Appropriations Act, 2017 (P.L. 115-31) and Consolidated Appropriations Act, 2019 (P.L. 116-6).

24 The Countering America's Adversaries through Sanctions Act, 2017 (P.L. 115-44), The National Defense Authorization Act for Fiscal Year 2018 (P.L. 115-91), The North Korean Human Rights Reauthorization Act, 2017 (P.L. 115-198), The John S. McCain National Defense Authorization Act for Fiscal Year 2019 (P.L. 115-232), The Department of Defense and Labor, Health and Human Services, and Education Appropriation Act, 2019 (P.L.115-245), The Hizballah International Financing Prevention Amendments Act, 2018 (P.L. 115-272), The Iraq and Syria Genocide Relief and Accountability Act, 2018 (P.L. 115-300), The Countering of Weapons of Mass Destruction Act, 2018 (P.L. 115-387).

25 Energy, Water, Legislative Branch, and Military Construction and Veterans Affairs Appropriations Act, 2019 (P.L. 115-244), The Save Our Seas Act, 2018 (115-265), Nuclear Energy Innovation and Modernization Act, 2019 (P.L. 115-439).

26 *See* the data collected by J.M. de Figuereido & E.H. Stiglitz, *Signing Statements and Presidentializing Legislative History*, NBER Working Paper No. 23951, October 2017, Figure 2, p. 13.

of preferred topics. Anyway, if it is true that signing statements, besides being a means of communication with Congress, administrative agencies and the general public, are generally oriented to concurring in the legislative history of a statute, in order to influence courts in construing the meaning of the text, recent studies[27] demonstrate that the rate of judicial citations of signing statements is very low, that congressional legislative history is by far preferred, that citations are generally used to buttress conclusions reached through other reasonings and that judges indulge to cherry-picking, "finding their friends in the crowd". In other words, Presidents have failed in the aim of conditioning legislative history and influencing the judiciary.

1.3 The Use of the Congressional Review Act

An unexpected way to reduce the allegedly overwhelming mass of agency regulations approved in previous years has been the resort to the Congressional Review Act (CRA).[28] Approved in 1996, as the Contract with America Advancement Act,[29] it had introduced a chance for Congress to veto agency rules, after *INS v. Chada*[30] and its holding of unconstitutionality of the so-called legislative veto in all the forms not implying the approval by both Houses and the presentment to the President. All rules announced by agencies, before being promulgated, need to be submitted, together with a cost-benefit analysis and a definition of the rule as a major one or not, to both Houses and to the Comptroller General of the General Accountability Office. A resolution of disapproval passed in the simplified forms authorized by the Act, including, in the Senate, the waiving of all the points of order against the resolution, the preclusion against filibustering and the requirement of a simple majority, and consisting in a standard declaration, can veto a major regulation within 60 days from the submission of a report by the Comptroller General or from the publication in in the Federal Register. Non-major regulations, not having significant effects on prices or the economy, enter into force after 60 days from the submission by the agency to Congress, in the absence of the double deliberation of the Houses. This mechanism had been used only once in 20 years, in 2001,[31] so that it seemed dormant, if not obsolete.[32] All of a sudden, it woke up from its long sleep in the 114th Congress, when the Republican

27 Id., 2017, p. 13.
28 5 U.S.C. §§ 801-802 (2012).
29 §251, Pub. L. No. 104-121, 110 Stat. 847, 868-74.
30 462 U.S. 919 (1983).
31 When the Ergonomics Program, 65 Fed. Reg 68, 262, had been disapproved by Pub. L. No. 107-5, 115 Stat. 7 (2001).
32 *See also* M. Rosenberg, 'Whatever Happened to Congressional Review of Agency Rulemaking?: A Brief Overview, Assessment, and Proposal for Reform', *Admin. L. Rev.*, Vol. 51, No. 4, 1999, p. 1051; Note, 'The Mysteries of the Congressional Review Act', *Harv. L. Rev.*, Vol. 122, No. 8, 2009, pp. 2162-2183.

majority resorted to it five times, without results owing to Obama's vetoes. At the beginning of the 115th Congress the Republicans had another chance of deleting all rules submitted to Congress after 30 May 2016. Since, for rules submitted to Congress in the last 60 session or legislative days before the end of a session, the Houses have 60 days after the 15th day of the next Congress, the Republican majority had plenty of time to eliminate regulations belonging to the last months of the Obama administration. Fourteen regulations fell under resolutions of disapproval.[33] It must be added that CRA also prohibits the renewed adoption of other rules having substantially the same form, whatever meaning the judiciary will award to this clause in future litigation.

1.4 Appointments and Recess Power

Another important chapter of the relationship between President and Congress is the ability of the first to obtain the consent and advice of the Senate required by art. II of the Constitution for the appointment of his nominees to federal judicial and executive posts.[34] President Trump has been helped in reaching good results by both the gridlock generated by the high polarization rate in the Senate and the failure of President Obama to handle the appointment of his nominees in the Senate during the 115th Congress.[35]

The sudden death of Justice Antonin Scalia on 13 February 2016 led to the nomination of Columbia District Court of Appeals Merrick B. Garland. The Senate Judiciary Committee announced a delay of the hearings for him and all the Obama nominees to the November presidential elections, after a letter signed by all its 11 Republican members. At least since 1955 senator-nominee meetings and public hearings in the Judicial Committee had been a consolidated tradition in the Senate practice,[36] although vacancies tend to last longer in times of divided government. Judge Garland had dozens of one-to-one meetings, but, notwithstanding several floor speeches up to the first half of March, the Judiciary Committee

33 Some of the vetoed regulations concerned class-action arbitrations on financial matters, Internet privacy, controls on selling firearms to mentally retarded. *See* P.J. Larkin Jr., 'Reawakening the Congressional Review Act', *Harv. J.L. & Pub. Pol.y*, Vol. 41, No. 1, 2018, pp. 187-252 and S. Santulli, 'Use of the Congressional Review Act at the Start of the Trump Administration: A Study of Two Vetoes', *Geo. Wash. L. Rev.*, Vol. 86, No. 1, 2015, pp. 1373-1391.

34 *See, generally,* S. Binder, F. Maltzman, *Advice and Dissent: The Struggle to Shape the Federal Judiciary*, Brookings Institution Press, Washington, DC, 2009.

35 A.J. Madonna, J.E. Monogan & R.L. Vining, 'Confirmation Wars, Legislative Time, and Collateral Damage: The Impact of Supreme Court Nominations on Presidential Success in the US Senate', *Pol. R. Q.*, Vol. 69, No. 4, 2016, p. 746.

36 *See, e.g.*, P.M. Collins Jr. & L.A. Ringhand, 'The Institutionalization of Supreme Court Hearings', *L. & Soc. Inquiry*, Vol. 41, No. 1, 2016, pp. 126-151 and M.E. Owens, 'Changing Senate Norms: Judicial Confirmations in a Nuclear Age', *Profession Symposium, American Political Science Association*, Vol. 51, No. 1, 2018, pp. 119-123.

never met, resulting in the longest delay in American constitutional history. Three potential defections in the Republican ranks were reabsorbed after political pressures. It is reported that President Obama in his second term got the lowest percentage of confirmation hearings since 1981 and that only 40% of his nominees received a hearing in that period.[37] But even 30 nominees that the Judiciary Committee had cleared did not receive the confirmation vote, together with 29 else.[38]

President Trump, therefore, had the opportunity to nominate about 100 federal judges on vacant seats and nominated Neil Gorsuch about one year after Scalia's death. The Senate Democrats opposed a filibuster, which, according to a long-standing rule could be blocked only by a floor supermajority vote of three-fifths or 60 invoking cloture. Then 52 Republican Senators voted to switch to a norm of majority control for all judicial nominations, the so-called 'nuclear option'. The same option had been triggered by a Democratic majority in November 2013 in order to force the vote on lower courts and executive nominations. As a consequence, Judge Gorsuch was confirmed on 8 April 2017. In the same way, at the retirement of Justice A.M. Kennedy at the end of July 2018, District of Columbia Court of Appeal Judge Brett M. Kavanaugh was confirmed by a 50 to 48 vote (the lowest margin since 1881) on 6 October, after some delay due to allegations of sexual assault by three women.

In the first year of presidency, of the 19 persons nominated to circuit court judgeships, 12 have been confirmed (63%) with an average length of 115 days; of the 49 individuals nominated to district court judgeships, only six were confirmed (12%). As a consequence, the number of vacancies decreased from 17 to 16 at the circuit level and increased from 86 to 124 (18.4% of the total number of the appeal judges). None of the nominees have been confirmed by unanimous consent or voice vote: all needed a roll call vote, and nine received more than 40 nay votes, 11 more than 20.[39] In comparison with the former Presidents, the average number of days from nomination to confirmation has slightly diminished from Obama's first year (137 to 115); however a cloture motion has almost always been used, while it has almost never been necessary in the past, though it became routine in Obama's subsequent years, mainly after the reinterpretation of Rule XXII, *i.e.* the nuclear option for the appointment of federal judges other than the Supreme Court's.[40] The frequent, if not usual, resort to cloture motion and roll call vote and the relative length of the procedure, together with the surprising presence of a certain number of ratings of non-qualified

37 Owens, 2018, pp. 119-123.

38 M.J. Gerhardt & R.W. Painter, 'Majority Rule and the Future of Judicial Selection', *Wis. L. Rev.*, Vol. 2017, No. 2, 2017, pp. 263-284.

39 B.J. McMillion, *U.S. Circuit and District Court Nominations during President Trump's First Year in Office: Comparative Analysis with Recent Presidents*, Congressional Research Service, Washington, DC, 2 May 2018.

40 McMillion, 2018.

by the American Bar Association, imply that, despite the Republican majority in the Senate, President's Trump relationship with Congress, and even with his own party, is somewhat ambiguous.

1.5 Administrative Control over Policy

President Trump has been constantly trying to strengthen the structure of the Executive in order not only to avail of an efficient and faithful machine, as it is imposed by the quicker and quicker decision processes in both foreign and domestic policy, but also to be able to bypass Congress and the complexity and length of its procedures. This approach has followed several different lines.

Therefore, first of all, he has kept alive the Obama policy of nominating 'czars', *i.e.* strong officers accumulating robust administrative powers in consolidated competence areas.[41] However, there have been complaints[42] that he would have been slower than most of his predecessors in naming many political appointees, perhaps because of the need to look for persons unrelated to the traditional party system and ready to share new administrative practices under his direct control. The result might have been to create a kind of vacuum in the relationship between presidency and Congress and to make congressional independence grow, which could be much of a problem after the 2018 mid-term elections, with the shift of the House to a Democratic majority. The frequent removal of chief officers and even of chiefs of independent agencies might have contributed to this effect. The most important case was the firing, in May 2017, of James B. Comey, the current FBI director, whose ten-year term had started in September 2013. The early dismissal of an FBI director is not without precedent, and President Clinton's firing of William Sessions in 1993, due to ethical and financial improprieties, was recent enough.[43] Yet, Comey was responsible for the investigation concerning possible behaviours of members of the presidential staff in the so-called Russiagate: this circumstance was alleged as influential by the press, while the officially declared reason for the removal was the asserted mishandling of the other investigation regarding Hillary Clinton's use of a private e-mail server during her term as Secretary of State.

---

41 M.A. Sollenberger & M.J. Rozell, *The President's Czars: Undermining Congress and the Constitution*, University Press of Kansas, Lawrence, 2012; J.S. Vaughn J.D. Villalobos, *Czars in the White House: The Rise of Policy Czars as Presidential Management Tools*, University of Michigan Press, Ann Harbor, 2015.

42 Bergner, 2017, p. 102.

43 *See* A. Vermeule, 'Conventions of Agency Independence', *Colum. L. Rev.*, Vol. 113, No. 5, 2013, pp. 1163-1238.

Second, the production of executive orders has continued, steady and fluent. During his presidency, Barack Obama had published between 30 and 40 orders yearly, on average,[44] and seven even in 2017, a number slightly lower than George W. Bush's.[45] President Trump has published 55 in 2017,[46] 37 in 2018[47] and six in the first three months of 2019.[48] The increasing presidential use of executive orders is obviously amenable to the constant growth of the "presidential administration",[49] namely the continuous attempts to reinforce executive power, within the ambiguous framework of its constitutional definition.[50] Scholars from different ideological backgrounds[51] share the opinion that the Reagan Administration had initiated a trend towards directing and authoritatively influencing administrative rule-making, beginning with the famous Executive Order 12, 291, which authorized the prescription of policy goals to non-independent agencies, to impose the carrying out of cost-benefit analyses and to review all administrative action through the Office of Information and Regulatory Affairs (OIRA), part of the Office of Management and Budget (OMB). The Clinton presidency forced a further expansion of the control of administrative agencies by presidential offices, issuing formal directives to executive officials and leading to an almost total identification between White House and administrative agencies, politics and expertise, perhaps increasing the effectiveness of the regulatory action, accountability and transparency but arousing doubts in the perspective of separation of powers and potentially diminishing the pluralist character of the system of government. The Bush Administration expanded the interpretation of the executive power, aiming at complete unity between presidential and administrative offices, allegedly reducing both the accessibility and openness of the administrative action and the chances of efficient control on the side of Congress.[52]

---

44 38 in 2009, 36 in 2010, 34 in 2011, 39 in 2012, 20 in 2013, 31 in 2014, 29 in 2015. Source: Federal Register per annum.

45 54 in 2001, 31 in 2002, 41 in 2003, 45 in 2004, 26 in 2005, 27 in 2006, 32 in 2007, 30 in 2008 and 5 in 2009.

46 From EO 13765 through EO 13819.

47 From EO 13820 through EO 13856.

48 From EO 13857 through EO 13862.

49 This term was successfully used first by Elena Kagan, much before being appointed to the Supreme Court, in an influential and much-cited article: E. Kagan, 'Presidential Administration', *Harv. L. Rev.*, Vol. 114, No. 8, 2001, pp. 2245-2385.

50 *See, e.g.*, J.L. Mashaw, *Creating the Administrative Constitution: The Lost One Hundred Years of American Administrative Law*, Yale University Press, New Haven, 2012.

51 *See, e.g.*, P.L. Strauss, 'Overseer or "The Decider"?, The President in Administrative Law', *Geo. Wash. L. Rev.*, Vol. 75, No. 4, 2007, pp. 696-760; A. Vermeule, 'Our Schmittian Administrative Law', *Harv. L. Rev.*, Vol. 122, No. 4, 2009, pp. 1095-1150; D.J. Levinson, 'Forward: Looking for Power in Public Law', *Harv. L. Rev.*, Vol. 130, No. 1, 2016, p. 31.

52 To this period C. Savage (*Power Wars: Inside Obama's Post 9/11 Presidency*, Back Bay Books, New York, 2012, and *Power Wars: The Relentless Rise of Presidential Authority*, Little, Brown and Company, New York, 2015) brings back the one-way ratchet theory: "Executive power tends to act like a ratchet: a president does something unprecedented that seems like the new outer boundary, but then a successor treats that as a baseline and goes even further."

According to Jerry L. Mashaw and David Berke,[53] the "experience of the later Obama and early Trump Administration [...] provides examples of both hyper-partisan divided and hyper-partisan unified government". The Deferred Action for Childhood Arrivals (DACA) and the Deferred Action for Parents of Americans (DAPA) are probably among the best examples of the attitude of the Presidents towards the administrative offices and their will to keep an important policy under strict control, preventing congressional action. DACA was announced in June 2012 in a memorandum by the Department of Homeland Security (DHS) Secretary as a 'temporary stopgap' intended to be superseded by a statute. It directed DHS officials, in the exercise of their discretion, to avoid the deportation of some young undocumented immigrants who had entered the United States as children and had not committed crimes. Before the presidential elections of November 2016 more than 1 million immigrants had enjoyed its application. DAPA came in November 2014 and again consisted of instructions included in a memorandum, also meant to be absorbed into a statute, directing DHS personnel to defer deportation of parents of US citizens or lawful permanent residents, in the absence of special reasons for enforcement: this time the population concerned amounted to about 4 million persons. DACA failed to pass through Congress in the form of the so-called 'Dream Act'; DAPA was announced before the presidential elections of November 2012, though implemented two years later, and the pertinent bill was also blocked in the House. DAPA was declared invalid by the 5th Circuit Court of Appeals[54] for violation of the notice-and-comment requirement prescribed by the Administrative Procedure Act of 1940 for all rule-making with the exception of non-binding general statements of policy. The Trump Administration first cancelled some Obama immigration instructions through a memorandum;[55] later on, it published two more executive orders,[56] immediately included and detailed in memoranda from the DHS redirecting the deportation policy and ordering more largeness with 'expedited removal' of aliens, without prior hearing before an immigration judge. Summing up, both Presidents have resorted to executive orders, memoranda and proclamations to have their immigration policies implemented by line officers, circumventing Congress and nullifying the distance between political appointees and down-to-the ground administration, although in an area where the prerogative powers of the President have traditionally been generously interpreted. Obama had to confront a divided government context, Trump a unified one, but

53 J.L. Mashaw & D. Berke, 'Presidential Administration in a Regime of Separated Powers: An Analysis of Recent American Experience', *Yale J. on Reg.*, Vol. 35, No. 2, 2018, pp. 549-616.

54 *Texas v. United States*, 809 F.3d 134 (5th Circuit 2015), affirmed by an equal divided Court, 136 S. Ct. 2271 (2016).

55 Memorandum from John Kelly, Secretary, Department of Homeland Sec., to Kevin McAleenan, Acting Comm., USCBP, Feb. 20, 2017.

56 Enhancing Public Safety in the Interior of the United States, Exec. Order No. 13,768 (30 January 2017); Border Security and Immigration Enforcement, Exec. Order No. 13,767 (30 January 2017).

the results have been more or less the same, in terms of the nature of the legal sources applied, of lacking or insufficient statutory base, of the relationship with Congress. Even judicial review is being stimulated by the novelty of this kind of administrative action: usually a broad discretion conferred on administrative authorities by some statutory provision is hardly subject to judicial control, while general presidential statements fully devoid of normative foundation and leaving wide margins of evaluation with the line officers may provoke judicial review.

Another example of this type of administrative action strictly guided by the President and his political appointees is the case of the so-called travel ban, introduced with Executive Order 13,769, suspending immigration and alien travel from seven Arab and some other countries and favouring for future admissions refugee claims founded on religious persecutions towards individuals belonging to minority religious groups in their respective countries of nationality. The Order had been elaborated by a White House team presided over by Steve Bannon, with no involvement of either the Defense Department or the DHS and with a last day opinion of the Office of Legal Counsel (OLC), and soon amended to exclude permanent residents. The Order was quickly enjoined by a federal judge,[57] replaced by another one,[58] soon modified, and also enjoined by two federal district judges and by the Courts of Appeals for the Fourth and Ninth Circuits due to breach of the Establishment Clause,[59] superseded by a Presidential Proclamation[60] and, finally, upheld by the Supreme Court.[61] In this case too the courts emphasized the difference between the wording of the orders and the parallel presidential declarations about their real purposes, in order to apply judicial review setting aside the precedents where administrative discretion founded on statutory provisions or even orders conferring broad discretion on the officers in care of the application of the rule were deemed unreviewable or hardly reviewable, as distinguished by general political statements directly addressing the administrative officials. The case of the Obama climate change policy and of its reversal by the Trump Administration also reflects the preference of both Presidents for unilateral executive actions, carried out almost completely outside of Congress, often after the failure of former bills of the same content.[62] President Obama, after an abortive congressional bill, directed the Environmental Protection

57 *Washington v. Trump*, No. C17-0141JLR (W.D. Wash., 3 February 2017).

58 Executive Order No. 13,780, Protecting the Nation from Foreign Terrorists Entry into the United States (9 March 2017).

59 *Hawaii v. Trump*, 859 F.3d 741 (9th Circuit 2017); *Int'l Refugee Assistant Project v. Trump*, 857 F.3d 554 (4th Cir. 2017), as amended (31 May 2027), vacated and remanded, Trump *v.* Int'l Refugee Assistance Project, 138 S. Ct. 353 (2017).

60 No. 9645, Enhancing Vetting Capacities and Processes for Detecting Attempted Entry into the United States by Terrorists or Other Public-Safety Threats, 24 September 2017.

61 *Trump v. Hawaii*, No. 17-965, 585 U.S._ (2018).

62 *See* Y. Hoshijima, 'Note, Presidential Administration and the Durability of Climate Consciousness', *Yale L. J.*, Vol. 127, No. 1, 2017, pp. 1-245 and again Mashaw & Berke, 2018, p. 579.

Agency[63] to adopt rules aiming at the reduction of emissions from power plants and vehicles, under the Clean Air Act, in order to have his Clean Power Plan (CPP) implemented. Such regulations flexibly required the States to formulate their own agendas, with the final goal of reducing carbon emissions by one-third before 2030. The President vetoed an attempt by the Senate to apply the CRA[64] to invalidate the Environmental Protection Agency (EPA) rules. Yet a highly divided Supreme Court, with a determinant vote by Justice Scalia just a few days before his death, granted a stay[65] while the case was pending in the D.C. Circuit. Meanwhile, President Obama signed the Paris Agreement, a parallel version of the CPP asking the 196 signing parties to adopt measures aimed at curbing greenhouse gas emissions in order to reduce the global temperature increase. Knowing since the beginning that the necessary majority in the Senate could not be reached, he resorted to an executive agreement, though founded on the UN Framework Convention on Climate Change ratified in 1992. The incoming President first appointed Edward Scott Pruitt, former Attorney General of Oklahoma and fervent denier of the human causation of climate change, at the head of EPA.[66] Then he adopted an Executive Order[67] directing the Agency to "as soon as practicable, suspend, revise, or rescind" the CPP, while the D.C. Circuit Court suspended the case in the imminence of the new regulations. The only presidential effort that has turned out unsuccessful has been the huge EPA fund cut that could have made the functioning of the Agency almost impossible: the Republican-controlled Congress took no action on this side, confirming that not even a unified government can break the trend towards an administrative presidentialism. The President also withdrew from the Paris Agreement at the beginning of June 2017, reaching one of his main political goals but causing international chagrin. At that point, the deconstruction or removal of Obama's environmental policy was complete, and the result has been obtained in exactly the same way the deconstructed policy had been implemented, through exclusively administrative action. Congress is almost completely bypassed and can hardly carry out its vetting functions; the work of the agencies is strictly dependent on presidential directives and bewilders citizens and operators; litigation grows in quantity but becomes more uncertain in the results.

From a more general perspective, President Obama heavily relied on "czars",[68] consolidated the rule-making process strengthening the role of the OIRA and reinforcing the

63 Power Sector Carbon Pollution Standards, 78 Fed. Reg. 39, 535.

64 *See supra*, para. 3.

65 *West Virginia v. EPA*, 36 S. Ct. 1000 (2016).

66 From 16 February 2017 to 6 July 2018. His deputy, Andrew R. Wheeler, lawyer and coal lobbyist, has then been appointed as his successor and assumed office on 28 February 2019.

67 Promoting Energy Independence and Economic Growth, Executive Order No. 13,783 (31 March 2017).

68 *See, e.g.*, K. Sholette, Note, 'The American Czars', *Cornell J. L. & Pub. Pol'y*, Vol. 20, No. 1, 2010, pp. 219-242; G.E. Metzger, 'Agencies, Polarization, and the States', *Colum. L. Rev.*, Vol. 115, No. 7, 2015, pp. 1739-1788.

cost-benefit analysis inserting non-economic values,[69] and tried to increase transparency and information to the public and to favour adjudication in the interest of consumer protection. President Trump has tried to deconstruct, at least in part, the administrative machinery recently reorganized. Executive Order 13,771[70] has imposed the elimination of two regulations for any new one, while a few weeks later Executive Order 13,777[71] has ordered the identification of regulations to be repealed through the creation of 'Regulatory Reform Task Forces'. Among other things, these provisions could collide with the Administrative Procedure Act in that it requires reasons in order to cancel existing rules, with explicit reference to the authorizing statute. Referring to this and other trends, some scholars talk of a real deconstruction of the administrative state.[72] At the least, the taxonomies of the presidential powers formulated by several scholars in the last ten years[73] have been put to a hard testing after these events.

1.6 ADMINISTRATIVE CONTROL OVER PERSONNEL

Another Executive Order, No. 13781,[74] provides the reorganization of the federal administrative machinery: the immediate aim is the elimination of inefficient agencies and outdated programmes; the final goal is allegedly to make federal government more efficient and in charge of only services not already available in the market or already provided by local or state governments. Immediately after the publication of the EO, the OMB Director, Mick Mulvaney, launched a "smart-hiring" plan[75] designed to ask the agencies to ensure that their personnel policies conformed with the President's America First Budget Blueprint. The reorganization of the use of public employees implies the authorization to fill vacancies

69 Executive Orders Nos. 13,497 (4 February 2009) and 13,563 (21 January 2011).
70 30 January 2017.
71 24 February 2017.
72 *E.g.* G.E. Metzger, '1930s Redux: The Administrative State under Siege', *Harv. L. Rev.*, Vol. 131, No. 1, 2017, pp. 1-95.
73 Such as G. Lawson, 'Ordinary Powers in Extraordinary Ties: Common Sense in Times of Crisis', *B.U.L. Rev.*, Vol. 87, No. 2, 2007, p. 289; S.B. Prakash, 'A Taxonomy of Presidential Powers', *B.U.L. Rev.*, Vol. 88, No. 2, 2008, pp. 327-340; B.A. Kleinerman, *The Discretionary President: The Promise and Peril of Executive Power*, University Press of Kansas, Lawrence, 2009; A.L. Warber, *Executive Orders and the Modern Presidency: Legislating from the Oval Office*, Lynne Rienner Publishers, Boulder, Col., 2006; J. Goldsmith, *Power and Constraint: The Accountable presidency after 9/11*, W.W. Norton & Company, New York, 2012; R.H. Fallon Jr., 'Constitutional Constraints', *Cal. L. Rev.*, Vol. 97, No. 4, 2009, pp. 975-1038 and R.H. Fallon Jr., 'Interpreting Presidential Powers', *Duke L.J.*, Vol. 63, No. 2, 2013, pp. 347-392; C.A. Bradley & T.W. Morrison, 'Essay, Presidential Power, Historical Practice, and Legal Constraint', *Colum. L. Rev.*, Vol. 113, No. 4, 2013, pp. 1097-1162. But *see also* K. Mayer & K. Price, 'Unilateral Presidential Powers: Significant Executive Orders, 1949-1999', *Pres. St. Q.*, Vol. 32, No. 2, 2002, p. 375.
74 13 March 2017.
75 A Comprehensive Plan for Reforming the Federal Government and Reducing the Federal Civilian Workforce, 11 April 2017.

and add new posts to some administrations and the obligation not to fill vacancies and to reduce total employment for others. The plan and the press briefing asked the public for participation, in order to get proposals from all sides. The timeline implied working on the proposals before September 2017 and starting to implement the plans in 2018, in order to have them 'hardwired' into the 2019 budget. Some cooperation between President and Congress is foreshadowed, but, at the same time, a measure of disagreement is also foreseen. As of March 2019, the number of federal civilian employees was about the same as at the end of Obama's second term.[76]

However, there is literature about the alleged hostility of the presidency towards career bureaucrats, sometimes defined as the "deep state".[77] During the campaign and immediately after his election, President Trump, like all his predecessors, had to experiment that the 'fine-tuned machine' is more complex and sophisticated than any other organization in the world. The Presidential Transitions Improvements Act of 2015[78] was conceived exactly to facilitate information sharing between candidates and agencies, to make the handover between outgoing President and winner more effective and to help the new team to start off efficiently. Trump first named New Jersey Governor Chris Christie responsible for the transition operations but removed him soon after his election and chose Mike Pence and Jared Kushner to take his place. The pace of the appointments was reported to be slow; some posts remained vacant; some mistakes in the initial designations, together with the demanding nature of the jobs, compelled a higher turnover; the staff number is still significantly lower than Obama's, which was already about 11% lower than Bush's.[79] After two years, it is clear that President Trump, despite his origins as a 'successful business executive', is no centralizer. He is said to prefer an "open, combative, and freewheeling structure", a "stuff with blurred and overlapping jurisdictions".[80]

1.7 EMERGENCY POWERS

The government shutdown that started on 1 October 2018 and lasted longer than any other in American constitutional history is both a representative sample of the relationship between separated powers in times of unified government (at least up to the installation of the 117th Congress) and an unprecedented cross-sectional example of interaction

76 *See* www.governing.com/gov-data/federal-employees-workforce-numbers-by-state.html.
77 *See, e.g.*, H. Kitrosser, 'Accountability in the Deep State', *U.C.L.A. L. Rev.*, Vol. 65, No. 6, 2018, p. 1532.
78 Pub. L. 114-136.
79 *See* the data in D.E. Lewis, P. Bernhard & E. You, 'President Trump as Manager: Reflections on the First Year', *Pres. St. Q.*, Vol. 48, No. 3, 2018, pp. 480-501; J. O'Connell, 'After One Year in Office, Trump's Behind on Staffing but Making Steady Progress', *Brookings Report*, 23 January 2018.
80 *See* again Lewis *et al.*, 2018, p. 493 and M. Wolff, *Fire and Fury: Inside the Trump White House*, Henry Holt & Co., London, 2018.

between the budget process, the presidential policy in the areas of national security and foreign policy and the use of the presidential emergency power.

A wealth of academic literature has described how the spending power has evolved, since the initial combination of the pertinent articles of the Constitution[81] up to the congressional reforms of 1865, 1885, 1921 and to the present legislative principles, introduced by the Congressional Budget and Impoundment Control Act, 1974.[82] This last statute has streamlined both the budget process and the appropriations process. The different cases of possible shutdown due to lack of agreement between President and Congress have been classified long ago,[83] also in the light of the instructions by the Government Accounting Office and the OMB, and even a famous legal opinion by then Attorney General Benjamin Civiletti, dated 1980, although constitutional and political practice does not stop enriching their number. The two most famous shutdowns till now had been the 1995-1996 one, during the Clinton presidency, which lasted 27 days in all,[84] and the 2013 one during the second Obama term, which lasted 16 days, and was aimed at sinking the continuing appropriations concerning Obamacare and was concluded thanks to the Continuing Appropriations Act, 2014, drafted after an agreement between the two Senate leaders, Harry Reid (D-NV) and Mitch McConnell (R-KY).[85]

Despite the scholarly efforts towards preventing the reiteration of new shutdowns,[86] President Trump has triggered the longest and perhaps most important shutdown in American constitutional history, which could be correctly defined as the "perfect storm of contemporary politics".[87] He insists on one of his electoral promises – the building of a wall or a fence along the Mexican border – which the Democrats in the House of Representatives are not willing to finance, invoking moral reasons. About 350,000 federal workers have been furloughed since 22 December; another half-million are working for

---

81 Art. I, s. 9, §7 and s. 7, §1 and Art. I, s. 7, § 2.

82 Pub. 93-344, 88 Stat. 297; *See, e.g.*, J. Sasser, *Budget Process Law Annotated*, U.S. Government Printing Office, Washington, DC, 1991; R.T. Meyers, *Handbook of Government Budgeting*, Jossey-Bass, San Francisco, 1998; J.V. Saturno, *The Congressional Budget Process: A Brief Overview*, Congressional Research Service, Washington, DC, 2001; A. Schick, *The Federal Budget, Politics Policy, Process*, 3rd edn, Brookings Institution Press, Washington, DC, 2008; I. Morgan, *The Age of Deficits: Presidents and Unbalanced Budgets from Jimmy Carter to George W. Bush*, University Press of Kansas Lawrence, 2009.

83 *See* C.T. Brass, *Shutdown of the Federal Government: Causes, Processes, and Effects*, Congressional Research Service, Washington, DC, 2013.

84 *See* R.A. Gephardt, 'The Congressional Budget Impasse', *St. Louis U. Pub. L. Rev.*, Vol. 16, No. 1, 1996, pp. 5-16.

85 *See* Office of Management and Budget, *Impacts and Costs of the October 2013 Federal Government Shutdown*, Washington, DC, 2013 and D. Curren, 'Government Contracting in the Shadow of the October 2013 Federal Government Shutdown', *Pub. Cont. L. J.*, Vol. 44, No. 2, 2015, p. 349; J.H. Woodard & F.W. Bacon, 'Government Shutdown: A Test of Market Efficiency', *J. Bus. & Behav. Sci.*, Vol. 27, No. 2, 2015, p. 71.

86 *See, e.g.*, D.S. Louk & D. Gamage, 'Preventing Government Shutdowns: Designing Default Rules for Budgets', *U. Colo. L. Rev.*, Vol. 86, No. 1, 2015, pp. 181-258.

87 Louk, 2015, pp. 181-258.

free, contributing to make essential services keep on. The alleged cost for the US economy should be at least 3.6 billion dollars, or even up to 23, as admitted by Kevin Hassett, chief of the Council of Economic Advisers, while the wall should cost about 5.7 billion. The tones of the political debate have changed from impasse to real turmoil. The dividing line in the polarized Congress is becoming larger, while the appeals for a truce have remained unheard.

The President, after menacing this move several times, has then used the weapon of last resort, the emergency declaration under the National Emergencies Act of 1976,[88] in order to be able to use funds appropriated by Congress for other purposes, possibly from the Department of Defense, to build the wall, qualified as a military construction project. This move is anything but new, since it is reported that since 1979 American Presidents have resorted to states of emergency 59 times and that 31 of them are still ongoing. Obama declared several national emergencies, the most famous being the order 'blocking the property of certain persons engaging in significant malicious cyber-enabled activities'. Trump himself had already invoked the National Emergency Act three times. However, this is the first time that this instrument has been used in order to solve a conflict between Congress and the President, albeit with a high risk of aggravating the juxtaposition and unleashing a first-rate institutional crisis. Actually, the House of Representatives passed a resolution disapproving the declaration on 26 February by a 245 to 182 vote, with 13 Republican dissenters, while the Senate also reacted by a 59 to 41 vote, with 11 Republican dissenters, on 14 March. The same day President Trump promptly put a veto, after announcing it with a tweet. An unprecedented congressional challenge to a President's authority to invoke emergency powers is thus open. Now it remains to be seen whether Congress will garner the two-third majority necessary to override the veto. In whatever case, an incredible climax of ideological conflict has been reached. In the last two years, Republican sources had accused Obama of several 'lawless' actions and of being 'unethical', while some scholars had accused Trump of undermining the American exceptionalism.[89] Now a group of Yale professors of law and political science – among them Bruce Ackerman and Owen Fiss – have declared against the American constitutional tradition the President's use of the military to enforce domestic law.[90] However the story ends, American democracy is being put to a hard proof.

88 Pub. L. No. 94-412, 90 Stat. 1255 (1976), codified as 50 U.S.C. §§1601-1651. *See* its congressional history in G. Slater, 'The National Emergency Act of 1976 – End of Emergency Government', *Iustitia*, Vol. 4, No. 2, 1977, pp. 50-73; antecedents and first applications in M.R. Belknap, 'New Deal and the Emergency Powers Doctrine', *Tex. L. Rev.*, Vol. 62, No. 1, 1983, pp. 67-109.

89 N. Smith, 'Against Walls: How President's Trump's Walling Initiatives Undermine American Exceptionalism', *Geo. Immigr. L. J.*, Vol. 31, No. 3, 2017, pp. 623-664.

90 Yale News, 17 January 2019.

1.8 THE PRESIDENT AS COMMANDER-IN-CHIEF

Foreign relations powers are notoriously shared between executive and legislative branches, the command of the military being assigned exclusively to the President and the regulation of foreign commerce to Congress. Some tension over the respective competences is a natural consequence of the constitutional design.[91] From this viewpoint the transition from the Obama to the Trump Administration has shown traits of both continuity and radical change.

The so-called "unipolar model",[92] following the end of the Cold War and founded on the presence of only one superpower on the global scene, came to an end in 2001:[93] earlier, Presidents Bush Sr. and Clinton enjoyed relative ease in conceiving and implementing armed interventions in Iraq (1991), Bosnia (1995) and Kosovo (1999). Since then, the United States has lost its freedom of political and strategic manoeuvre, while China has become a serious global hegemonic competitor, its industry has taken away the world primacy from America, and its economy has reached 15% of the total world GDP from 6% in 1995, the US GDP remaining substantially the same, around 23%. The absence of strong counterparts had rendered more difficult the work of the international organizations that had supported the American order and even the institutional relationships between the United States and its traditional allies.[94] At the same time, unipolarity made easier but less necessary the maintenance of the international orders and of global markets.[95] Finally, the end of the Cold War had lessened the links between foreign policy, and the menace represented by the logic of blocks, and domestic policies, leaving foreign policy options more open and indeterminate, but also controversial and unbound.[96]

The Obama administration declaredly tried to return to traditional multilateralism, to revitalize the role of international organizations and to resort to force in a more cautious and shared way,[97] in other words to go back to the long-standing traditions of cooperative security and liberal hegemony dating back to the 1990s. Most commentators, however, concluded that Obama's efforts had not been successful, that his pragmatic preference for

91 A recent detailed analysis of the relationship between President and Congress in this area in R.A. Spivak, 'Co-Parenting War Powers: Congress's Authority to Escalate Conflicts', *W. Va. L. Rev.*, Vol. 121, No. 1, 2018, pp. 135-194.

92 *See, e.g.*, C. Krauthammer, 'The Unipolar Moment', *Foreign Affairs*, Vol. 70, No. 1, 1990/1991, p. 23.

93 *See* C. Layne, 'This Time It's Real: The End of Unipolarity and the Pax Americana', *Int'l Stud. Q.*, Vol. 56, No. 1, 2012, pp. 203-213.

94 D. Skidmore, 'The Obama Presidency and U.S. Foreign Policy: Where's the Multilateralism?' *Int'l Stud. Perspect.*, Vol. 13, No. 1, 2012, p. 43.

95 J.G. Ikenberry, M. Mastanduno & W.C. Wolforth (Eds.), *International Relations Theory and the Consequences of Unipolarity*, Cambridge University Press, Cambridge, 2011.

96 *See* J.G. Ikenberry, 'The Plot against American Foreign Policy. Can the Liberal Order Survive?', *Foreign Affairs*, Vol. 96, No. 3, 2017, pp. 2-9.

97 *See* H.R. Nau, 'Obama's Foreign Policy', *Pol. Rev.*, Vol. 160, 2010, pp. 27-47.

facing threats case by case ('war by necessity') concealed the lack of capacity to foresee serious dangers for national security and revealed a 'non-doctrine doctrine'.[98] The renewed engagement in Afghanistan in 2009 and the attack on Libya in 2011 revealed the impossibility of reversing a long-term trend and the ambiguity of the new approach. The 114th Congress passed, for instance, statutes on North Korea sanctions and electronic surveillance and overrode a presidential veto against a law authorizing victims of international terrorists to sue foreign governments; it also often denied the use of funds to transfer prisoners out of the Guantanamo military prison.

President Trump's foreign policy has been prevalently neo-isolationist, though activist. The revision of several commercial treatises, from NAFTA to the Trans-Pacific Partnership, the apparent reconciliation with Russia followed by a sudden change of attitude during the Ukrainian crisis, the ambiguous approach towards NATO and EU, the troop evacuation from Iraq and Afghanistan have been interpreted as a not quite coherent 'principled realism'.[99] All the President's moves have been carried out almost completely outside Congress, while Obama sought its support, above all during his second term. The launch of cruise missiles against Syrian military airfields in April 2017 was decided by the President alone, and many other actions similarly.

1.9 Openness and Freedom of Information

It is reported that during his campaign President Obama promised to have 'the most transparent administration in history' and to make transparency the touchstone of his presidency,[100] and indeed he made a start or improved some policies oriented in that direction. However, he was also compelled or chose to take steps apparently contradicting the logic of transparency. On one side, on his very first day at the White House, he issued a memorandum requiring federal agencies to apply the Freedom of Information Act (FOIA) faithfully and to stick to a presumption of favour towards any information requests, 'erring on the side of openness'.[101] His Executive Order 13,489, published on the same date, reversed

98 *See, e.g.*, D.W. Daniel, 'Does Obama Have a Grand Strategy?', *Foreign Affairs*, Vol. 90, No. 4, 2011, p. 57; M.S. Indyk, K.G. Lieberthal & M.E. O'Hanlon, 'Scoring Obama's Foreign Policy: A Progressive Pragmatist Tries to Bend History', *Foreign Affairs*, Vol. 91, No. 3, 2012, p. 29; N. Danforth, 'Thank Goodness There's No Obama Doctrine', *Foreign Policy*, 12 January 2016; R. Ingber, 'The Obama War Powers Legacy and the Internal Forces That Entrench Executive Power', *Am. J. Int'l L.*, Vol. 110, No. 4, 2016, pp. 680-700.

99 I. Tharoor, 'Trump's "Principled Realism" Is an Incoherent Mess', *The Washington Post*, 20 September 2017; an overview of Trump's foreign policy in E. Engle, 'Trump's Foreign Policy: Realist Economic Nationalism', *Loy. U. Chi. Int'l L. Rev.*, Vol. 91, No. 2, 2016, pp. 91-132.

100 *See* T.C. Ellington, 'The Most Transparent Administration in History? An Assessment of Official Secrecy in the Obama's Administration First Term', *Pub. Integrity*, Vol. 15, No. 2, 2013, pp. 133-148.

101 Memorandum for the heads of executive departments and agencies. Subject: Freedom of Information Act, 21 January 2009.

the previous Bush's Executive Order 13,233,[102] ordering full disclosure of his personal records and those of his family. In 2011 he called for an Open Government Partnership, in order to have full cooperation towards transparency from states and private organizations. During his eight years the number of subjects authorized to declare information classified for security reasons dropped by more than 405 and the number of classification decisions reached the minimum level ever.[103] The number of documents to be declassified yearly grew to more than 40 million, and Executive Order 13,526[104] founded the National Declassification Center and prescribed a uniform system of classification and declassification. On the other hand, the Obama administration continued in the prosecution of public-interest leakers under the Espionage Act of 1917,[105] which had begun under the Bush Presidency, reaching a peak equivalent to all cases started by all previous Presidents. It also kept on invoking the state secret doctrine, another practice begun under the Bush Administration, in order to withhold evidence in civil or criminal lawsuits owing to possible detriment to national security or to seek dismissal altogether.

The Trump Administration has not changed such policies. The President had let his orientation towards transparency be known during the campaign, although he apparently supported WikiLeaks revelations about the campaign of his opposer.[106] No bill has been introduced in Congress in order to alter the legislative framework, nor has any Executive Order been published.

However, the change in attitude towards leaks has been evident:[107] all unauthorized release of information, above all when classified, has been publicly declared criminal, even if committed by journalists;[108] the Director of National Intelligence, Daniel R. Coats, has issued a directive defining the concept of leak of classified information in very broad terms;[109] in a signing statement concerning an appropriation provision, the President claimed to be able to withhold information from Congress, contrasting the prohibition of

102 Signed on 1 November 2001, by George W. Bush.

103 T.C. Ellington, 'Transparency under Trump: Policy and Prospects', *Pub. Integrity*, Vol. 21, No. 2, 2019, pp. 127-140.

104 29 December 2009. All the data from 1998 to 2017 are published in Information Security Oversight Office (ISOO), 2017 Report to the President, Washington, D.C., July 2018.

105 Pub. L. 65 – 24, 40 Stat. 217. About its application, *see, e.g.*, S.M. Kohn, *American Political Prisoners: Prosecutions under the Espionage and Sedition Acts*, Praeger, Westport, 1994; K. Freuer, 'Protecting Government Secrets: A Comparison of the Espionage Act and the Official Secrets Act', *Boston Coll. Int'l and Comp. L. Rev*, Vol. 38, No. 1, 2015, p. 91; M. Fenster, *The Transparency Fix: Secrets, Leaks and Uncontrollable Government Information*, Stanford Law Books, Stanford, 2017.

106 *See* Fenster, 2017, p. 173.

107 *See, e.g.*, N. Schoenberger, 'Access to Information in the Age of Trump', *Emerging Library & Information Perspectives*, Vol. 1, 2018, pp. 6-33; unfriendly newspapers talk of a 'war on leaks'.

108 About precedents, *see* G. Schoenfeld, *Necessary Secrets: National Security, the Media and the Rule of Law*, W.W. Norton & Company, New York, 2010.

109 Intelligence Community Directive 701, Unauthorized disclosure of classified national security information, 22 December 2017).

using public funds for special access programmes before 30 days from notification to the congressional defence commission;[110] there were rumours in the newspapers of the removal of much information from the White House website, above all with reference to climate change and environmental matters,[111] a move that groups of scientists would have countered by saving the pertinent files (the so-called guerrilla archiving); some newspapers also mentioned a list of terms that the Centers for Disease Control and Prevention would have been prevented from using officially;[112] finally, he has kept his tax returns secret, derogating to a practice that could be considered traditional, at least after Watergate, and that some scholars label a constitutional convention.[113]

On the other side, the declassification of documents concerning incidents implying the exposure of US military to toxic substances has been included in a bipartisan attachment to the National Defense Authorization Act;[114] and President Trump uses social media posting very often, so much so that a Democratic Representative (Mike Quigley, Ill.) has even proposed to include them in the presidential records to be preserved (so-called COVFEFE Act, 2017). No measure has been taken either on the application of FOIA in the presidential offices[115] or about the organization of the intelligence agencies and their relationship with the public.[116]

---

110 Statement by President Donald J. Trump on signing H.R. 244 into law, 5 May 2017.

111 T. Etty *et al.*, 'Transnational Environmental Law on the Threshold of the Trump Era', *Transnat'l Env. L.*, Vol. 6, No. 1, 2017, pp. 1-10.

112 *Washington Post*, 15 December 2017.

113 *See* N.S. Siegel, 'Political Norms, Constitutional Conventions, and President Donald Trump', *Ind. L. J.*, Vol. 93, No. 1, 2018, pp. 177-206; H. Huq, T. Ginsburg, 'How to Lose a Constitutional Democracy', *U.C.L.A. L. Rev.*, Vol. 65, No. 1, 2018, pp. 78-169.

114 Pub. L. 114-328.

115 *See* D. Cohen, 'FOIA in the Executive Office of the President', *N.Y.U. J. Legis. & Pub. Pol.y*, Vol. 21, No. 1, 2018, pp. 203-236.

116 *See* A.B. Zegart, *Eyes on Spies: Congress and the United States Intelligence Community*, Hoover Institution Press, Stanford, CA, 2011; S.J. Rascoff, 'Presidential Intelligence', *Harv. L. Rev.*, Vol. 129, No. 3, 2016, pp. 633-717 and T.T. Gibson, 'Multiple Principals and the (Lack of) Intelligence Oversight', *Natl. Sec. L. J.*, Vol. 5, No. 2, 2017, p. 239-276.

Bibliography

Belknap, M.R., 'New Deal and the Emergency Powers Doctrine', *Tex. L. Rev.*, Vol. 62, No. 1, 1983, pp. 67-109.

Bergner, J., 'The Congressional Apprentice. How Trump Is Approaching Capitol Hill', *Foreign Affairs*, September./October. 2017, p. 99.

Binder, S., Maltzman, F., *Advice and Dissent: The Struggle to Shape the Federal Judiciary*, Washington, DC: Brookings Institution Press, 2009.

Bradley, C.A., Morrison, T.W., Essay, 'Presidential Power, Historical Practice, and Legal Constraint', *Colum. L. Rev.*, Vol. 113, No. 4, 2013, p. 1097-1162.

Brass, C.T., *Shutdown of the Federal Government: Causes, Processes, and Effects*, Washington, DC: Congressional Research Service, 2013.

Bruff, H.H., 'The President and Congress: Separation of Powers in the United States of America', *Adel. L. Rev.*, Vol. 35, No. 1, 2014, pp. 205-224.

Bump, P., '60 Percent of the Bills Trump Has Signed into Law Have Been One Page Long', *Washington Post*, 5 July 2017.

Campbell, J.E., 'Explaining Electoral Change in the 2018 US Midterm Elections: The Three Components of Electoral Mandates', *The Forum*, Vol. 16, No. 4, 2018, p. 513.

Carson, J.L., Hitefield, A.A., 'Donald Trump, Nationalization, and the 2018 Midterm Elections', *The Forum*, Vol. 16, No. 4, 2018, p. 531.

Cohen, D., 'FOIA in the Executive Office of the President', *N.Y.U. J. Legis. & Pub. Pol'y*, Vol. 21, No. 1, 2018, pp. 203-236.

Collins Jr., P.M., Ringhand L.A., 'The Institutionalization of Supreme Court Hearings', *L. & Soc. Inquiry*, Vol. 41, No. 1, 2016, pp. 126-151.

Corwin, E.S., *The President, Office and Powers: History and Analysis of Practice and Opinion*, New York: New York University Press, 1941.

Curren, D., 'Government Contracting in the Shadow of the October 2013 Federal Government Shutdown', *Pub. Cont. L. J.*, Vol. 44, No. 2, 2015, p. 349.

Dan Wood, B., Jordan, S., *Party Polarization in America: The War over Two Social Contracts*, Cambridge: Cambridge University Press, 2017.

Danforth, N., 'Thank Goodness There's No Obama Doctrine', *Foreign Policy*, 12 January 2016.

Daniel, D.W., 'Does Obama Have a Grand Strategy?', *Foreign Affairs*, Vol. 90, No. 4, 2011, p. 57.

De Figuereido, J.M., Stiglitz, E.H., *Signing Statements and Presidentializing Legislative History*, NBER Working Paper No. 23951, October 2017, Figure 2, p. 13

Edwards III, G.C., 'No Deal: Donald Trump's Leadership of Congress', *The Forum*, Vol. 15, No. 3, 2017, pp. 451-497.

Edwards III, G.C., *All the Margins: Presidential Leadership of Congress*, New Haven: Yale University Press, 1990.

Ellington, T.C., 'The Most Transparent Administration in History? An Assessment of Official Secrecy in the Obama's Administration First Term', *Pub. Integrity*, Vol. 15, No. 2, 2013, pp. 133-148.

Ellington, T.C., 'Transparency under Trump: Policy and Prospects', *Public Integrity*, Vol. 21, No., 2019, pp. 127-140.

Engle, E., 'Trump's Foreign Policy: Realist Economic Nationalism', *Loy. U. Chi. Int'l L. Rev.*, Vol. 91, No. 2, 2016, pp. 91-132.

Etty, T., *et al.*, 'Transnational Environmental Law on the Threshold of the Trump Era', *Transn.tl Env. L.*, Vol. 6, No. 1, 2017, pp. 1-10.

Fallon Jr., R.H., 'Constitutional Constraints', *Cal. L. Rev.*, Vol. 97, No. 4, 2009, pp. 975-1038.

Fallon Jr., R.H., 'Interpreting Presidential Powers', *Duke L.J.*, Vol. 63, No. 2, 2013, pp. 347-392.

Fenster, M., *The Transparency Fix: Secrets, Leaks and Uncontrollable Government information*, Stanford: Law Books, 2017.

Ferrari, G.F. (2011). 'The Obama Presidency (2008-2016)', *in* G.F. Ferrari (Ed.), *The American Presidency after Barack Obama*, Leiden: Eleven International Publishing, p. 13.

Freuer, K., 'Protecting Government Secrets: A Comparison of the Espionage Act and the Official Secrets Act', *Boston Coll. Int. Comp. L. Rev*, Vol. 38, No. 1, 2015, p. 91.

Gephardt, R.A., 'The Congressional Budget Impasse', *St. Louis U. Pub. L. Rev.*, Vol. 16, No. 1, 1996, pp. 5-16.

Gerhardt, M.J., Painter, R.W., 'Majority Rule and the Future of Judicial Selection', *Wis. L. Rev.*, Vol. 2017, No. 2, 2017, pp. 263-284.

Gibson, T.T., 'Multiple Principals and the (Lack of) Intelligence Oversight', *Natl. Sec. L. J.*, Vol. 5, No. 2, 2017, pp. 239-276.

Goldgeier, J.M., Saunders, E.N., 'The Unconstitutional Presidency: Checks and Balances Eroded Long Before Trump', *Council on Foreign Relations*, 14 August 2018.

Goldsmith, J., *Power and Constraint: The Accountable presidency after 9/11*, New York: W.W. Norton & Company, 2012.

Hoshijima, Y., Note, 'Presidential Administration and the Durability of Climate Consciousness', *Yale L. J.*, Vol. 127, No. 1, 2017, pp. 1–245.

Huq, H., Ginsburg, T., 'How to Lose a Constitutional Democracy', *U.C.L.A. L. Rev.*, Vol. 65, No. 1, 2018, pp. 78-169.

Ikenberry, J.G, Mastanduno, M., & Wolforth W.C. (Eds.), *International Relations Theory and the Consequences of Unipolarity*, Cambridge: Cambridge University Press, 2011.

Ikenberry, J.G., 'The Plot against American Foreign Policy. Can the Liberal Order Survive?', *Foreign Affairs*, Vol. 96, No. 3, 2017, pp. 2-9.

Indyk, M.S., Lieberthal, K.G., & O'Hanlon, M.E., 'Scoring Obama's Foreign Policy: A Progressive Pragmatist Tries to Bend History', *Foreign Affairs*, Vol. 91, No. 3, 2012, p. 29.

Ingber, R., 'The Obama War Powers Legacy and the Internal Forces That Entrench Executive Power', *Am. J. Int'l L.*, Vol. 110, No. 4, 2016, pp. 680-700.

Jacobson, G.C., 'Party Polarization in American Politics', *Pres. St. Q.*, Vol. 43, No. 4, 2013, pp. 688-708.

Kabaservice, G., *Rule and Ruin: The Downfall of Moderation and the Destruction of the Republican Party, From Eisenhower to the Tea Party*, Oxford: Oxford University Press, 2012.

Kagan, E., 'Presidential Administration', *Harv. L. Rev.*, Vol. 114, No. 8, 2001, pp. 2245-2385.

Kelley, C.S., 'Rhetoric and Reality? Unilateralism and the Obama Administration', *Soc. Sc. Q.*, Vol. 93, No. 5, 2012, pp. 1146-1160.

Kelley, C.S., Marshall, B.W., & Watts, D.J., 'Assessing the Rhetorical Side of Presidential Signing Statement's', *Pres. Studies Q.*, Vol. 43, No. 2, 2013, pp. 274-298.

Kessler, G., 'No, President Trump. You Haven't Signed More Bills than Any Other President', *Washington Post*, 17 July 2017.

Kitrosser, H., 'Accountability in the Deep State', *U.C.L.A. L. Rev.*, Vol. 65, No. 6, 2018, pp. 1532-1551.

Kleinerman, B.A., *The Discretionary President: The Promise and Peril of Executive Power*, Lawrence: University Press of Kansas, 2009.

Kohn, S.M., *American Political Prisoners: Prosecutions under the Espionage and Sedition Acts*, Wesport: Praeger, 1994.

Krauthammer, C., 'The Unipolar Moment', *Foreign Affairs*, Vol. 70, No. 1, 1990/1991, p. 23.

Krent, H.J. *Presidential Powers*, New York: New York University Press, 2005.

Larkin Jr., P.J., 'Reawakening the Congressional Review Act', *Harv. J.L. & Pub. Pol.y*, Vol. 41, No. 1, 2018, pp. 187-252.

Lawson, G., 'Ordinary Powers in Extraordinary Ties: Common Sense in Times of crisis', *B.U.L. Rev.*, Vol. 87, No. 2, 2007, p. 289.

Layne, C., 'This Time It's Real: The End of Unipolarity and the Pax Americana', *Int. Stud. Q.*, Vol. 56, No. 1, 2012, pp. 203-213.

Lee, F.E., *Beyond Ideology: Politics, Principles, and Partisanship in the U.S. Senate*, Chicago: The University of Chicago Press, 2009.

Levinson, D.J., 'Forward: Looking for Power in Public Law', *Harv. L. Rev.*, Vol. 130, No. 1, 2016, p. 31

Lewis, D.E., Bernhard, P., & You E., 'President Trump as Manager: Reflections on the First Year', *Pres. St. Q.*, Vol. 48, No. 3, 2018, pp. 480-501

Louk, D.S., Gamage, D., 'Preventing Government Shutdowns: Designing Default Rules for Budgets', *U. Colo. L. Rev.*, Vol. 86, No. 1, 2015, pp. 181-258.

Madonna, A.J., Monogan, J.E., & Vining, R.L., 'Confirmation Wars, Legislative Time, and Collateral Damage: The Impact of Supreme Court Nominations on Presidential Success in the US Senate', *Pol. R. Q.*, Vol. 69, No. 4, 2016, p. 746.

Mann, T.E., Ornstein, N.J., *It's even Worse than It Looks: How the American Constitutional System Collided with the Politics of Extremism*, New York: Basic Books, 2012.

Mashaw J.L., Berke, D., 'Presidential Administration in a Regime of Separated Powers: An Analysis of Recent American Experience', *Yale J. on Reg.*, Vol. 35, No. 2, 2018, pp. 549-616.

Mashaw, J.L., *Creating the Administrative Constitution: The Lost One Hundred Years of American Administrative Law*, New Haven: Yale University Press, 2012.

Mayer, K., Price, K., 'Unilateral Presidential Powers: Significant Executive Orders, 1949-1999', *Pres. St. Q.*, Vol. 32, No. 2, 2002, p. 375.

McMillion, B.J., *U.S. Circuit and District Court Nominations during President Trump's First Year in Office: Comparative Analysis with Recent Presidents*, Washington, DC: Congressional Research Service, 2 May 2018.

Metzger, G.E., '1930s Redux: The Administrative State under Siege', *Harv. L. Rev.*, Vol. 131, No. 1, 2017, pp. 1-95.

Metzger, G.E., 'Agencies, Polarization, and the States', *Colum. L. Rev.*, Vol. 115, No. 7, 2015, p. 1739-1788.

Meyers, R.T., *Handbook of Government Budgeting*, San Francisco: Jossey-Bass, 1998.

Milkis, S.M. Nelson, M., *The American Presidency. Origins and Development, 1776-2014* (7th ed.), Washington, DC: Sage Publishing, 2015.

Morgan, I., *The Age of Deficits: Presidents and Unbalanced Budgets from Jimmy Carter to George W. Bush*, Lawrence: University Press of Kansas, 2009.

Nau, H.R., 'Obama's Foreign Policy', *Pol. Rev.*, Vol. 160, 2010, pp. 27-47.

Neureuther, J., *The Quiet Revolution. What the Evolution of the Presidential Veto Power Can Tell Us about the Modern Use of Presidential Signing Statements*, Saarbrücken: VDM Verlag Dr. Müller, 2011.

Newland, E., 'Executive Orders in the Court', *Yale L. J.*, Vol. 124, No. 6, 2015, pp. 2026-2099.

Note, 'The Mysteries of the Congressional Review Act', *Harv. L. Rev.*, Vol. 122, No. 8, 2009, pp. 2162-2183.

O'Connell, J., 'After one year in office, Trump's behind on staffing but making steady progress', *Brookings Report*, 23 January 2018.

Office of Management and Budget, *Impacts and Costs of the October 2013 Federal Government Shutdown*, Washington, D.C., 2013.

Ornstein, N. 'The Other Devil's Bargain', *Politics*, 21 August 2017.

Owens, M.E., 'Changing Senate Norms: Judicial Confirmations in a Nuclear Age', *Profession Symposium, American Political Science Association*, Vol. 51, No. 1, 2018, pp. 119-123.

Patterson, C.P., *Presidential Government in the United Sates: The Unwritten Constitution*, North Carolina: University of North Carolina Press, 1947.

Prakash, S., 'Regulating Presidential Powers', *Cornell L. Rev.*, Vol. 91, No. 1, 2005, pp. 215-258.

Prakash, S.B., 'A Taxonomy of Presidential Powers', *B.U.L. Rev.*, Vol. 88, No. 2, 2008, pp. 327-340.

Rascoff, S.J., 'Presidential Intelligence', *Harv. L. Rev.*, Vol. 129, No. 3, 2016, pp. 633-717.

Rodriguez, D.B, Stiglitz, E.H., & Weingast, B.R., 'Executive Opportunism, Presidential Signing Statements, and the Separation of Powers', *J. of Leg. An.*, Vol. 8, No. 1, 2016, pp. 95-119.

Rosenberg, M., 'Whatever Happened to Congressional Review of Agency Rulemaking? A Brief Overview, Assessment, and Proposal for Reform', *Admin. L. Rev.*, Vol. 51, No. 4, 1999, p. 1051.

Rossiter, C., *The American Presidency*, New York: Harcourt, 1956.

Rudalevige, A., 'Old Laws, New Meanings: Obama's Brand of Presidential Imperialism', *Syracuse L. Rev.*, Vol. 66, No. 1, 2016, p. 1.

Santulli, S., 'Use of the Congressional Review Act at the Start of the Trump Administration: A Study of Two Vetoes', *Geo. Wash. L. Rev.*, Vol. 86, No. 1, 2015, pp. 1373- 1391.

Sasser, J., *Budget Process Law Annotated*, Washington, DC: U.S. Government Printing Office, 1991.

Saturno, J.V., *The Congressional Budget Process: A Brief Overview*, Washington, DC: Congressional Research Service, 2001

Savage, C., *Power Wars: Inside Obama's Post 9/11 Presidency*, New York: Back Bay Books, 2012.

Savage, C., *Power Wars: The Relentless Rise of Presidential Authority*, New York: Little, Brown and Company, 2015.

Schaffner, B.F., 'Party Polarization', *in* G.C. Edwards III, F.E. Lee & E. Schickler (Eds.), *The Oxford Handbook of the American Congress*, Oxford: Oxford University Press, 2011.

Schaffner, B.F., Macwilliams, M., & Nteta, T., 'Understanding White Polarization in the 2016 Vote for President: The Sobering Role of Racism and Sexism', *Pol. Sc. Q.*, Vol. 133, No. 1, 2018, pp. 9-34.

Schick, A., *The Federal Budget, Politics Policy, Process* (3rd ed.), Washington, DC: Brookings Institution Press, 2008.

Schoenberger, N., 'Access to Information in the Age of Trump', *Emerging Library & Information Perspectives*, Vol. 1, 2018, pp. 6-33.

Schoenfeld, G., *Necessary Secrets: National Security, the Media and the Rule of Law*, New York: W.W. Norton & Company, 2010.

Sholette, K., Note, 'The American Czars', *Cornell J. L. & Pub. Pol.y*, Vol. 20, No. 1, 2010, pp. 219-242.

Siegel, N.S., 'Political Norms, Constitutional Conventions, and President Donald Trump', *Ind. L. J.*, Vol. 93, No. 1, 2018, pp. 177-206.

Sinclair, B., *Unorthodox Lawmaking: New Legislative Processes in the U.S. Congress* (5th ed.), Washington, DC: CQ Press, 2015.

Skidmore, D., 'The Obama Presidency and U.S. Foreign Policy: Where's the Multilateralism?' *Int'l Stud Perspect.*, Vol. 13, No. 1, 2012, p. 43.

Skopckol, T., Williamson, V., *The Tea Party and the Remaking of Republican Conservatism*, New York: Oxford University Press, 2012.

Slater, G., 'The National Emergency Act of 1976 – End of Emergency Government', *Iustitia*, Vol. 4, No. 2, 1977, pp. 50-73.

Smith, N., 'Against Walls: How President's Trump's Walling Initiatives Undermine American Exceptionalism', *Geo. Immigr. L. J.*, Vol. 31, No. 3, 2017, pp. 623-664.

Sollenberger, M.A., Rozell, M.J., *The President's Czars: Undermining Congress and the Constitution*, Lawrence: University Press of Kansas, 2012.

Spivak, R.A., 'Co-Parenting War Powers: Congress's Authority to Escalate Conflicts', *W. Va. L. Rev.*, Vol. 121, No. 1, 2018, pp. 135-194.

Stathis, S.W., 'Enough Posturing: Congress should embrace veto override', *The Hill*, 1 January 2019

Strauss, P.L., 'Overseer or "The Decider"?, The President in Administrative Law', *Geo. Wash. L. Rev.*, Vol. 75, No. 4, 2007, pp. 696-760.

Tharoor, I., 'Trump's "Principled Realism" Is an Incoherent Mess', *The Washington Post*, 20 September 2017.

Theriault, S.M., *Party Polarization in Congress*, Cambridge: Cambridge University Press, 2008.

Ura, J.D., Ellis, C.R., 'Partisan Moods: Polarization and the Dynamics of Mass Party Preferences', *J. Pol.*, Vol. 74, No. 1, 2012, pp. 1-15.

Vaughn, J.S., Villalobos, J.D., *Czars in the White House: The Rise of Policy Czars as Presidential Management Tools*, Ann Harbor: University of Michigan Press, 2015.

Vermeule, A., 'Conventions of Agency Independence', *Colum. L. Rev.*, Vol. 113, No. 5, 2013, pp. 1163-1238.

Vermeule, A., 'Our Schmittian Administrative Law', *Harv. L. Rev.*, Vol. 122, No. 4, 2009, pp. 1095-1150.

Warber, A.L., *Executive Orders and the Modern Presidency: Legislating from the Oval Office*, Boulder: Lynne Rienner Publishers, 2006.

Williamson, R.D., 'Evaluating Candidate Positioning and Success in the 2018 Midterm Elections', *The Forum*, Vol. 16, No. 4, 2018, p. 653.

Wolff, M., *Fire and Fury: Inside the Trump White House*, London: Henry Holt & Co., 2018.

Woodard, J.H., Bacon, F.W., 'Government Shutdown: A Test of Market Efficiency', *J. Bus. & Behav. Sciences*, Vol. 27, No. 2, 2015, p. 71.

Zegart, A.B., *Eyes on Spies: Congress and the United States Intelligence Community*, Stanford: Hoover Institution Press, 2011.

2 Tiptoeing on the Edge of the Law: How Trump Is Fighting the Regulatory State

Nausica Palazzo

2.1 Introduction

President Donald J. Trump, acting on his campaign promise to curb agencies' powers and regulatory excesses, initiated a radical reform of the regulatory state. Crucially, he asserted a presidential and agency power to reverse previous policies with little, if any, constraint. However, in delivering his promise to undo Obama-era rules and put the brakes on the regulatory state, he encountered many established practices and laws that, in principle, limit his authority to change policies at will.

The result of this 'uncomfortable encounter' led him (and appointed heads of agencies) to twist existing legal rules, whether procedural, administrative or constitutional, and overlook consolidated practices in unprecedented ways. The central claim of this chapter, thus, is that in the first two years of Trump's presidency a major departure from consolidated case law and conventional practices has been registered. The following points are outlined to buttress this central claim:

i. an unprecedented recourse to the Congressional Review Act (CRA) to undo previous regulations;
ii. the agencies' inaction following executive order 13.771 on 'Reducing Regulation and Controlling Regulatory Costs';
iii. agencies' policy shifts following statutory abnegation claims;
iv. recent attempts on the part of agencies to waive the *Chevron* deference.

The recourse to the CRA indicates a departure from a praxis (that of *not* using the CRA is such an aggressive way to dismantle previous policies) and from the law in providing an interpretation of the Act itself that is against the black letter of the law. Likewise, the points under (ii), (iii) and (iv) denote a departure from administrative and constitutional laws and doctrines. They indeed raise serious constitutional issues. For instance, they put under pressure the long-established principle of the separation of powers. This principle acquires special meaning in the United States, such a system being the first in the history of establishing a carefully drafted system of checks and balances. They also run roughshod over basic principles of administrative law, and this conflict will be the principal focus of the analysis.

In Sections 2.2, 2.3, 2.4 and 2.5, this chapter intends to outline the four trends concerning, respectively, the 'aggressive' use of the CRA, the executive order 13.771, statutory abnegation claims and the *Chevron* waiver. In Section 2.6, the chapter sets out to problematize the regulatory actions following executive order 13.771, the *Chevron* waiver and statutory abnegation claims. The recourse to the CRA, while far more bold compared with the past, 'merely' departs from a praxis. By contrast, my contention is that in the cases under (ii), (iii) and (iv) a departure from statutory requirements and case law is occurring. In Section 2.6, the chapter will thus outline the main legal hurdles that the President encounters in putting in place unconventional deregulatory actions that do not comply with administrative law.

2.2 DISMANTLING PRIOR RULES THROUGH THE CRA

The CRA is a legislative tool enabling Congress to overturn a final rule issued by a federal agency.[1] This congressional oversight of agencies' rule-making is carried out by:

i. imposing reporting duties to each house of Congress and to the Comptroller General of the Government Accountability Office (GAO);
ii. providing for a fast-track legislative procedure[2] that allows Congress to issue a resolution of disapproval within 60 days (or more if Congress is adjourning,) which prevents agencies from issuing the rule, and from issuing prospective rules in "substantially the same form".[3]

As to the covered rules, these are mainly 'major rules'.[4] The virtual applicability to all major rules, however, must come to grips with political reality: it is unlikely for a President to let Congress overthrow his or her agencies' rules, nor is Congress likely to do so when the majority party is ideologically aligned with the President. This renders the Act inherently unsuitable for most major rules. By contrast, its appeal increases during presidential transitions, especially when this corresponds to a transition from a Democratic to a

1 Congressional Review Act, 5 U.S.C. §§ 801-802 (2012). On which, *see* M.P. Carey, A.M. Dolan & C.M. Davis, 'Congressional Review Act: Frequently Asked Questions', *Cong. Res. Serv.*, R43992, 2016, p. 14.

2 The expedited procedure under the Act, while complying with two requirements under Chadha of bicameralism and presentment, still allows for bypassing a filibuster and passing the resolution by a simple majority. *See* 5 U.S.C. § 802(d)(1). As to the presentment and bicameralism requirements, applying to legislative vetoes, *see Immigration and Naturalization Service v. Chadha*, 462 U.S. 919 (1983).

3 5 U.S.C. § 801(b)(2).

4 The definition of 'major rules' is patterned after the definition set forth in the Administrative Procedure Act (APA).

Republican president and vice versa.[5] The newly established Congress estimated that all the rules issued after 30 May 2016 were potentially eligible for review, considering that the 60-day period to submit and disapprove a rule 'resets' in the next session of Congress.[6]

Since its enactment in 1996, only once has the Act been successfully used to repeal a final rule. This occurred in 2001, in the aftermath of Bush's election, when Congress repealed the Occupational Safety and Health Administration (OSHA) ergonomics rule,[7] issued at the tail end of the Clinton's administration.[8] The rule would have required employers to implement safety measures to reduce workers' exposure to factors leading to musculoskeletal disorders. Yet the Bush administration considered it as too costly for enterprises.

Tellingly, Congress only sparingly used the CRA to block agencies' regulations and, even when attempts were made, the President vetoed the Congress resolution issued under the CRA. For instance, the 114th Congress issued five resolutions of disapproval.[9] Yet all of them were vetoed by Obama, and none could eventually block an agency rule.[10]

By contrast, President Trump has pleaded to use the Act more aggressively, to limit the excesses of the regulatory state under the Obama administration. Since its inauguration, the 115th Congress has used the Act to overthrow 14 agency regulations.[11] These regulations concerned, among others, the Securities and Exchange Commission 'Disclosure of Payments by Resource Extraction Issuers'[12] (providing for disclosure duties to restrict companies in the energy sector from bribing foreign governments), the Department of the Interior 'Stream Protection Rule'[13] (restricting coal companies from dumping mining debris into streams), the Social Security Administration rules implementing the National Instant Criminal Background Check System (NICS) Improvement Amendments Act[14] (on background checks for the purchase of firearms by mentally impaired people,) the 'Arbitration

5 S. Santulli, 'Use of the Congressional Review Act at the Start of the Trump Administration: A Study of Two Vetoes', *Geo. Wash. L. Rev.*, Vol. 86, 2018, p. 1373.

6 Memorandum from M.P. Carey, C.M. Davis & C. Burgat, '"Major" Obama Administration Rules Potentially Eligible to Be Overturned under the Congressional Review Act in the 115th Congress', *Cong. Res. Serv.*, 17 November 2016, p. 2, available at https://fas.org/sgp/crs/misc/major-rules-cra.pdf.

7 Ergonomics Program, 65 Fed. Reg. 68,262 (Nov. 14, 2000), disapproved by Pub.L. 107-5, 115 Stat. 7 (2001).

8 Santulli, 2018, p. 1380.

9 Carey *et al.*, 'Congressional Review Act', 2016, p. 5.

10 Id.

11 For a list of these regulation, *see* E. Lipton & J.C. Lee, 'Which Obama-Era Rules Are Being Reversed in the Trump Era', *New York Times*, 18 May 2017, available at: www.nytimes.com/interactive/2017/05/01/us/politics/trump-obama-regulations-reversed.html (accessed 20 February 2019).

12 Pub.L. 115-4, H.J.Res. 41 (14 February 2017).

13 Pub.L. 115-5, H.J.Res. 38 (16 February 2017).

14 Pub.L. 115-8, H.J.Res. 40 (28 February 2017) ("Providing for congressional disapproval ... of the rule submitted by the Social Security Administration relating to Implementation of the NICS Improvement Amendments Act of 2007").

agreements' of the Bureau of Consumer Financial Protection,[15] several rules from the Department of Education,[16] the Department of Labor,[17] the Secretary of Health and Human Services[18] and the Department of Defense.[19]

This unconventional use of the legislative tool did not go unnoticed, leading prominent columnists to speak of a 'new Republican plan to deregulate America'.[20] Congress has indeed gone well beyond the run-of-the-mill interpretation of the Act by holding that any rule that has not been submitted for congressional oversight in the past is amenable to be vetoed. While the Act only allows for overturning rules within 60 days from their submission, the new interpretation assumes that when a rule has not been submitted, the new agency shall do so (and this is when the 60-day period starts ticking). This 'adventurous use'[21] of CRA led Congress to withdraw a 2013 guidance from the Consumer Financial Protection Bureau, prohibiting racial discrimination in auto lending.[22] The rule had not been submitted in the past, since it was a mere policy statement on the enforcement of a previous rule by the Bureau. Therefore, it does not qualify as a 'rule' under the Act.[23] The new interpretation thus exposes hundreds of non-submitted rules from previous administrations to resolutions of disapproval, including Obamacare regulations,[24] thereby creating a deep uncertainty about their fate.

---

15 Pub.L. 115-74, H.J.Res. 111 (1 November 2017).

16 Pub.L. 115-13, H.J.Res. 57 (27 March 2017) ("Providing for congressional disapproval ... of the rule submitted by the Department of Education relating to accountability and State plans under the Elementary and Secondary Education Act of 1965"); Pub.L. 115-14, H.J.Res. 58 (27 March 2017) ("Providing for congressional disapproval ... of the rule submitted by the Department of Education relating to teacher preparation issues.").

17 Pub.L. 115-17, H.J.Res. 42 (31 March 2017) ("Disapproving the rule submitted by the Department of Labor relating to drug testing of unemployment compensation applicants."); Pub.L. 115-21, H.J.Res. 83 (3 April 2017) ("Disapproving the rule submitted by the Department of Labor relating to 'Clarification of Employer's Continuing Obligation to Make and Maintain an Accurate Record of Each Recordable Injury and Illness'").

18 Pub.L. 115-23, H.J.Res. 43 (13 April 2017) ("Providing for congressional disapproval ... of the final rule submitted by Secretary of Health and Human Services relating to compliance with title X requirements by project recipients in selecting subrecipients").

19 Pub.L. 115-11, H.J.Res. 37 (27 March 2017) ("Disapproving the rule submitted by the Department of Defense, the General Services Administration, and the National Aeronautics and Space Administration relating to the Federal Acquisition Regulation").

20 D. Scott, 'The New Republican Plan to Deregulate America, Explained', *Vox*, 25 April 2018, available at www.vox.com/policy-and-politics/2018/4/25/17275566/congressional-review-act-what-regulations-has-trump-cut.

21 Id., quoting Professor Nicholas Bagley.

22 GAO, B-330736, Bureau of Consumer Financial Protection: Disclosure of Loan-Level HMDA Data, available at https://www.gao.gov/assets/700/697072.pdf (accessed 21 February 2019).

23 For a rule to qualify for submission and congressional oversight it must be: "1) an agency statement, 2) of future effect, and 3) designed to implement, interpret, or prescribe law or policy."

24 C. Jacobs, 'New Precedent Allows Congress to Dismantle (Some of) Obamacare', *The Federalist*, 23 April 2018, available at http://thefederalist.com/2018/04/23/new-precedent-allows-congress-dismantle-obamacare/ (arguing that only the Obamacare rules that the administration has officially submitted for review are now safe).

2.3 Freezing Agencies: Executive Order 13.771

As announced, one of the first moves of the Trump administration was to curb the excesses of the regulatory state, by forcing agencies to scrutinize all their pending and future actions. To this end, the President enacted on 30 January 2017 an executive order titled 'Reducing Regulation and Controlling Regulatory Costs'.[25] The order introduced two major innovations:

i. the so-called 'two-for-one rule' for prospective regulations, requiring that whenever an agency proposes or promulgates a new rule, it must point to at least two regulations to repeal;[26]
ii. the cap on incremental costs of regulations, directing that an agency may issue a new rule only if, together with repealed regulations, the total incremental costs are $0 for fiscal year 2017 and below $0 for fiscal year 2018.[27] As a consequence, agencies are supposed to meet the requirement by offsetting the incremental cost of each new rule with the savings gained from wiping off old rules.

The Office of Management and Budget (OMB) of the White House then issued two guidance documents to clarify the scope of the order: the so-called Interim Guidance[28] and the 'Guidance Implementing Executive Order 13771'.[29] They both reinforce the idea that agencies cannot account for benefits in calculating the cost of a rule (nor cost savings). For instance, the Interim Guidance maintains that the cost savings vis-à-vis energy that consumers would enjoy if manufacturers were to produce more cost-efficient equipment do not count for purposes of the calculation. It, furthermore, rules out the possibility of considering the 'sunk costs' of regulations considered for elimination (*i.e.* those already incurred at the time of the promulgation of the rule). The only possibility left is thus that of considering the future costs of these regulations (the practical implication being that agencies will often need to repeal more than two regulations to meet the requirement). The second guidance goes one step further in requiring something that is plainly against the letter of the law: it states that even if "a statute prohibits consideration of cost in taking a particular regulatory action", agencies are still "required to offset the costs of such regu-

25 Exec. Order No. 13,771, 82 Fed. Reg. 9339 (3 February 2017) (EO 13771).
26 EO 13771, §2(a).
27 EO 13771, §2(b).
28 Memorandum from Dominic J. Mancini, Acting Adm'r, Office of Info. & Regulatory Affairs, to Regulatory Policy Officers at Exec. Dep'ts & Agencies & Managing & Exec. Dirs. of Certain Agencies & Comm'ns (2 February 2017).
29 Memorandum from Dominic J. Mancini, Acting Adm'r, Office of Info. & Regulatory Affairs to Regulatory Policy Officers at Exec. Dep'ts & Agencies & Managing & Exec. Dirs. of Certain Agencies & Comm'ns (5 April 2017).

latory actions through other deregulatory actions taken pursuant to statutes that do not prohibit consideration of costs".[30]

As specified in the Interim Guidance, the order covers significant rules, which are mainly those that "have an annual effect on the economy of $100 million or more or adversely affect in a material way the economy".[31] Besides non-significant rules, the order itself exempts some categories, such as those falling within the realm of national security, military and foreign affairs, purely internal rules (concerning the agency management and personnel) and those exempted by the OMB Director. Furthermore, the order does not apply to independent agencies and thus only applies to executive agencies.

The result of EO 13.771 was that of freezing agencies. Ample evidence confirms that hundreds of agency actions were withdrawn, suspended or delayed as a result of compliance with the order.[32] For instance, the Environmental Protection Agency (EPA) Acting Principal Deputy Assistant Administrator for Water released a statement in March 2017 according to which the order 'tied up' the dental effluent rule of the Clean Water Act that would have prevented mercury from being dumped in municipal water systems.[33]

It should be no surprise that the executive order and its subsequent guidance documents were promptly challenged in court. Interest groups argued that a withdrawal, suspension or weakening of the agencies' rule-making activity amounted to a palpable injury to their members.[34] The civic organization Public Citizens and other plaintiffs sought declaratory and injunctive relief against the order. On 8 February 2019, the reviewing Court denied defendants' motion to dismiss.[35] Thus, as of May 2019, the litigation is still ongoing.

---

30 Id., p. 8, Q.18.

31 The definition of 'significant rule' can be found in §3(f) of Exec. Order No. 12,866, 58 Fed. Reg. 51,735 (4 October 1993). In addition to those with an annual effect of over $100 million on the economy, a rule is significant if it creates serious inconsistencies with actions taken by other agencies; significantly alters the budget of entitlements, grants, user fees or loan programs, or the rights and obligations descending from them; raises novel legal or policy issues.

32 OMB, 'Current Regulatory Plan and the Unified Agenda of Regulatory and Deregulatory Actions', *RegInfo.gov*, 14 December 2017, available at https://web.archive.org/web/20171215071216/https:/www.reginfo.gov/public/do/eAgendaMain (accessed 27 February 2019); OMB, 'Regulatory Reform: Two-for-One and Regulatory Cost Caps', 14 December 2017, available at www.reginfo.gov/public/do/eAgendaEO13771 (accessed 27 February 2019) (listing the 'results' of implementing EO 13.771).

33 Plaintiffs' memorandum in support of motion for partial summary judgment and in opposition to defendants' motion to dismiss, *Public Citizen v. Trump*, No. 17-253 (D.D.C. 4 June 2018), p. 6 (citing to: 'Trump "Two For One" Deregulatory Order Halts EPA's Dental Amalgam Rule', 38 Inside EPA Weekly Report 12, 2017 WLNR 8997168, 24 March 2017).

34 Id., p. 5 ("The Executive Order is preventing, delaying, and weakening new rules that would protect public health, safety, and the environment, to the detriment of plaintiffs and their members").

35 In February 2018, the District Court of Columbia granted a motion to dismiss, holding that plaintiffs lacked standing. Yet it gave a deadline to amend the initial complaint on the standing issue and later granted the leave to the proposed amendments. It then denied the second motion to dismiss. Thus, the case is still pending.

Plaintiffs oppose Trump's new order on several statutory and non-statutory grounds. First, plaintiffs lament that all the regulatory and deregulatory actions entered into by agencies in compliance with the order contrast with the Administrative Procedure Act (APA) and with governing statutes. None of these statutes allegedly authorize that, in delaying or amending regulations, agencies consider rescinding old regulations or comply with an arbitrary cap on incremental costs.[36] In this sense, each of these regulatory actions is arbitrary and capricious, an abuse of discretion, and not in accordance with the law (a typical standard under which it is possible to strike down a rule under the APA).[37]

Second, in seeking to impose requirements that neither the organic statute nor APA set forth, the executive order itself runs roughshod on the Constitution. In particular, it exceeds the President's authority under Article II, violates the presidential duty "to take care that the law be faithfully executed" under Article II§3 and encroaches upon the legislative power of Congress under Article I.[38]

2.4 AGENCY STATUTORY ABNEGATION CLAIMS

Under the Trump administration, many policy reversals occurred in yet another manner: through summary and thumbnail repeals by agencies maintaining that they lack the authority to govern the matter.

Georgetown law professor William Buzbee called these summary and thumbnail repeals "agency statutory abnegation claims".[39] They consist in an allegation that the agency lacks power to regulate a matter, despite such power having previously been asserted. This kind of claim was commonplace in policy reversals that occurred in the years 2017 and 2018.

The examples in this regard are many. The first concerns a new interpretation of EPA statutory authority to issue the Clean Power Plan (CPP).[40] As reported on EPA website, this Obama-era policy "established emission guidelines for states to follow in limiting carbon dioxide (CO_2) emissions from existing power plants".[41] The new interpretation aims at asserting a lack of authority to regulate the matter with a view to repealing the

36 Second Amended Complaint for Declaratory and Injunctive Relief, *Public Citizen v. Trump*, No. 17-253 (D.D.C. April 2018), p. 3, §5 ("Second Amended Complaint").
37 *See* Administrative Procedure Act (APA) §706(2)(A).
38 Second Amended Complaint, p. 4, §8.
39 W.W. Buzbee, 'The Tethered President: Consistency and Contingency in Administrative Law', *B.U. L. Rev.*, Vol. 98, 2018, pp. 1357, 1371.
40 Repeal of Carbon Pollution Emission Guidelines for Existing Stationary Sources: Electric Utility Generating Units, 82 Fed. Reg. 48,035, 48,037 (proposed 16 October 2017). The new interpretation touches upon the agency power to regulate the matter under Section 111(d) of the Clean Air Act (on which the targeted policy was based).
41 EPA website, available at www.epa.gov/stationary-sources-air-pollution/electric-utility-generating-units-repealing-clean-power-plan (accessed 1 March 2019).

Cpp. Examples of EPA policy reversals are conspicuous and range from issues such as the reclassification of major sources as area sources (material to determining the safety standard vis-à-vis toxic air pollutant) to caps on air emissions from refurbished trucks and engines.[42] A second example concerns the Federal Communications Commission's (FCC's) repeal of the net neutrality policy.[43] On that occasion the reasoning boiled down to the assertion that the agency had no power to regulate the Internet, as it 'unaptly' did in 2015.

Agency statutory abnegation claims are not 'new' in the sense that when an agency wants to shift its position on a prior issue it could well be the case that it reasons around its authority to regulate it under the organic statute. What, again, is genuinely new is the frequency with which agencies seem to use this argumentative tool and the fact that an abnegation claim is extremely cursory. Put differently, what seems to be missing is a thorough analysis of facts, data and new circumstances warranting a policy shift, as required by the APA and consolidated case law. This point is elaborated on in the last section.

2.5 WAIVING THE *CHEVRON* DEFERENCE

The *Chevron* deference[44] is the standard of review for certain types of agencies' rules, namely those "carrying the force of law".[45] It sets out the boundaries for the agency's discretion in interpreting the enabling statute (both the organic statute that creates the agency and delimits its authoritative powers, and the substantive law an agency rule is supposed to implement). The standard is fairly deferential,[46] as it tends to rule out only those agencies' interpretations that are patently wrong.[47] This point has two practical implications. The

42 Buzbee, 2018, n. 103 and accompanying text.

43 Restoring Internet Freedom, 82 Fed. Reg. 25,568, 25,573 (proposed 2 June 2017) (Codified at 47 C.F.R. pts. 8, 20).

44 *Chevron, U.S.A., Inc v. Natural Resources Defense Council, Inc*, 467 US 837 (1984). The *Chevron* question arises where an agency issues: (1) a rule interpreting a statutory term or rule as a matter of 'genuine interpretation': *e.g.* what the statutory term 'take' means, (2) a legislative rule filling a vacuum or an unclear passage of the statute, under the assumption that Congress wanted the agency to fill it.

45 *United States v. Mead Corp*, 533 US 218 (2001).

46 The broad discretion agencies enjoy in implementing statutes without interference from judicial review led former 'czar' of the Obama administration and administrative law scholar Cass Sunstein to speak of *Chevron* as the 'counter-Marbury for the administrative state'. *See* C.R. Sunstein, 'Chevron Step Zero', *Va. L. Rev.*, Vol. 92, 2006, pp. 187, 188-189. Besides, the principal hint of the breadth of this discretion is the success rate of agencies before courts applying the standard. *See* K. Barnett & C.J. Walker, 'Chevron in the Circuit Courts', *Mich. L. Rev.*, Vol. 116, 2017, p. 3031 (noting that the success rate in circuit courts when agencies invoke *Chevron* is 77% as compared with a 54% rate in the cases in which such courts do not apply *Chevron*).

47 To oversimplify what seems to be a rather complex and multilayered doctrine, under *Chevron* step one, the reviewing court asks: "Has Congress directly spoken to the precise question at issue?" At step 1 the question is not whether the word 'modify' is clear/unambiguous but rather whether an agency's interpretation is clearly precluded. *See MCI Telecommunications Corporation v. American Telephone & Telegraph Company*, 512 US 218 (1994). Under *Chevron* step two, the reviewing court asks: "If the statute is silent or ambiguous,

first implication is that only rules meeting certain (procedural) conditions can enjoy the deferential standard (and the ample leeway in interpreting statutes thereto attached). The second implication is that *Chevron* is routinely invoked by agencies, which are usually interested in shielding their rules from administrative challanges.[48]

The latter point brings us to the crux of the problem addressed in this paragraph: an anomalous use of the *Chevron* doctrine by an administrative agency, namely the FCC.[49] The case *Global Tel*Link v. Federal Communications Commission*[50] was filed under the Obama administration and decided in the aftermath of Trump's election. It concerned an order[51] issued under the Obama administration aimed at reducing the high costs associated with interstate inmate calling services (ICS) calls. Back then, the regulatory purpose was achieved by setting permanent rate caps and ancillary fee caps. As a previous FCC order noted, the cost of such services was as high as $17.30 for a 15-minute long-distance call in some states.[52] It was likely so for reasons related to site commissions and security concerns.[53] Yet the Trump administration did not seem to share the same concern the Obama administration had, and was quick to side with service providers. Once the new five FCC members were appointed by the newly elected President, the Commission signalled a different position on rate caps,[54] and the case was briefed accordingly.[55]

is the agency's answer based on a permissible construction of the statute?" This step requires courts to make a spectrum of potential meanings and to exclude those patently unsustainable. *See Food and Drug Administration v. Brown & Williamson*, 529 US 120 (2000).

48 An agency action can be challenged under (1) the Constitution; (2) the organic statute; (3) the Administrative Procedure Act (APA). APA § 706 sets forth the 'Scope of Review' of the reviewing court. An agency action/finding/conclusion can be set aside, among the others, if it is 'otherwise not in accordance with law' (APA § 706 (A)). This contrast with the statutory law will trigger either the *Chevron* deference or the *Skidmore* deference (a much less deferential standard) depending on certain factors listed in the *Mead* case. These factors, especially in subsequent case law, all boil down to (in which case the *Chevron* deference is triggered).

49 The Court itself observes that "the current posture of this case is unusual since counsel for the FCC has advised the court that the agency will not oppose two of the principal challenges raised by petitioners" (among which was the lack of authority in setting rate caps). Global Tel*Link, 866 F3d p. 406.

50 866 F3d 397 (DC Cir. 2017).

51 Rates for Interstate Inmate Calling Services, 80 Fed Reg 79136, 79137 (2015). The Court eventually stayed the order with respect to 47 C.F.R. § 64.6030 (imposing interim rate caps). *See* the Court order available on the FCC website: www.fcc.gov/document/court-order-granting-partial-stay-global-tellink-v-fcc-dc-cir (accessed: 20 February 2019).

52 Report and Order and Further Notice of Proposed Rulemaking, In the Matter of Rates for Interstate Inmate Calling Services, 28 FCC Rec 14107, 14126 (2013).

53 J.D. Rozansky, 'Waiving Chevron', *Chi. L. Rev.*, Vol. 85, 2018, pp. 1927, 1931 ("One reason rates are so high is that service providers compete for contracts at correctional facilities, often by bidding up site commissions, the shares of revenue that go to the correctional facility. Rates are also higher inside prisons and jails because of security concerns.")

54 Letter, *Global Tel*Link v. Federal Communications Commission*, No. 15-1461, *1 (DC Cir. filed 31 January 2017).

55 The final reply brief was submitted on 14 November 2016, one week after the elections.

Thus, the anomalous use of the doctrine occurred in the context of an ongoing litigation. In a nutshell, a change in the agency heads resulted in a change in policy, which in turn resulted in a change in the litigation strategy within the ongoing litigation. On that occasion, the agency decided not to avail itself of the broad discretion *Chevron* warrants. This is what legal scholarship calls the '*Chevron* waiver'. A *Chevron* waiver means that the agency does not intend to defend the rule.

The admissibility of a *Chevron* waiver, a 'novel' and 'interesting' issue, as it has been defined,[56] is now inflaming a vivid debate among administrative and constitutional law researchers.[57] While a court's debate over whether the *Chevron* deference can be waived was already underway, the recent move of the Trump administration made the issue all the more relevant as it materialized in an unprecedented way. The novelty consists in the fact that the agency has deliberately downplayed, if not waived, the argument so as to allow the reviewing court to strike down the Obama-era rule, instead of going through the lengthy administrative procedure required for its repeal.[58] By contrast, the run-of-the-mill scenarios were: (1) one where both parties assumed without arguing the applicability of *Chevron* or (2) one where the agency pressed more convincing arguments than the *Chevron*-based arguments, and waived the deference to avoid wasting time on unpersuasive arguments.

The first scenario consists in waiving the *Chevron* step zero analysis, set forth in *Mead*, according to which courts must preliminarily assess whether an agency action is reviewable under *Chevron* or under a much less deferential standard of review set out in *Skidmore*.[59]

56 A. Nielson, 'D.C. Circuit Review—Reviewed: A New Step for Chevron?', *Yale J. on Reg.*: Notice & Comment, Vol. 36, 16 June 2017, available at https://perma.cc/95AF-HRKS (defining it as a novel and major issue, and calling for law students to write student notes on it).

57 J. Durling & E.G. West, 'May Chevron Be Waived?', *Stan. L. Rev. Online*, Vol. 71, 2019, p. 183; Rozansky, 2018; A. Bernstein, 'Who Is Chevron For?', *Yale J. on Reg.*, Notice & Comment, Vol. 36, 24 August 2017, available at http://yalejreg.com/nc/who-is-chevron-for-by-anya-bernstein/ (accessed: 20 February 2019); A. Nielson, 'D.C. Circuit Review—Reviewed: A New Step for Chevron?', Yale J. on Reg.: Notice & Comment, Vol. 36, 16 June 2017, http://yalejreg.com/nc/d-c-circuit-review-reviewed-a-new-step-for-chevron/ (accessed 20 February 2019).

58 These issues in the end touch upon the nature and latitude of the power to rescind previous policies in courts, rather than through legislative rules. Compare it with the possibility to withdraw the DOJ defensive claims altogether in cases challenging rules from the previous administration.

59 *Skidmore v. Swift & Co.*, 323 U.S. 134 (1944). Under this more stringent standard, interpretative deference is warranted after considering the "thoroughness evident in its consideration, the validity of its reasoning, its consistency with earlier and later pronouncements, and all those factors which give it power to persuade, if lacking power to control". Suffice it to say that in the case *Martin v. SSA*, 903 F.3d 1154 (2018), the 11th Circuit Court noted circuit courts split on the issue, without resolving it. On the one side are those courts maintaining that it is a non-jurisdictional argument, and as such a waivable argument. *See Lubow v. Dep't of State*, 783 F.3d 877, 884, 414 U.S. App. D.C. 379 (D.C. Cir. 2015) (stating that "The applicability of the *Chevron* framework does not go to our court's jurisdiction, and a party can therefore forfeit an argument against deference by failing to raise it."); Humane Soc'y of the *U.S. v. Locke*, 626 F.3d 1040, 1054 n.8 (9th Cir. 2010); *Kikalos v. C.I.R.*, 190 F.3d 791, 796 (7th Cir. 1999) (a case recognizing the waiver before the Supreme Court laid out the step zero analysis). On the other side are those courts stating that the argument is not waivable, since it is a standard of review. As such, courts are called to independently assess it. *See*

By contrast, the second scenario consists in a litigation position that results in *Chevron* forfeiture, rather than waiver, since agencies deliberately decide not to brief *Chevron* arguments to press alternative – and more persuasive – legal arguments.[60]

Put differently, the novelty consists in the *political* use of the *Chevron* waiver on the part of an agency, whereby the agency relinquishes a previously raised *Chevron* argument, that, if pushed and accepted, would have likely prevented the rule from being struck down by a court.

This issue of the waiver is surely controversial. In the Court's opinion, the majority seemed to concede that a waiver occurred.[61] Yet after a few days the Court made repairs of the potential implications of its decision and issued an order 'amending' and 'clarifying' the decision. It still invalidated Obama's order on ISCs. Yet now it did so by 'assuming' that the action would be impermissible even if the *Chevron* deference were to apply.[62] This move allowed the Court not to rule on the permissibility of the waiver. Thus, the *Chevron* waiver is still a potential option for agencies eager to strike down previous policies in court rather than repealing them through the burdensome notice-and-comment procedure or other formal administrative procedures.[63]

Sierra Club v. United States DOI, 899 F.3d 260, 2018 WL 3717067, p. *17 (4th Cir. 2018); *Mushtaq v. Holder*, 583 F.3d 875, 876 (5th Cir. 2009) (rejecting the *Chevron* standard even if both parties agreed on its application).

60 *MBIA Insurance Corp v. Federal Deposit Insurance Corp*, 708 F3d 234, 240 (DC Cir. 2013) (observing that the FDIC did not seek deference, probably because the regulation at stake was not interpreting the statute); *Lawson v. FMR LLC*, 670 F3d 61, 82 (1st Cir. 2012) (stating that the agency was correct in arguing that no deference was warranted); *Oklahoma Natural Gas Co, a Division of ONEOK, Inc v. Federal Energy Regulatory Commission*, 940 F2d 699, 740 (DC Cir. 1991) (saying that an agency correctly did not seek deference for a jurisdictional interpretation, that the Supreme Court had not yet established to warrant deference). For a complete list of cases *see*: Rozansky, 2018, n. 73.

61 *Global Tel*Link*, 866 F3d, p. 408 (stating it "would make no sense for this court to determine whether the disputed agency positions advanced in the Order warrant *Chevron* deference when the agency has abandoned those positions".).

62 Id., p. 416 (Clarification and Amendment of the Majority Opinion).

63 This alternative clearly only applies to notice-and-comment (or informal) rule-making and to formal adjudication because these are the 'easy' and topical cases in which the *Chevron* step zero doctrine warrants an application of *Chevron* (rather than the less deferential *Skidmore*). This is to say that when a 'simple' and not burdensome procedure has been used, there is no reason to go to court and risk an adverse ruling, since it is easier to go through the same 'simple' procedure to repeal the rule. By contrast, when burdensome procedures apply, it is understandable that some agencies might want to roll the dice and ask the court to invalidate the rule. However, this clearly poses a problem of circumvention of APA rules.

2.6 Tiptoeing on the Edge of the Law: The Limited Role of Politics as a Rationale for Policy Shifts

As argued in the introductory note, the regulatory actions following the executive order 13.771, the *Chevron* waiver, statutory abnegation claims and the acts of disapproval under the CRA are problematic. The recourse to the CRA denotes a departure from both an established praxis and from the most basic canons of statutory interpretation. Likewise, when it comes to the *Chevron* waiver, statutory abnegation claims, and compliance with the EO 13.771, there is a clear departure from current laws and doctrines.

As a premise, this chapter shares the view that the agency power "to pursue whatever policy whim rule the day"[64] is problematic. The so-called whim theory was codified by Justice Gorsuch when sitting on the bench of the 11th Circuit Court; it sees the agency power to shift policies at will, and at the expenses of its various stakeholders, as constitutionally problematic. While this theory largely overlooks the fact that policy change usually takes several years,[65] over which agencies go through lengthy administrative procedures, gather data and findings and address comments submitted by stakeholders, it is on point when it comes to deregulatory attempts that bypass such procedures, or major steps thereof.

Building upon recent case law and legal scholarship, this chapter suggests that for a policy change to be successful, agencies cannot bypass the relevant procedures under the governing statute and the APA and cannot do so merely on the basis of political reasons. Obvious as this might seem, in reality it is not, as recent events have shown.

There is no need to linger on the CRA resolutions as they are based on an interpretation that goes against the black letter of the law (particularly the attempt to consider as 'rule' any rule that has not been submitted in the past, including those that would not qualify as 'rule' under the Act). This problem vis-à-vis statutory interpretation is quite self-evident.

More crucially, for purposes of this analysis, one should take the example of the *Chevron* waiver. The FCC litigation strategy runs contrary to administrative law principles and doctrines. In particular, it circumvents APA procedural rules[66] and allows agencies to state reasons anew (contrary to the principle of the so-called closed reasons).[67] It also raises constitutional concerns, "scratching at the heart of the notion of sovereignty under the rule of law",[68] in that it conflates the position of the agency, formally expressed in an order,

---

64 *See, e.g., Gutierrez-Brizuela v. Lynch*, 834 F.3d 1142, 1149-58 (10th Cir. 2016) (Gorsuch, J., concurring), p. 1153.

65 Buzbee, 2018, p. 1371.

66 *See* n. 21 and accompanying text.

67 *Under Securities and Exchange Commission v. Chenery Corporation*, 318 U.S. 80 (1943) (Chenery I), neither the court nor the DOJ lawyers can supply/substitute justifying reasons on behalf of the agency. In this case, the agency lawyer is likely substituting with his or her reasons, the reasons underlying agency action at the time it was taken.

68 Bernstein, 2017.

with the position of agency staff.[69] According to others, it runs roughshod on the separation of powers in that only the judicial and legislative power can decide if an action warrants deference.[70]

Likewise, when it comes to deregulatory actions complying with E0 13.771 and statutory abnegations claims, the problems are multifarious.

Repeals of prior rules must follow the same procedures provided for issuing a new rule. Therefore, if the rule had to undergo the notice-and-comment process under the APA (so-called informal rule-making) its repeal must undergo the very same procedure. The most important rules that Trump tried to undo were the result of informal rule-making. As a consequence, they are subject to hard look review in courts.[71] Hard look review demands that agency decisions must be logically sound, supported by facts and thoroughly considered. Under this test, an action is arbitrary and capricious if: (1) it was not based on a consideration of the relevant factors (*i.e.* considered statutorily impermissible factors or totally failed to consider an important aspect of the problem); and (2) there is a clear error of judgment (since the decision does not match the considerations and is thus logically inconsistent).[72]

Subsequent case law further specifies the circumstances under which an action is to be considered as arbitrary and capricious.

i. First, the requirement of a closed record demands that an action is contrary to APA if the agency 'showed the wrong homework': *i.e.* if there is lack of the relevant record including all material you considered *ex ante* to reach a decision (by contrast, any post hoc rationalization is irrelevant).[73]
ii. Likewise, an action is arbitrary and capricious if the agency did not show homework at all, and there is a failure to disclose the scientific data relied on.[74]
iii. A complete failure to state reasons is also a ground for declaring the rule invalid.[75]

69 Id.

70 Durling & Garrett West, 2019, p. 185.

71 R.M. Levin, 'Hard Look Review, Policy Change, and Fox Television', *U. Miami L. Rev.*, Vol. 65, 2011, pp. 555, 570-573.

72 *Motor Vehicle Mfrs. Ass'n v. State Farm Mut. Auto. Ins. Co.*, 463 U.S. 29, 43 (1983).

73 *Citizens to Preserve Overton Park v. Volpe*, 401 U.S. 402 (1971); *Portland Cement Ass'n v. Ruckelshaus*, 486 F2d 375 (DC Cir. 1973).

74 *United States v. Nova Scotia Food Products Corp.* 568 F.2d 240 (2d Cir. 1977) ("If the failure to notify interested persons of the scientific research upon which the agency was relying actually prevented the presentation of relevant comment, the agency may be held not to have considered all 'the relevant factors' … One cannot ask for comment on a scientific paper without allowing participants to read the paper … To suppress meaningful comment by failure to disclose the basic data relied upon is akin to rejecting comment altogether").

75 Overton Park, 401 U.S. (holding that a rule proposing a route for a six-lane, high-speed expressway was contrary to APA because the court cannot decide whether an action is arbitrary and capricious unless there is a record to assess, and unless the agency clearly states the reasons for reaching a decision).

iv. Another ground for invalidation is the failure to consider the right statutory factors (*e.g.* if you carry out a cost-benefit analysis when prohibited).[76]
v. A failure to consider different claims/approaches to the issue is also fatal to a rule. In this regard, it is all the most relevant that the Supreme Court in reaching its decision in *State Farm* maintained that politics cannot factor into reaching administrative decisions (only technocratic reasons can.)[77]
vi. Finally, a failure to comply with the procedural steps set forth in the APA will make a decision arbitrary and capricious.

The previous list clarifies that actions such as EPA repeal of the CPP would be arbitrary and capricious under the current doctrine of hard look review. The cursory statement according to which EPA lacks an authority that it had asserted in the past, the decision not to address prior findings by EPA concerning the electricity sector nor the reported results of implementing the CPP, the decision to limit public comments, the lack of a thorough assessment of the costs to environment and health caused by the repeal[78] all point to the same direction: the likelihood that under current doctrines the repeal of the rule is arbitrary and capricious. The rule repealing the CPP is indeed vulnerable to legal challenges that pivot on a failure to state reasons, to show data and findings (closed record) to comply with APA procedural rules and to address the agency's previous approach to the issue with a view to justifying its current inadequacy.

Likewise, all regulatory and deregulatory actions taken pursuant to the EO 13.771 that are entered into without addressing material comments, showing scientific evidence, stating reasons, addressing alternative approaches (including the approach of the previous administration) or that factor only political reasons into reaching a decision are likely to breach the APA.

2.7 CONCLUDING REMARKS

The chapter scrutinized the recent attempts on the part of the Trump administration to curb the regulatory state. Some moves seem to run contrary to administrative and constitutional law. Especially problematic is the assertion of a presidential and agency power to get rid of old rules with little constraint. This assertion assumes that one can undo old rules based solely on new political considerations. This is problematic per se, given the Supreme Court position in *State Farm*, according to which politics alone cannot be said

76 *Overton Park*, 401 U.S.; *State Farm* 463 U.S.
77 *State Farm* 463 U.S.
78 Buzbee, 2018, pp. 1387-1388.

to factor into reaching administrative decisions. Yet this is even more troublesome if one considers established administrative law doctrines requiring agencies to scrutinize all the relevant facts and data before issuing a decision, to engage with comments, thoroughly assess previous policies and state the reasons for their inadequacy or the changed circumstances that warrant a repeal of the rule.

What seems to be uncontroversial is that there is no such thing as an unfettered power to undo what has previously been done. Without going so far as to bring up the Constitution (which, yet, seems to be engaged in these practices), an elementary analysis of administrative law warrants the conclusion that Trump is tiptoeing on the edge of legality and that his actions would be precarious if challenged in courts.

3 President Trump's Appointments in Four Keywords

*Paolo Passaglia**

3.1 Introduction

According to Article II, Section 2, Clause 2, of the Constitution (the so-called Appointments Clause), the President of the United States is empowered to appoint a wide range of public officials. Depending on the level of the officials, the appointment process requires either the 'advice and consent' of the Senate or, simply, an individual decision by the President him/herself. Among the officials whom the President is entitled to appoint, the most significant positions within the Executive and the Judiciary are established either by the Constitution or by legislation.[1]

Owing to its scope, the power of appointment is one of the most significant powers to define a president, not only in relation to the immediate impact of his or her policies but also with regard to his or her capacity to influence the public apparatus for decades following the end of his or her mandate. This applies especially to the judicial branch, as Article III, Section 1, of the Constitution protects judges from removal, granting them the power to "hold their offices during good behavior". Therefore, judges appointed by a president can (and generally do) remain in office even for many years, throughout the terms of subsequent presidents.

Of course, the great power allocated to the President in theory may have different practical outcomes, depending on the circumstances and the context in which it is exercised and on how the President decides to act.

With regard to the first two years of President Trump's term, it is fair to state that the political context surrounding the appointments afforded him, at least in theory, significant freedom to choose appointees, because in the 2016 elections, Republicans maintained a

* Full Professor of Comparative Law, University of Pisa. *Pro-tempore* Scientific Coordinator of the Comparative Law Division of the Research Department, Constitutional Court of the Italian Republic.

1 Art. II, Section 2, Clause 2, of the Constitution reads as follows: "[The President] shall nominate, and by and with the Advice and Consent of the Senate, shall appoint Ambassadors, other public Ministers and Consuls, Judges of the Supreme Court, and all other Officers of the United States, whose Appointments are not herein otherwise provided for, and which shall be established by Law: but the Congress may by Law vest the Appointment of such inferior Officers, as they think proper, in the President alone, in the Courts of Law, or in the Heads of Departments."

majority of seats in the Senate (52, reduced to 51 one year later[2]). Indeed, despite the narrowness of their majority, Republicans were able to support presidential nominations and, as a general rule, no compromise with Democrats seemed to be needed, as the House of Representatives too had a Republican majority – and a comfortable one at that, with 241 seats against Democrats' 194.[3]

Such a favourable situation could have provided ample space to design special policies governing the selection of appointees. Actually, however, the power of appointment, as President Trump has exercised it to date, is difficult to analyse in light of a particular policy that the President intended to execute. Unlike President Obama, for example, who committed to the implementation of diversity in the federal administration and judiciary,[4] President Trump has not expressly asserted a particular purpose when making his nominations, but has adopted, rather, as far as an external observer can see, a case-by-case approach.

It is probably this approach that explains why it is extremely hard to identify reference points against which the first few years of Trump's presidency may be analysed. This accords with the approach that was adopted; nevertheless, I must note that the task of even broadly outlining the exercise of the power of appointment turned out to be as ambitious as it was hazardous.

To sketch some features that may be of interest, I will start by listing some keywords that could help to describe some of the most notable aspects of the appointments made over the last two years. In particular, these are: (1) turnover; (2) politics; (3) vacancies; and (4) two-speed nominations.

In the following paragraphs, I will examine these keywords with reference to different sectors of the federal government to which presidential appointments are made.

3.2 Turnover in the Highest Ranks of the Executive Branch

One of the most significant features of the Executive branch in the first two years of Trump's presidency is the high turnover rate in the individuals occupying the roles of advisers and

2 In February 2017, Senator Jeff Sessions, of the Republican Party, resigned. In the elections held in December 2017 in Alabama to replace Senator Sessions, Doug Jones (Democratic Party) was elected.

3 The situation may change in the near future. In fact, after the mid-term elections, Republicans strengthened their majority in the Senate (53 seats), but in the House of Representatives, Democrats gained a majority (235 seats, with 199 seats for Republicans). Therefore, the appointment to federal office could be sometimes considered, as a compromise to ensure that some measures issued by the White House will be passed by the lower chamber.

4 *See* below, para. 4. I analysed President Obama's appointments policy in P. Passaglia 'Change We Can Believe in." The Case of President Obama's Appointments', *in* G.F. Ferrari (Ed.), *The American Presidency after Barack Obama*, The Hague, Eleven, 2018, p. 81 ff. I implicitly refer to this article, and to the bibliographical references that it includes, with regard to many of the issues examined here.

secretaries to the President. The turnover rate became the focus of particular attention from the very first few months of the presidential term, such that several in-depth analyses of the changes were soon conducted. One of the most interesting studies in this vein was presented by the Governance Studies program at the Brookings Institution in January 2018;[5] it was later updated and developed, with a second report published in January 2019.[6] The data on turnover in President Trump's administration referred to in this presentation is drawn mainly from this second report.

A first set of data focuses on the most important members of the Executive Office of the President,[7] identified on the basis of the 'Decision Makers' editions of the National Journal.[8]

There are estimated to be 65 'decision makers' in Trump's administration, slightly more than the average number in previous presidencies since 1981. In fact, the average number of decision makers in the five previous presidencies was 60.6; it was only during the Clinton years that the number (70) exceeded that of Trump's administration today. Two other presidencies were close to Trump's total: Reagan's administration had 60 such positions, and G.W. Bush had 63. There is a significant gap only with the 57 positions in place during G.H.W. Bush's presidency and, in particular, with the 53 positions during Obama's term.

The crucial factor, however, is the turnover rate. In the first two years of Trump's term, 42 positions out of 65 went through turnover, which is equivalent to almost 65%: 22 positions changed hands during the first year (34%) and 20 during the second (31%). During the previous presidencies, the only rate exceeding 40% occurred under Reagan (57%); under all other presidents, there was limited turnover, with rates ranging from 38% (Clinton) to 25% (Obama). The most striking comparison can be drawn with reference to the Presidents' first year, in which turnover is generally very limited: while President Trump

5 *See* K.D. Tenpas, 'Why Is Trump's Staff Turnover Higher than the 5 Most Recent Presidents?', *The Brookings Institution*, 19 January 2018, available at www.brookings.edu/research/why-is-trumps-staff-turnover-higher-than-the-5-most-recent-presidents/.

6 *See* K.D. Tenpas, 'Tracking Turnover in the Trump Administration', *The Brookings Institution*, January 2019, available at www.brookings.edu/research/tracking-turnover-in-the-trump-administration/. The 2018 report considered only the President's most influential staff, whereas the 2019 report also takes Cabinet positions into account.

7 The Executive Office of the President, overseen by the White House Chief of Staff, has had a key role since its establishment in 1939. In fact, many of the President's closest advisers are part of this Office. Senate confirmation is required only for some advisers, whereas most of them are appointed by the President at his own discretion.

8 From 1981 to 2009, the National Journal published these figures during each President's first year. The criteria that were used to select the most influential advisers are explained in 'How the 250 Decision Makers Were Selected', *National Journal*, 16 July 2013, available at https://www.nationaljournal.com/s/75992/how-250-decision-makers-were-selected.

changed more than one-third of his highest advisers, all of the other Presidents changed less than 10% of their appointees to the posts, except for Reagan (17%) and Clinton (11%).

The distance between the practices followed by previous Presidents and that of President Trump is remarkable. This is all the more so if it is considered that 12 of the 42 positions in which change occurred underwent *serial* turnover: over the past two years, the position of Deputy National Security Adviser has been covered by five persons; four persons have exercised the function of Deputy Chief of Staff; and four persons were appointed to the role of Communications Director. Nine other positions underwent two replacements each, and in some cases, the third person had yet to be appointed as of January 2019.

The rate of change occurring at the highest level of the Executive branch is corroborated by the rate of turnover in the Cabinet. President Trump made three changes during his first year in office and ten during the second. Taking the last four presidencies into account, it is easy to see that during their first year, neither Clinton nor G.W. Bush nor Obama made any changes, while during their second year, there was turnover but to a relatively limited extent: six changes were made under Clinton, one under G.W. Bush and four under Obama. As a result, in the space of two years, President Trump made more changes to his Cabinet than did his three predecessors in the entire span of their first terms (Clinton, 12; G.W. Bush, 4; Obama, 9).

The high turnover rate has multiple reasons. With regard to the most influential members of the Executive Office, 17 out of 42 changes (40%) were due to a promotion of the person who held the position, while the other 25 were the result of resignations. Among the resignations, 14 were defined as 'resignations under pressure', although there are no clear criteria to describe when this situation occurs other than "the general sentiment at the time of [the] departure" of the person holding the office.[9] As for turnover in the Cabinet, promotions were the cause in only three out of 13 cases; eight of the ten resignations were defined as having been tendered 'under pressure', and one was an explicit 'protest resignation'.[10]

Every case of departure from office, of course, is the result of specific reasons and circumstances. It is impossible to analyse each case individually, also because of the lack of information required to provide a reliable overview. Considered as a whole, however, the changes that have occurred so far in the Trump administration – especially compared with

9 *See* Tenpas, note 6: "The departure status was difficult to determine in some cases because media reports were often at odds with an individual's claim that they were resigning. In the end, I decided to create the category 'resigned under pressure', which I believe captures the general sentiment at the time of their departure."

10 Indeed, the resignation of the Secretary of Defense, Jim Mattis, can be considered an explicit 'protest resignation' because of his resignation letter tendered to President Trump on 20 December 2018, in which the retired general objected to the United States' withdrawal from Syria and criticized the President's attitude towards the NATO and the country's traditional allies.

the practice followed by previous Presidents – appear to show a clear innovation that can be explained, in part, by the high number of outsiders to traditional political membership and careers appointed. However, the main reason that may underlie the turnover rate is probably related to the concentration of executive power in the hands of the President, who tends to act as a true 'Commander-in-Chief', such that his advisers and secretaries are subject to a sort of accountability based on their alignment to the President's policies. The second part of the presidential term will clarify whether this is an ongoing attitude or whether it is a feature to be linked to President Trump's atypical entry into politics, which made a period of adjustment necessary to strengthen the stability of his staff.

3.3 The Weight of Politics in Ambassadorial Appointments

The ambassadors of the United States are nominated by the President, and their appointment must be confirmed by the Senate.

To date, President Trump has appointed a significant number of ambassadors. The updated list as of 25 January 2019 includes 102 appointments and 25 nominations that are awaiting confirmation by the Senate. Five other nominations were returned to the White House on 3 January 2019, whereas three nominations made in 2018 were withdrawn.[11]

Taking into account the number of appointments alone, President Trump's pace of appointment (51 per year) is roughly equal to that of his predecessors: President Obama appointed 416 ambassadors in eight years (52 per year),[12] President Clinton appointed 417 (52.125),[13] President Reagan appointed 420 (52.5),[14] and President Carter appointed 202, albeit in four years (51).[15] Only President G.W. Bush, who made 460 appointments in eight years (57.5),[16] and President G.H.W. Bush, who made 214 appointments in four years (53.5),[17] present a significantly higher rate. Of course, the 25 pending nominations may change this analysis, to the point that President Trump's term may eventually be characterized by an even more pronounced degree of activism in choosing ambassadors than his immediate Republican predecessors.

In any case, the total number of ambassadorial appointments does not appear to be a distinguishing feature of President Trump's policy. However, a point that certainly deserves

11 The full list is available on the website of the American Foreign Service Association http://www.afsa.org/appointments-donald-j-trump. The data referred to in the text is the result of a reprocessing based on the table available on the website.

12 *See* http://www.afsa.org/appointments-barack-obama.

13 *See* http://www.afsa.org/appointments-william-j-clinton.

14 *See* http://www.afsa.org/appointments-ronald-reagan.

15 *See* http://www.afsa.org/appointments-jimmy-carter.

16 *See* http://www.afsa.org/appointments-george-w-bush.

17 *See* http://www.afsa.org/appointments-george-h-w-bush.

special mention, which does appear to characterize the current presidency, is the high rate of political appointments. The choice between appointing a career diplomat or an outsider falls within the President's margin of discretion. In the last 40 years, however, most ambassadors were chosen from among diplomats. Even if Democratic presidents appeared to be slightly more willing to value career experience than Republicans, the general trend was to reserve no more than one-third of appointments for political choices: the most 'diplomat-oriented' President was Carter, only 26.24% of whose ambassadorial appointments were selected on a political basis; President Clinton's rate was 28.06%, President Obama's 30.05%, President G.H.W. Bush's 31.3% and President G.W. Bush's 31.8%. Only President Reagan, probably the least 'conventional' president of those considered here, gave greater consideration to political choices, which constituted 37.6% of his total appointments. President Trump's choices are in the same vein of President Reagan's and go even further, as 42 of his 102 appointed ambassadors (41.18%) were not chosen from the diplomatic corps. Therefore, today, political selection bears unprecedented weight. In this regard, if one takes the 25 pending nominations into consideration, the weight of politics gains additional momentum, as only one-fifth of these nominees are diplomats. Assuming that all 25 nominations will be confirmed, 62 of the 127 ambassadors appointed by Trump would not be career diplomats, a rate (48.82%) that is almost equal to the more traditional way of selecting representatives of the US abroad. This data seems to confirm the unconventionality of President Trump's choices and may suggest a link with the idea of an executive apparatus that tends to be oriented, more than in the past, towards an administration that strengthens personal links instead of most neutral forms of selecting officers.

3.4 A Huge Number of Vacancies

The President of the United States has yet to appoint a large number of federal officers, both to the Executive branch and to the Judiciary.

The number of appointments is relatively standardized, partly owing to the spoils system that characterizes the Executive branch. When it comes to the Judiciary, however, the number of vacancies changes depending on the circumstances and, in particular, on judges' retirement. Indeed, as noted in the Introduction, judges are appointed without time limits on their term in office and remain in office 'during good behaviour'.

President Trump, at the beginning of his term, had a significant number of vacancies to fill, not only in the Executive branch, but also in the Judiciary. Filling all of the vacancies is a difficult task that obviously requires time; indeed, two years later, this work is still in progress.

In this section, I will address the issue of the appointment of executive officers, while the next section will deal with judicial appointments from a general point of view, without neglecting, however, the noteworthy issue of the pace at which vacancies are filled.

The *Washington Post* newspaper, together with *Partnership for Public Service*, a nonprofit, nonpartisan organization founded in 2001,[18] is tracking the confirmation process of 707 key Executive branch nominations. This constitutes a significant proportion of the approximately 1,200 positions that require Senate confirmation.[19]

As at 11 February 2019 the number of nominations confirmed by the Senate amounted to 431, approximately three-fifths of the 707 key positions (60.96%), while 127 nominations were still to be confirmed (17.96%). For six other positions, the name of the nominee had been announced (0.85%), but the nomination had yet to be officially made. 143 vacancies were still to be filled, which means that one-fifth (20.23%) of key executive positions were not occupied at the middle of President Trump's term.

The situation changes depending on the department taken into account. Eighty-three percent of the key positions in the Department of Veterans Affairs are filled, and 78% of those in the Department of Energy. However, in the latter case, the remaining positions were occupied by nominees awaiting confirmation. In three further departments, individuals had been appointed to over 70% of the key positions: Health and Human Services, 76%; Defence, 75%; and Commerce, 71%. On the other hand, less than 50% of key positions were filled in three departments: Labour, 43%; Justice, 41%; and Interior, 41%.

Among the positions for which not even an announcement of a nomination was made, the most important was the Secretary of Defense, after Jim Mattis' resignation. Two other first-rank nominations had only been announced, namely Heather Nauert, as United States Representative to the United Nations,[20] and David Bernhardt, as Secretary of the Interior.[21] For two further positions, Senate confirmation was pending: William P. Barr, as Attorney General,[22] and Andrew Wheeler, as Administrator of the Environmental Protection Agency.[23]

---

18 *See* the organization's website: https://ourpublicservice.org.

19 "These positions include Cabinet secretaries, deputy and assistant secretaries, chief financial officers, general counsel, heads of agencies, ambassadors and other critical leadership positions." *See* 'PowerPost. Tracking How Many Key Positions Trump Has Filled So Far', *The Washington Post*, 11 February at 9:39 a.m., available at www.washingtonpost.com/graphics/politics/trump-administration-appointee-tracker/database/?utm_term=.f9139aa96f61.

20 The nomination was announced on 7 December 2018 and awaited referral to the Foreign Relations Committee.

21 The nomination, announced on 4 February 2019, awaited referral to the Energy and Natural Resources Committee.

22 His appointment was announced on 7 December 2018. On 7 February 2019, the Judiciary Committee of the Senate reported favourably.

23 His appointment was announced on 16 November 2018, but only on 5 February 2019 did the Environment and Public Works report favourably.

The number and significance of the vacancies cannot be neglected, as they are likely to affect the effectiveness of the Executive's policies in some way: as other chapters will explore this issue, I will simply mention it briefly. As far as the appointments policy is concerned, what deserves particular attention is the length of time required to fill vacancies, a length that could be observed from the very first days of President Trump's term. With regard to the confirmation of his initial Cabinet nominees, an interesting comparison may be carried out between President Trump and his three most recent predecessors.[24]

The last four Presidents all began their first term succeeding a president of the opposite party, such that the need to make staff changes could be considered to exist on an equal footing. Moreover, all four Presidents could count on a majority of senators of their own party, although in all four cases this was an absolute majority that did not reach the threshold of 60 senators. The only major difference in this regard consists in the 'nuclear option'. To overcome filibustering in the advice and consent process, on 21 November 2013, the Senate's Democratic majority adopted a reinterpretation of U.S. Senate Rule XXII, according to which the Senate was allowed to pass a cloture motion with a simple majority of those voting, instead of with three-fifths of the members of the Senate.[25] The new interpretation also applied to the confirmation of Cabinet nominees, such that, in principle, President Trump had a clear advantage compared with his predecessors: in 2017, Republicans had a highly effective tool to overcome Democrats' filibustering, even though their majority did not reach 60 senators.

This advantage notwithstanding, only two Cabinet nominees were confirmed on President Trump's Inauguration Day, one less than those of President Clinton, and far from the confirmations made under President Obama (6) and President G.W. Bush (7).

The existence of early troubles was confirmed by the protracted confirmation process. President G.W. Bush filled his Cabinet on 30 January 2001; however, controversies over his election prevented him from announcing members of the Cabinet before mid-December. All but one of President Clinton's Cabinet members were confirmed in two days; therefore, it was only because of problems arising from the choice of Attorney General that his Cabinet was filled only on 11 March, 1993. President Obama certainly faced greater difficulties, in particular with the nomination of the Secretary of Commerce: after a withdrawal operated by President Obama before his Inauguration Day, the withdrawal of his

24 The analysis was conducted by K. Schaul & K. Uhrmacher, 'Trump's Wait for His Major Cabinet Picks Was Nearly the Longest in 30 Years', *The Washington Post*, 27 April 2017, available at www.washingtonpost.com/graphics/politics/how-long-confirmations-will-take/?tid=graphics-story, who also took into account the G.H.W. Bush presidency. I will not do so because of its peculiarities: on the one hand, President Bush Sr. succeeded a member of his own party and became President after having acted as Vice President, so that he could take advantage of his previous eight-year experience; on the other hand, the advantages in terms of his ability to select nominees were essentially balanced by the Democrat majority in the Senate and the resulting difficulties in obtaining some confirmations.

25 On the nuclear option, *see also* below, para. 4.

second candidate made it necessary to find a third choice, who was confirmed only in late March. Another withdrawal, by the person nominated to the position of Secretary of Health and Human Services, delayed the confirmation of the final nominee until 28 April 2009.

Completing the Cabinet took only one day less for President Trump than for President Obama. Early announcements of the nominees and the possibility to use the 'nuclear option' notwithstanding, the confirmation process was delayed by Democrats, but also by problems in collecting the paperwork concerning the business interests of certain nominees. Moreover, President Trump waited until March to submit to the Senate his nomination to the position of Secretary of Agriculture. This nomination was confirmed on 25 April 2017, while his first nomination for the post of Secretary of Labor was withdrawn, and the second nomination was confirmed on April 27.

Among the reasons that may explain the long time required to fill the Cabinet, the most interesting is probably that concerning the average waiting time between the nomination and the Senate's vote or withdrawal. Previous Presidents waited no more than two days (President Obama) or even less (President Clinton, 1; President Bush, 0), whereas President Trump had to wait 25 days on average: certainly, a remarkable amount of time.[26]

This remark leads us to focus on the advice and consent process, which, of course, plays a crucial role in the President's appointments policy, especially with regard to judicial appointments,[27] the subject of the next section.

3.5 Judicial Appointments and the Policy of Two-Speed Nominations

The data regarding vacancies in the federal judiciary at the beginning of a presidency shows that, in the long term, an 'increasing' trend may be identified. At the beginning of President Reagan's term, the number of vacancies was 38. These grew to 43 (+13.2%) at the beginning of President G.H.W. Bush's term. The increasing trend gained tremendous momentum during this term, culminating in as many as 109 vacancies (+153.5%) at the beginning of Clinton's presidency. During Clinton's presidency, the figure decreased slightly, so that President G.W. Bush had 92 initial vacancies to fill (–15.6%). His activism in making appointments produced a remarkable fall in the number of offices to be filled at the beginning of President Obama's first term: 59 (–35.9%).[28]

26 The data is even more significant if compared with the time needed for nominations by President G.H.W. Bush to be confirmed: even though he had to face a Democrat majority in the Senate, his median wait was approximately half of that of President Trump (13 days).

27 On this subject, *see* J. Sample, 'The Agnostic's Guide to Judicial Selection', *DePaul L. Rev.*, Vol. 67, 2018, p. 219.

28 This data was collected comparing the number of vacancies at the beginning of February of the relevant years, as provided by the Federal Judiciary on the U.S. Courts website, in the "Archive of Judicial Vacancies" section: www.uscourts.gov/judges-judgeships/judicial-vacancies/archive-judicial-vacancies (accessed

During President Obama's years, the number of vacancies swelled dramatically (by 98.3%), mainly because of the Republican Senate majority's tenacious opposition in the last two years of his presidency. As a result, at the beginning of his term, President Trump had 117 vacancies to fill, which constituted more than one-eighth (13.1%) of all 890 federal judge offices.

With a Republican majority in the Senate, circumstances were extremely favourable for strengthening the proportion of conservative judges within the federal judiciary and to ensure long-standing influence in several circuits and districts.

Certainly aware that "[t]he judges a president appoints may be his most important legacy," given that "[j]udges serve long after the appointing president leaves office",[29] thanks to the activism of Senator Mitch McConnell, the Majority Leader in the Senate, President Trump was able, in two years, to appoint as many as 85 federal judges. The overall number is interesting in itself, as it shows that the pace of President Trump's appointments was slightly higher than that of President Obama (42.5 appointments per year versus 41.75) and equal to that of President G.W. Bush. To find better 'performances', one must go back to President Clinton (48.38) or to President G.H.W. Bush (49.25), not to mention President Reagan (50.25).

The real reason why this data is interesting, however, appears only after 'dividing' (*a*) from one another the two years and (*b*) the categories of judges that were appointed, because on both sides of this 'partition', a sort of two-speed nomination policy may be identified.

(*a*) The pace of appointment changed significantly between the first and second years of President Trump's term: in 2017, 19 judges were appointed, while in 2018 the appointees were 66 (+247.4%), well beyond the average number of 56 appointments made during the second year of presidency of Trump's predecessors. This rate becomes even more remarkable if it is considered that the Democrats in the Senate struggled to delay confirmations as long as possible, to the point that a cloture motion was needed to confirm President Trump's nominations in 46 cases. In previous presidencies, in the first two years, confirmations rarely prompted a cloture vote: on two occasions in President Obama's years, on three during G.W. Bush's presidency and on one during the Clinton years, while no cloture vote was recorded in the first years of the mandates of Presidents G.H.W. Bush and Reagan.[30]

---

14 February 2019). On judicial vacancies at the beginning of President Trump's term, *see* J. Marion, 'So Many Seats to Fill: The Future of the Federal Judiciary', *San Francisco Attorney*, Vol. 43, 2017, p. 36.

29 *See* T. Jipping, 'A New Way of Tracking Trump's Judicial Nominees', *The Heritage Foundation*, 13 November 2018, available at www.heritage.org/courts/commentary/new-way-tracking-trumps-judicial-nominees.

30 Id.

The dramatic increase in the number of cloture votes is certainly the result of the greater ease of using the nuclear option.

As can be observed for all of the other presidents considered, harsh confrontations between the majority and the opposition in the Senate during the advice and consent process also took place during the first two years of Trump's presidency. And, as in the past, while senatorial opposition resorted to filibustering, the majority sought to contain time-wasting as much as possible, so as to obtain the expected result and also, possibly, speed up the appointment process.

Since President Obama's mandate, the frequency of cloture motions has become a key element of the entire confirmation process: to clear the hurdle of the vigorous filibustering conducted against President Trump's nominations, the Republicans were increasingly compelled to end the debate by using a 'clean-cutting' measure. The use of these motions was greatly facilitated, compared with the past, because the interpretation of U.S. Senate Rule XXII, Paragraph 2, underwent a major change. According to this rule, in order to pass a cloture motion, the question "Is it the sense of the Senate that the debate shall be brought to a close?" "shall be decided in the affirmative by three-fifths of the Senators duly chosen and sworn – except on a measure or motion to amend the Senate rules, in which case the necessary affirmative vote shall be two-thirds of the Senators present and voting". To end the debate and stop filibustering, the support of 60 senators is required to pass the motion.[31]

On 21 November 2013, the Democratic majority in the Senate adopted a reinterpretation of the rule with specific regard to the advice and consent process concerning both executive and judicial appointments, with the sole exception of nominations to the U.S. Supreme Court, the process for which was left unaltered. The new interpretation allowed the Senate to pass a cloture motion with a simple majority of those voting, instead of three-fifths of the members of the Senate.[32] The impact of this interpretation is clearly demonstrated by its definition as the 'nuclear' option.

In the last two years, therefore, the advice and consent process was characterized by frequent implementation of the 2013 innovation; actually, the innovation even expanded its scope, with the removal of the sole exception that remained in the confirmation process. The sudden death of Justice Antonin Scalia, on 13 February 2016, had triggered a harsh confrontation between President Obama and the Republican majority in the Senate, a

31 In a two-party system, this 'supermajority' cannot be gained easily: in fact, the last Congress during which a party obtained at least 60 seats in the Senate was the 95th (19771979). In recent years, only the 111th Congress (2009-2011) was close to producing a supermajority in the Senate: Democrats had 57 seats and Republicans 41; the two remaining seats were occupied by independents both caucusing with the Democrats.

32 The power to override the written rule was based on an opinion written by Richard Nixon in 1957 (when acting as vice president and therefore as President of the Senate), according to which the Senate had the power to make a ruling that derogated from the Rules and thus establish a new, different practice.

confrontation that led to a deadlock in which Obama's nominee, Judge Merrick Garland, was never even given a Senate hearing. When President Trump took office, he soon announced (on 30 January 2017) the nomination of Neil Gorsuch. As a reaction to the Republicans' attitude towards President Obama's nominee, the Democrats strongly opposed President Trump's nomination and filibustered the advice and consent process. To overcome the Democrats' opposition, Republicans invoked the need to extend the nuclear option also to nominations to the U.S. Supreme Court and, on 6 April 2017, this extended method was actually used to pass a cloture motion. The next day, Neil Gorsuch was confirmed with 54 votes against 45.[33] The extension of the nuclear option was reiterated on 5 October 2018, for the confirmation of the second Supreme Court Justice appointed by President Trump, Brett Kavanaugh. The criticism levelled against Kavanaugh, especially concerning sexual assault allegations, had led Democrats to a fierce opposition.[34]

The use of the nuclear option certainly had a major effect on the advice and consent process for Supreme Court nominees. More generally, however, it is fair to state that this procedural means greatly contributed to a particularly high rate of confirmations of judicial nominations, especially in 2018, when the pace of confirmation was so fast that it could be defined as 'historic'.[35]

(*b*) Some remarks can also be made with regard to the categories of judges that President Trump has appointed to date.

The double appointment to the Supreme Court has already been mentioned earlier. It is noteworthy that, in only two years, President Trump was able to appoint the same number of Justices that Presidents Obama, G.W. Bush and Clinton appointed in eight years and President G.H.W. Bush appointed in four years. Since President Kennedy's term, only President Reagan (three appointments) and President Nixon (four appointments) had a greater impact on the Supreme Court's composition.

Of course, the choice of new justices particularly captures the attention of observers. Nevertheless, the impact on case law of appointments to circuit courts is far from negligible, especially taking into account the firm case selection policy carried out by the Supreme Court. In this regard, President Trump appointed 12 circuit judges in 2017 and 18 in 2018, which means that in the space of a mid-term, the rate of circuit judges chosen was

---

33 On the appointment of Justice Gorsuch, *see* M. Goldhaber, 'American Presidency: The Conundrum of Justice Gorsuch's Supreme Court Appointment', *IBA Global Insight*, June/July 2017, p. 13 ff.

34 With regard to the appointment of Justice Kavanaugh, *see* P.J. Aschenbrenner, 'United States of America: Nomination of DC Circuit Judge Brett Kavanaugh to the United States Supreme Court Ignites Public Firestorm over Allegations of Sexual Misconduct, Alcohol-Fuelled Misbehaviour and Lack of Judicial Temperament – Nominee Brutally Describes Senate Judiciary Proceedings: "This Is a Circus"', *Public Law*, January 2019, p. 220 ff.

35 *See* C. Johnson, 'Trump's Judicial Appointments Were Confirmed at Historic Pace in 2018', *National Public Radio*, 2 January 2019, available at www.npr.org/2019/01/02/681208228/trumps-judicial-appointments-were-confirmed-at-historic-pace-in-2018?t=1550148178005.

approximately half of the total number of appointments made in eight-year presidencies by Obama (58), G.W. Bush (72) and Clinton (73); and it was not far from the total number of appointments made in G.H.W. Bush's four-year presidency (44). Two years were sufficient to appoint one-sixth of the total number of circuit judges (179), not to mention that, in January 2019, there were still 12 remaining vacancies, such that President Trump's 'score' is likely to increase considerably this year: as a matter of fact, nine circuit judges were nominated on 23 January 2019, and three further judges were nominated on February 6.

The special attention that the current Administration pays to filling circuit courts is certainly due to the impact that these courts can have on case law, such that an enduring legacy can be ensured, in particular by appointing relatively young judges, who are likely to serve for a long time.[36]

Considering the appointments made so far, it is indisputable that President Trump focused on appellate judges. The number of district judges is, in fact, relatively low. In 2017, only six judges were nominated, while in 2018 the number of appointments reached 47. On the whole, 53 appointments in two years (27.5 per year) are well below the annual rate of previous Presidents: President Obama appointed 270 district judges (33.7 per year), President G.W. Bush 264 (33 per year), President Clinton 307 (38.4 per year) and President G.H.W. Bush 150, in four years (37.5 per year). Probably, once the circuit courts have been filled, President Trump will begin to focus on district courts. And, in this regard, he will have great opportunities for activism, given that at the beginning of 2019 there were 119 vacancies to fill, namely more than one-sixth of the 677 judges (17.6%). For this purpose, a significant number of nominations were made in the initial weeks of 2019: six on 17 January, 37 on 23 January and four on 6 February, such that in the following weeks the Senate had to confirm 47 district judge nominees.

The deep impact on the federal judiciary that President Trump's appointments have already had, which is even more significant if the choices that are yet to be made are considered, has given rise to analyses of the type of appointees selected over the past two years. In this respect, observers have expressed criticism, especially with regard to diversity. The most prominent feature of President Obama's appointment policy was, most likely, his commitment to diversity,[37] a commitment that produced significant changes in general

36 *See* C. Johnson & R. Klahr, 'Trump Is Reshaping the Judiciary. A Breakdown by Race, Gender and Qualification', *National Public Radio*, 15 November 2018, available at www.npr.org/2018/11/15/667483587/trump-is-reshaping-the-judiciary-a-breakdown-by-race-gender-and-qualification.

37 The attention paid to diversity and its implementation was defined as a key aspect of President Obama's administrative action, aimed at strengthening civil rights (in this regard, on the White House's website, the presentation of the 'Empowerment through Diversity' initiative was extremely revealing; the presentation, once at page www.whitehouse.gov/issues/civil-rights/empowerment, last accessed November 2016, is no longer available).

attitudes towards minorities compared with his predecessors' practices. In fact, surveys agreed on defining Obama's administration as the most diverse in American history.[38]

On the contrary, President Trump's policy has been, to date, characterized by a non-negligible reduction of diversity.[39] In terms of gender, President Obama's nominations featured a strong injection of women into the judiciary (42.3% of all nominations), whereas women count for only 22.4% of President Trump's nominees,[40] a proportion that, in any event, is higher than that of previous Republican presidents.[41] A comparison between the last two Presidents shows that Trump tends to select slightly younger judges: the average age at the time of nomination was 51 years for Obama, as against 50 years for Trump.

As for race, almost four-fifths of President Trump's nominees are white (78.9%), a rate that is much higher than that which characterized President Obama's years (63.0%). If appointments of Asian Americans have seen a minimal increase (6.8% for President Trump, 6.6% for President Obama), the rate of African Americans and Hispanics has fallen to 2.5%, while the rates of nominations by President Obama were 18.6% of African Americans and 9.2% of Hispanics.

Some critics have expressed concerns about some of Trump's appointees, at times because of doubts as to their qualifications. Among President Trump's nominees, 55.9% were rated 'well qualified' by the Standing Committee on the Federal Judiciary of the American Bar Association,[42] and 29.8% were rated 'qualified', which means that almost 85% of nominations were well received; actually, only 3.7% were considered 'not qualified'.[43] The good performance of these candidates does not reach, however, that of President Obama's choices, which were better received, as 64.0% were rated 'well qualified' and 36.0% 'qualified'.

---

38 *See* A.J. O'Connell, 'Obama Ups Diversity in Appointees', *UC Berkeley Law/The Washington Post*, 20 September 2015, available at www.washingtonpost.com/politics/obama-ups-diversity-in-appointees/2015/09/20/5b042aac-5ffb-11e5-8e9e-dce8a2a2a679_graphic.html (accessed 14 February 2019).

39 *See* R. Solberg & E.N. Waltenburg, 'Trump's Presidency Marks the First Time in 24 Years that the Federal Bench Is Becoming Less Diverse', *The Conversation*, 11 June 2018, available at https://theconversation.com/trumps-presidency-marks-the-first-time-in-24-years-that-the-federal-bench-is-becoming-less-diverse-97663.

40 Data was provided by Johnson and Klahr, note 36. The article was published in November 2018, but the tables have been updated to 5 February 2019: *see* https://docs.google.com/spreadsheets/d/1O0ZUP-Kogqk1PMoJn50_gdbdBwyj54i-RqHUDFQ7Z5E8/edit#gid=1242775320.

41 *See* J. Gramlich, 'Trump Has Appointed a Larger Share of Female Judges than Other GOP Presidents, but Lags Obama", *Pew Research Center*, 2 October 2018, available at http://www.pewresearch.org/fact-tank/2018/10/02/trump-has-appointed-a-larger-share-of-female-judges-than-other-gop-presidents-but-lags-obama/.

42 The 'well-qualified' candidates include both of the Associate Justices appointed to the Supreme Court.

43 On 5 February 2019, 10.6% of nominees were not rated. The complete list of the American Bar Association's ratings is available at https://www.americanbar.org/content/dam/aba/uncategorized/GAO/Web%20rating%20Chart%20Trump%20115.pdf (115th Congress) and at https://www.americanbar.org/content/dam/aba/uncategorized/GAO/WebratingChartTrump116.pdf (116th Congress; 14 February 2019).

Nonetheless, the most controversial issue was not related to qualification, but rather to the political orientation of President Trump's appointees, who were generally described by critics as 'hard-right' judges,[44] most of them being members of the Federalist Society[45] and 'anti-choice, anti-union, anti-immigrant and pro-gun'.[46]

It is probably too soon to try any assessment of President Trump's choices, as the attitude of any judge, irrespective of his or her political orientation, can be analysed only by reading his or her judgments. In any case, the *stare decisis* rule appears to be an efficient guarantee of stability in the case law on the majority of the most debated issues.

3.6 CONCLUSION

I began this chapter by noting that it is difficult to identify a policy behind President Trump's appointments. The different topics that were discussed briefly appear to confirm this idea, because of the wide variety of outcomes in the choice of federal officers. Activism in certain fields and periods (in particular, the appointments of superior courts' judges and the judicial appointments made in 2018) act as a counterweight to a significant proportion of the vacancies yet to be filled in other sectors of the Judiciary and of the Executive. The selection of qualified or even well-qualified judges may be a counterpoint to the frequent appointments of 'outsiders' as ambassadors. The search for stability in courts' membership, thanks to appointments of relatively young judges, must be compared with the high rate of turnover in the Executive.

The next two years will certainly help to find longer-term trends in the appointments policy and, with particular regard to the Judiciary, will allow for objective assessment of the personal choices made by the President. For the moment, it is wisest to wait and see, trying to verify, on the basis of the future nominations, whether the concerns expressed by critics will be confirmed or refuted. Waiting for the moment when the American people,

---

44 *See* S.A. Scheindlin, 'Trump's Hard-Right Judges Will Do Lasting Damage to America', *The Guardian*, 31 May 2018, available at https://www.theguardian.com/commentisfree/2018/may/30/trump-judge-appointments-roe-v-wade-courts.

45 A report by Lambda Legal estimates that 85% of appointed judges are members of the Federalist Society, which is supposed to have been 'vocal about their desire to "pack the courts" with conservative judges to undo, what they call, the "Judicial Legacy of Barack Obama"': *see Trump's Judicial Assault on LGBT Rights, Lambda Legal*, 28 December 2018, available at www.lambdalegal.org/sites/default/files/publications/downloads/2018_eoy_judicial_report.pdf, p. 4. Also, J. Zengerle, 'How the Trump Administration Is Remaking the Courts', *The New York Times Magazine*, 22 August 2018, available at www.nytimes.com/2018/08/22/magazine/trump-remaking-courts-judiciary.html, admits that "[t]he Federalist Society for Law and Public Policy Studies, as it is officially known, has played a crucial role in putting conservative jurists on the bench".

46 *See* Scheindlin, note 44.

in less than two years, will have to judge its President and the Senate majority by his side so far.

4 PRESIDENT TRUMP'S POLITICAL AGENDA VIS-À-VIS THE SUPREME COURT

*Roberto Toniatti**

4.1 INTRODUCTION

The political agenda of President Trump – after the first two years of his Presidency – faithfully reflects the political agenda of Donald Trump as the Republican party's presidential candidate during the 2016 electoral campaign. In fact, many provocative statements of his as well as a radically innovative platform that had raised wide support by and among the populist segments of the voting population simply turned into presidential policies without any substantial change.

The evident continuity between the intensely ideological commitments and promises of the campaign – first, within the Republican party and, later, during the fight against the candidate of the Democratic party – and the subsequent presidential agenda emphasize the high degree of sharp polarization achieved by the political conflict in the United States. In fact, Trumpism departs even from traditional orientations of the Republican party itself and marks an unbalanced (and, to some extent, unexpected) outcome of political developments in the United States.[1]

The process of enhancement of the ideological division – it must be said – did not originally start with Trumpism. That ideological division extends beyond party politics and, at this stage, it affects society as a whole. However, Trumpism seems to be making it more visible and vitriolic: the traditional turn to a balanced mainstream domestic policy-

---

* Professor of Comparative Constitutional Law, Trento University.

1 On Trump, Trumpism and the Republican party *see* P. Wehner, 'What I've Gained by Leaving the Republican Party', *The Atlantic*, 6 February 2019, who explains his reasons for stepping out of the GOP and writes: "Today I see the Republican Party through the clarifying prism of Donald Trump, who consistently appealed to the ugliest instincts and attitudes of the GOP base"; and "I certainly don't have problems with those who decide to stay in a party in order to improve it. [...]. If the GOP were to embrace a humane, aspirational conservatism – one that seeks to defend truth rather than to deconstruct it – I would certainly be open to returning to the fold. But whether I ever do or not, what troubles me in the here and now are those who, having decided to stay in the Republican Party, are allowing that affiliation to seriously impair their moral judgments and intellectual standards; to lead them to enable those in power to do grave damage to our civic and political culture; and to encourage them to protect a Republican president for acting in ways that they would condemn in any Democratic president", available at www.theatlantic.com/ideas/archive/2019/02/i-left-gop-because-trump/581965/.

making normally practised by older-time Presidents after taking office has quite vanished, and the President appears today to choose not to act as the leader of the whole nation but, rather, to deliberately behave as the head of one faction of the population permanently against some other factions. Foreign and security policies tend to follow the same pattern of an aggressive discontinuity with the past, recent and less recent.

The contribution made by President Trump to further increasing the systemic ultra-polarization beyond the traditional cleavages may carry with it a heavy institutional cost: an excess of extremist policy attitudes may make the Presidency vulnerable and weaker and facilitate the trap of divided government, which is a permanent challenge in a dualist form of government. The constitutionally mandated mid-term elections are a significant indicator of the continuing support enjoyed by a President, and the electoral loss of a Republican majority in the House of Representatives experienced in November 2018 might suggest that more divided government is to come in the years ahead (in case of a re-election of Trump in 2020). Of course, the federal government working under the lame duck pattern is not exclusive of the current presidency, President Obama having experienced it to a very large extent. The only exception is, in fact, the period of two years after his first election. Nevertheless, it is an open question whether an extremely ideological presidency will be able to maintain citizens' and consequently congressional support for presidential policies, even from within the President's own party.

In other words, the twofold alternative hypothesis must be taken into account that Trumpism is only a temporary disease that will find its appropriate therapy and eventually – sooner or later – disappear or, rather, that it is *the* symptom of the change of a dominant cultural paradigm that may be there to last and shape an era. Furthermore, an open question concerns also the interpretation of Trumpism: is it an unexpected phenomenon belonging exclusively to the United States, or is it part of a wider network of populist leaders who are here to shape a new radically conservative worldview for the near future?

The response given by the judiciary to cases and controversies that are especially representative of Trump's public policies and set of public values may be able to reflect, at least in this short period, the resilience of mainstream constitutional paradigms of the United States – that even as foreign scholars we have grown accustomed to know, appreciate and make our own. Thus, an analysis of the case law that originated during the first two years of Trump's presidency may prove to be usefully indicative of further processes to come, stepping into one of the two alternative tracks indicated earlier.

At this stage, it is appropriate to highlight how President Trump's priorities – which transform his ideological commitments into federal official public actions – have been confronted by a fairly active judicial activity: among the substantive areas that proved to be open to almost immediate judicial challenge – by individuals, member states, organized interests directly affected and public interest non-governmental organizations[2] – immigration policy is certainly to be listed as the main field of collision, followed by the Trump Administration's interference with civil rights, with particular concern for the rights of the lesbian, gay, bisexual, transgender and intersex (LGBTI) community.

It is too early for an assessment of whether lower federal courts' response against presidential policies are to be properly qualified as *judicial activism*, with the implication that the judiciary is to be seen as engaged in a sort of judicial resistance not only to individual legislative and administrative initiatives by the Trump Administration but also as a form of thoroughly ideological opposition to Trumpism.

And it is too early also for an assessment of the interaction between Trump's policies, response by lower federal courts and the Supreme Court, both in general terms and also with specific regard to the effects on the Court's judgments of the two recent presidential appointments, considering the short time since Associate Justices Neil McGill Gorsuch and Brett Michael Kavanaugh took office (respectively, on 10 April 2017 and 6 October 2018). In fact, not all judicial cases started at the lower levels of the federal Judiciary have yet reached the Supreme Court.

Such an assessment may still rely on two possible interpretations: (i) the Supreme Court is reflecting the ideological polarization of the system, as evidenced by a set of 5-4 decisions, such a condition being likely to be overcome by the inevitable impact of more appointments to the Court of justices selected by Trump and his majority in the Senate; (ii) the Supreme Court is somehow mediating between a reactive or activist federal lower judiciary and its own institutional option in favour of a more balanced selection of cases when supporting presidential policy options.

At the moment, the first of the foregoing alternative interpretations appears to be winning, although indications supporting the second are not totally missing. Such an uncertain early evaluation is somehow sensitive to the circumstance that – more than any other members of the Judiciary – Justices of the Supreme Court are inclined to think of themselves in terms of the historical record they individually leave on the quality of the Court's jurisprudence rather than accepting the quite diminishing role of 'the President's Justices'. Such circumstance has recently crept into the public debate, when in response to President Trump's qualification of a federal judge as an 'Obama judge', Chief Justice Roberts (normally in the conservative majority) reacted by stating that

> We do not have Obama judges or Trump judges, Bush judges or Clinton judges […]What we have is an extraordinary group of dedicated judges doing their

2 A visit to the website of the American Civil Liberties Union (ACLU) is paradigmatic, available at www.aclu.org/.

level best to do equal right to those appearing before them [...] The independent judiciary is something we should all be thankful for.[3]

4.2 The Main Areas of Judicial Challenges to President Trump's Political Agenda

The substantive areas to be considered in more detail, as indicated earlier, are immigration policies and civil rights. While the latter is represented in particular by one topic, namely the admission of transgender personnel in the Armed Forces, within the wide field of immigration some main issues are to be singled out, the travel ban, the inclusion of a question on citizenship in the 2020 Census, the proclamation of a national emergency aimed at the construction of a wall at the national border with Mexico in spite of congressional denial of ad hoc funds, the recognition of the Special Status of Immigration Juveniles and the DACA Program.

4.2.1 *Immigration Policy: The 'Travel Ban Case'*

One of the very first presidential actions – taken during the first week in office – was the issuing of an Executive Order (EO1)[4] aimed at establishing a temporary suspension of granting visas for entry into the United States to nationals of seven countries with a Muslim majority.[5]

Judicial challenges quickly followed the adoption of the EO1, and courts granted preliminary injunctions barring enforcement of several of its provisions. The injunctions were

3 *See* A. De La Garza, 'President Trump's Spat with Chief Justice Roberts Isn't the First Time a President Has Sparred with the Supreme Court', *Time*, 22 November 2018: "President Donald Trump's recent public spat with Supreme Court Chief Justice John Roberts is unprecedented in contemporary political history – rarely has a sitting president criticized the judiciary so directly. However, it's hardly the first time that tensions between a President and the judiciary have boiled over into the public eye", available at http://time.com/5462066/trump-roberts-president-supreme-court-history/.

4 Executive Order No. 13769, Protecting the Nation from Foreign Terrorist Entry Into the United States, 82 Fed. Reg. 8977 (January 27, 2017). The E.O. requested the Secretary of Homeland Security to assess the information given on their own nationals wishing to enter the United States by their respective governments.

5 The suspension was to last for 90 days, and the seven countries were Iran, Iraq, Libya, Somalia, Sudan, Syria and Yemen. During the electoral campaign, candidate Trump had insisted on "a total and complete shutdown of Muslims entering the United States until our country's representatives can figure out what the hell is going on", although this statement was later removed from his campaign website: *see also* for further quotations 'The Supreme Court – Leading Cases', *Harvard Law Review*, 2018, 327. The circumstances related to the E.O. during the campaign are analysed quite in detail also in the Supreme Court's opinions in *Trump v. Hawaii*, as is to be recalled below in this paragraph.

upheld by Courts of Appeals. A new Executive Order (EO2)[6] was then issued, although it had the same short life because of a new set of judicial challenges. In particular, the lawsuits argued that "the order violates the Establishment Clause of the First Amendment because it was motivated not by concerns pertaining to national security, but by animus toward Islam", and it is on this constitutional ground that a nationwide preliminary injunction was granted barring the Government from enforcing the order. Nevertheless, the U.S. Supreme Court – without judging the merits yet – stayed the injunctions but only with respect to foreign nationals lacking a bona fide relationship with a person or entity in the United States.[7]

President Trump then issued a third Executive Order (EO3) – Proclamation No. 9645 Enhancing Vetting Capabilities and Processes for Detecting Attempted Entry into the United States by Terrorists or Other Public-Safety Threats[8] – banning the entry of nationals of eight countries.[9] The Proclamation contributed to making up what has been called 'the saga of the travel ban'.[10] Also, the Proclamation was soon challenged in court. In particular, the U.S. District Court for Hawaii issued a universal preliminary injunction that, on appeal, was stayed by the Ninth Circuit – following the Supreme Court's precedent – only with regard to foreign visitors having a bona fide relationship with a person or an entity in the United States.

This decision was reversed by the Supreme Court in *Trump v. Hawaii* (June 2018), in a 5-4 decision[11] that deserves to be analysed with regard to the Court's objections to the

6 Executive Order No. 13780 Protecting the Nation from Foreign Terrorist Entry into the United States, 82 Fed. Reg. 13.209 (March 9, 2017). Citizens of Iraq were exempted from the new ban.

7 *See* "The interest in preserving national security is "an urgent objective of the highest order [...] To prevent the Government from pursuing that objective by enforcing §2(c) against foreign nationals unconnected to the United States would appreciably injure its interests, without alleviating obvious hardship to anyone else. We accordingly grant the Government's stay applications in part [...]", in *Trump v. Int'l Refugee Assistance Project* (Supreme Court, 2017, Justice Thomas, with whom Justice Alito and Justice Gorsuch join, concurring in part and dissenting in part).

8 In 82 Fed. Reg. 45161 (September 24, 2017). Protection from terrorism has been the main purpose of this Proclamation as well ("Section 1. Policy and Purpose. (a) It is the policy of the United States to protect its citizens from terrorist attacks and other public-safety threats. Screening and vetting protocols and procedures associated with visa adjudications and other immigration processes play a critical role in implementing that policy. They enhance our ability to detect foreign nationals who may commit, aid, or support acts of terrorism, or otherwise pose a safety threat, and they aid our efforts to prevent such individuals from entering the United States").

9 In EO3 the countries concerned were Chad, Iran, Iraq, Libya, North Korea, Syria, Venezuela and Yemen.

10 *See* E.M. Maltz, 'The Constitution and the Trump Travel Ban', *Lewis & Clark L. Rev.*, 2018, p. 395.

11 ROBERTS, C. J., delivered the opinion of the Court, in which KENNEDY, THOMAS, ALITO and GORSUCH, JJ., joined. KENNEDY, J., and THOMAS, J., filed concurring opinions. BREYER, J., filed a dissenting opinion, in which KAGAN, J., joined. SOTOMAYOR, J., filed a dissenting opinion, in which GINSBURG, J., joined.

claims argued by the plaintiffs,[12] based on both statutory and constitutional grounds[13] and maintaining that the Proclamation entailed a violation of the Immigration and Nationality Act (INA)[14] and was inconsistent with the First Amendment (the Establishment Clause).

According to the opinion of the Court written by Chief Justice Roberts, INA's specific provision

> [b]y its plain language, [...] grants the President broad discretion to suspend the entry of aliens into the United States. The President lawfully exercised that discretion based on his findings – following a worldwide, multi-agency review – that entry of the covered aliens would be detrimental to the national interest. And plaintiffs' attempts to identify a conflict with other provisions in the INA, and their appeal to the statute's purposes and legislative history, fail to overcome the clear statutory language.[15]

The acknowledgement of a wide presidential discretion afforded by INA is used by the Court also as the ground for denying the plaintiffs' claim that the Proclamation was in violation of INA's prohibition of discrimination "in the issuance of an immigrant visa because of ... nationality".[16]

Reference to national security provides also sufficient justification for the majority of the Court ruling out any relevance to the plaintiffs' argument concerning violation of the Establishment clause, in part because "foreign nationals seeking admission have no constitutional right to entry into the U.S." ("the Court has engaged in a circumscribed judicial enquiry when the denial of a visa allegedly burdens the constitutional rights of a U.S. citizen"), in part because "admission and exclusion of foreign nationals is a fundamental sovereign attribute exercised by the Government's political departments largely immune

12 Plaintiffs in this case were the State of Hawaii (operating the University of Hawaii system, which recruits students and faculty from the designated countries), three individuals (who were US citizens or lawful permanent residents having relatives from Iran, Syria and Yemen applying for immigrant or non-immigrant visas) and the Muslim Association of Hawaii (a non-profit organization that operates a mosque in Hawaii).

13 *See* E.M. Maltz for a survey of judicial precedents supporting the majority's opinion.

14 Pub.L. No. 96-212, 94 Stat, 102. One of its most relevant provisions in this case is §1182(f).

15 Furthermore, the Court holds that "[t]he Proclamation falls well within this comprehensive delegation. The sole prerequisite set forth in §1182(f) is that the President 'find []' that the entry of the covered aliens 'would be detrimental to the interests of the United States'. The President has undoubtedly fulfilled that requirement here"; and that "Like its predecessors, the Proclamation makes clear that its 'conditional restrictions' will remain in force only so long as necessary to 'address' the identified 'inadequacies and risks' within the covered nations", *See Trump v. Hawaii*, p. 4.

16 *See* "Common sense and historical practice confirm that §1152(a)(1)(A) does not limit the President's delegated authority under §1182(f). Presidents have repeatedly exercised their authority to suspend entry on the basis of nationality. And on plaintiffs' reading, the President would not be permitted to suspend entry from particular foreign states in response to an epidemic, or even if the United States were on the brink of war", *Trump v. Hawaii, p. 4.*

from judicial control", and in part out of traditional judicial deference in matters of defence and foreign policy ("the Court cannot substitute its own assessment for the Executive's predictive judgments on such matters").[17]

Justice Breyer's dissenting opinion, quite to the contrary, refers mainly to the 'evidence of antireligious bias' and emphasizes that "the claim that the Proclamation is a "Muslim ban," rather than a "security-based" ban, becomes much stronger".[18] Also, Justice Sotomayor supports her dissent from the majority's opinion on the relevance of the First Amendment and maintains that "a reasonable observer would conclude that the Proclamation was driven primarily by anti-Muslim animus, rather than by the Government's asserted national-security justifications";[19] the Proclamation is also defined as a "religious gerrymandering"[20] and a "new window dressing [that] cannot conceal an unassailable fact: the words of the "president and his advisers create the strong perception that the Proclamation is contaminated by impermissible discriminatory animus against Islam and its followers".[21]

There is a main methodological difference between the majority's opinion and the two dissents.[22]

Justices Breyer (joined by Justice Kagan) and Sotomayor (joined by Justice Ginsburg) emphasize the relevance of both the text and the 'historical context' of the Proclamation (given President Trump's statements during the electoral campaign), and of the 'specific sequence of events' leading to it. The dissenting opinions go beyond the limits of a rational-basis scrutiny and, rather, rely on a more stringent standard of review[23], one that allows to see clearly "that the primary purpose of the Proclamation is to disfavour Islam and its adherents by excluding them from the country".[24]

---

17 The foregoing quotations are from the Syllabus of the decision. The Court further states that "[i]t cannot be said that it is impossible to 'discern a relationship to legitimate state interests' or that the policy is 'inexplicable by anything but animus.' [...] But because there is persuasive evidence that the entry suspension has a legitimate grounding in national security concerns, quite apart from any religious hostility, we must accept that independent justification. The Proclamation is expressly premised on legitimate purposes: preventing entry of nationals who cannot be adequately vetted and inducing other nations to improve their practices. The text says nothing about religion", pp. 33-34.

18 *See* J. Breyer's dissent, *Trump v. Hawaii*, p. 3.

19 *See* J. Sotomayor's dissent, *Trump v. Hawaii*, p. 10.

20 *See* J. Sotomayor's dissent, *Trump v. Hawaii*, p. 17.

21 *See* J. Sotomayor's dissent, *Trump v. Hawaii*, p. 13.

22 The methodological difference reflects a difference in attitude by the judiciary. A criticism of judicial activism in the circumstance is elaborated in E.M. Maltz, according to whom "[...] one point emerges clearly from *Trump v. Hawaii*. The majority unmistakably endorsed the view that, in almost all cases, decisions on the question of which noncitizens should and should not be allowed to enter the United States are best left to the political branches of the government, and that judges should rarely if ever invoke the Constitution to overturn such decisions", p. 412.

23 *See* J. Sotomayor's dissent, *Trump v. Hawaii* p. 15.

24 *See* J. Sotomayor's dissent, *Trump v. Hawaii*, p. 10.

Chief Justice Roberts, on the other hand, writing for the majority, adopts a more formal approach ("we must consider not only the statements of a particular President, but also the authority of the Presidency itself")[25] that allows the Court to avoid probing the sincerity of the stated justifications for the policy ("by reference to extrinsic statements – many of which were made before the President took the oath of office") and to give the Proclamation a qualification as 'facially neutral toward religion'.[26] The final remark is, therefore, that "the Government has set forth a sufficient national security justification to survive rational basis review".[27]

4.2.2 *Immigration Policy: The Wall and National Emergency*

Building a wall along the southern border between the United States and Mexico as a means of protection from illegal migration has been one of the constant and most inflated promises during Donald Trump's presidential campaign. Nevertheless, the final execution of the plan was delayed until after the 2018 mid-term elections, when the Democrats gained control of the House of Representatives.[28] The consequent divided government led to an arm-twist between the House and the President that affected – within and beyond the federal budget shutdown in 2018 and early 2019 – the appropriation of funds specifically requested by the President for having the Department of Homeland Security build the wall. Nevertheless, in February 2019, a deal over the issue was reached by majority and minority in Congress, based on a compromise (a significant reduction of funds and a variety of restrictions) that made bipartisan approval of the Border Security Act a reality.

In spite of the legislative achievement – although partial both in rules and funds – building the wall according to his own criteria and costs and irrespective of any compromise with the Democratic majority in the House continued being the Chief Executive's priority. President Trump, therefore, decided to proceed with his plans and, in order to be able to

---

25 *See Trump v. Hawaii*, 29.

26 *See Trump v. Hawaii*, 29.

27 *See Trump v. Hawaii*, 38. For a critical comment on the Court's approach ("The travel ban Court deviated from its usual approach to evaluating claims of unconstitutional motive. It remains unclear when the Court will take the same approach. The four questions that the travel ban case left unanswered will provide the fault lines along which courts will define its progeny") *see* Note, First Amendment, 336.

28 The electoral result attributed 235 seats to the Democrats and 199 seats to the Republicans, the former gaining a net total of 40 seats. In the Senate, however, the Republicans not only defended their previous majority but even gained two seats. Worthy of mention are also some results of state elections, the Democrats gaining seven state governorships and the first openly gay governor as well as the first openly bisexual senator having been elected.

divert billions of federal funds from their original destination and spend them for the wall, proclaimed a national emergency.[29]

The justification offered for such a declaration is the serious threat to national security that migration through the southern border had been creating[30] and that requires as serious an effort as to involve the deployment of the Armed Forces.[31] The normative ground for the declaration is "the authority vested in [the President] by the Constitution and the laws of the United States of America, including sections 201 and 301 of the National Emergencies Act (50 U.S.C. 1601 et seq.)".[32]

The political (first) and judicial (later) reaction to the declaration of a national emergency has been quite immediate and it has also reached some Republican congressmen.

The most direct challenge by Congress has been the adoption of Joint Resolution No. 46, which, in conformity with section 202 of the National Emergencies Act, terminates the effects of the declaration.[33] The Resolution was vetoed by Trump,[34] and the new vote

29 Proclamation 9844 (84 Fed. Reg. 4949). *See* J. Pramuk, C. Wilkie, 'Trump Declares National Emergency to Build Border Wall, Setting Up Massive Legal Fight', *CNBC*, 15 February 2019: "Trump had pushed for lawmakers to approve $5.7 billion to build his proposed border wall. Instead, the divided Congress passed only $1.375 billion to construct new bollard fencing on 55 miles of the U.S.-Mexico border. By declaring a national emergency, and taking other executive action, the White House hopes to create a pool of $8 billion to use for barriers," available at www.cnbc.com/2019/02/15/trump-national-emergency-declaration-border-wall-spending-bill.html.

30 *See* the text of the proclamation: "The current situation at the southern border presents a border security and humanitarian crisis that threatens core national security interests and constitutes a national emergency. The southern border is a major entry point for criminals, gang members, and illicit narcotics. The problem of large-scale unlawful migration through the southern border is long-standing, and despite the executive branch's exercise of existing statutory authorities, the situation has worsened in certain respects in recent years. In particular, recent years have seen sharp increases in the number of family units entering and seeking entry to the United States and an inability to provide detention space for many of these aliens while their removal proceedings are pending. If not detained, such aliens are often released into the country and are often difficult to remove from the United States because they fail to appear for hearings, do not comply with orders of removal, or are otherwise difficult to locate."

31 The text continues: "a national emergency exists at the southern border of the United States [...] To provide additional authority to the Department of Defense to support the Federal Government's response to the emergency at the southern border, I hereby declare that this emergency requires use of the Armed Forces."

32 The identification of normative foundation, limits, subordination to congressional oversight and to judicial review is an ongoing question in US constitutional law, due also to the silence of the text (with the exception of the habeas corpus clause) and the frequency of presidential declarations. *See* Congressional Research Service (CRS), 'National Emergency Powers', 27 February 2019, available at https://fas.org/sgp/crs/natsec/98-505.pdf.

33 The House voted on 26 February 2019 with a majority of 245 against 182. The Senate voted on 3 March 2019 with a majority of 59 to 41, 12 Republican senators joining a unanimous Democratic front. The 26 March vote in the House that could not achieve the termination of the emergency was 248 to 181.

34 The final part of the veto message reads: "Under current laws, court decisions, and resource constraints, the Government cannot detain families or undocumented alien children from Central American countries in significant numbers or quickly deport them. Instead, the Government is forced to release many of them into the interior of the United States, pending lengthy judicial proceedings. Although many fail ever to establish any legal right to remain in this country, they stay nonetheless. This situation on our border cannot be described as anything other than a national emergency, and our Armed Forces are needed to help confront

in the House failed to reach the two-thirds qualified majority requirement necessary for overturning presidential vetoes. Nevertheless, in spite of the bipartisan failure in achieving the termination of the national emergency,

> final passage of a measure to assert Congress's constitutional authority over spending is sure to bolster numerous lawsuits that maintain that Mr. Trump's declaration is an unconstitutional end run around Congress's lawful power of the purse.[35]

Yet another attempt by the House of Representatives to oppose the proclamation has taken the judicial path: the Bipartisan Legal Advisory Group, consisting of leaders from both parties in the House, has authorized filing a lawsuit challenging Trump's declared national emergency.[36] The complaint maintains that

> [a]bsent any applicable Congressional appropriation, the expenditure of up to $8.1 billion to construct a border wall – and the transfer of appropriated funds from other sources to pay for the wall – violates the Appropriations Clause and the constitutional separation of powers. The United States House of Representatives brings this civil action for declaratory and injunctive relief to halt the defendants' unconstitutional actions, which usurp the House's Article I legislative powers.[37]

Apart from Congress' political and judicial reaction, a plurality of lawsuits has been filed in court by other actors: an alliance of 17 states, led by California, whose respective Gover-

it. My highest obligation as President is to protect the Nation and its people. Every day, the crisis on our border is deepening, and with new surges of migrants expected in the coming months, we are straining our border enforcement personnel and resources to the breaking point. H.J. Res. 46 ignores these realities. It is a dangerous resolution that would undermine United States sovereignty and threaten the lives and safety of countless Americans. It is, therefore, my duty to return it to the House of Representatives without my approval."

35 From E. Cochrane, 'House Votes to Block Trump's National Emergency Declaration about the Border', *New York Times*, 26 February 2019, available at www.nytimes.com/2019/02/26/us/politics/national-emergency-vote.html.

36 *See* E. Cochrane & C. Savage, 'House Adds Lawsuit to Challenges against Trump's Emergency Declaration', *New York Times*, 5 April 2019, available at www.nytimes.com/2019/04/04/us/politics/national-emergency-act-lawsuit.html. The ground for the lawsuit is provided by the Appropriations Clause and its violation by the President's determination to diverting money from funds that have been already appropriated by Congress.

37 The full 45-page text of the House's lawsuit is available at www.speaker.gov/wp-content/uploads/2019/04/2019.04.05-ECF-No.-1-Complaint.pdf; quotation is at p. 6.

nors (with the exception of Maryland) are from the Democratic party,[38] a group of landowners from Texas along with an environmentalist group,[39] the Sierra Club and the Southern Border Communities Coalition, which are represented by the American Civil Liberties Union,[40] and many others.[41]

The controversy – needless to say – remains quite open at this stage, and only the final judgment of the Supreme Court will be able to set an authoritative word about the case.

4.2.3 *Immigration Policy: The 2020 Census*

Still another controversial issue indirectly affecting the field of immigration concerns the forthcoming 2020 Census. First, the state of California and, later, a coalition composed of both 18 states and some larger cities (including Washington, D.C.) as well as immigrants' rights groups have challenged the administrative decision to introduce a question concerning citizenship in the Census form that is sent to all households. The plaintiffs' allegation is that, since answers to all items are mandatory, the specific question on citizenship may make immigrants reluctant to give an answer, thus producing an undercount of the population.[42]

The reason for the Constitution mandating a census to be conducted every ten years is that its outcome provides for follow-up consequences as important as attributing to

38 The states are California Colorado, Connecticut, Delaware, Hawaii, Illinois, Maine, Maryland, Minnesota, Nevada, New Jersey, New Mexico, New York, Oregon, Virginia and Michigan.

39 The group is the Frontera Audubon Society, Their lawsuit is available at https://assets.documentcloud.org/documents/5742084/2-15-19-Alvarez-v-Trump-Complaint.pdf.

40 The plaintiffs request the U.S. District Court for the District of Columbia, inter alia, to "Declare the Declaration, and the President's direction that the Defense Department reallocate funds to support construction of a border wall under 10 U.S.C. §§ 284 and 2808, to be in excess of presidential authority under Article II of the Constitution, an infringement on legislative authority, and invalid"; full text available at https://www.aclu.org/sites/default/files/field_document/29._pi_motion_4.4.19.pdf.

41 *See* J. Thomsen, 'Trump Faces Mounting Legal Challenges to Wall', *The Hill*, 4 April 2019, available at https://thehill.com/policy/national-security/437949-trump-faces-mounting-legal-challenges-to-wall.

42 "In the New York case, the plaintiffs accused the administration of Republican President Donald Trump of adding the question to intentionally discourage immigrants from participating, which could lead to a population undercount – and possibly fewer seats in Congress – in places that tend to vote Democratic. Even people in the U.S. legally, they said, might dodge the census questionnaire out of fears they could be targeted by a hostile administration" [...] "Among other things, the judge said, Ross [the Secretary of Commerce, which designs the census] didn't follow a law requiring that he give Congress three years notice of any plan to add a question about citizenship to the census" [...] "When Ross announced the plan in March, he said the question was needed in part to help the government enforce the Voting Rights Act, a 1965 law meant to protect political representation of minority groups. Furman [the New York federal district judge], appointed to the bench by former President Barack Obama, said, 'Finally, and perhaps most egregiously, the evidence is clear that Secretary Ross's rationale was pretextual," meaning Voting Rights Act enforcement was not his real reason,' available at www.nbcnews.com/politics/politics-news/judge-bars-trump-administration-adding-citizenship-question-2020-census-n958786.

states the varying number of seats in the House of Representatives and in the Electoral College for presidential elections, as drawing up electoral districts, and allocating funds to local government under several federal programmes depending on the population. It is obvious that some states and cities would suffer serious damage were the census not faithfully reflective of the population, including immigrants.

In February 2019, the Supreme Court agreed to hear and decide the New York case,[43] both on grounds of conformity of the census' regulation with federal administrative law and on "whether the Secretary of Commerce's decision to add a citizenship question to the Decennial Census violated the Enumeration Clause of the U.S. Constitution, art. I, §2, cl. 3".[44] The Supreme Court acceded to the Department of Commerce's motion to expedite the process and give a judgment before June 2019, while appellate judgments would continue in front of lower courts,[45] the motion being justified by the time needed in order to organize the Census (starting from printing the questionnaires).

4.2.4 *Immigration Policy: The Special Status of Immigration Juveniles*

Yet another case (*R.F.M., T.D., S.W., D.A.F.A. & O.M.S. v. Kirstjen Nielsen, et al.*) was recently decided against the Trump Administration by a federal court, the U.S. District Court for the Southern District of New York (April 2019).

The controversy dealt with a change of policy by the U.S. Citizenship and Immigration Services (USCIS), a part of the Department of Homeland Security: according to the previous criteria, juveniles under the age of 18 who had been abused, abandoned or neglected by one or both parents were allowed to receive a green card by submitting to the USCIS the judge's order from a juvenile court, which determined that they had been abused, aban-

43 The case is *Department of Commerce, et al., v. New York, et al.*

44 *See* Orders in Pending Cases, 15 March 2019.

45 In April 2019, a 119-page judgement by the US District Court for the District of Maryland has meanwhile decided the case against the Department of Commerce on administrative ground, that is that according to the Court the fact of including a question concerning citizenship would be a violation of the Administrative Procedure Act and of the Enumeration clause. Quoting the criteria established by judicial precedents (*Motor Vehicles Manufacturers Association v. State Farm*, 463 US 29 (1983), the District Court judged that "[t]he decision to add a citizenship question to the 2020 Census was arbitrary and capricious in violation of the [Administrative Procedure Act]" and that the decision by the Administration "ran counter to the evidence before the agency, and was not based on facts, a different view, or agency expertise". Furthermore, the Court concluded that "the addition of the citizenship question would unreasonably compromise the distributive accuracy of the Census and the addition violates the Enumeration Clause". Nevertheless, "the evidence given for supporting the claim of a discriminatory animus of the Administration could not prove a violation of the Equal Protection Clause".

doned or neglected. The new policy did not allow the same effects when that class of individuals were above the age of 18 at the time of their application to the USCIS.[46]

Relying on statutory authority as well as on judicial precedents, the District Court concluded that the Agency's new procedure is a new policy and that, as such, the agency's new policy is in violation of the APA (Administrative Procedure Act).[47]

There is no action before the Supreme Court at the present time.

4.2.5 *Immigration Policy: Governmental Power of Detention of Legal Immigrants with a Criminal Record That May Lead to Deportation*

Another controversy dealt with the power of the government to detain legal immigrants with a criminal record not immediately after serving a criminal sentence but several years later (from 5 to 11 years). Inclusion in this category of immigrants might lead to deportation. Both the District Court and the Ninth Circuit ruled that such detention was illegal because it did not follow immediately upon having served the sentence. The Supreme Court reversed,[48] once again through a split 5-4 decision in *Nielsen, Secretary of Homeland Security, et al. v. Preap at al.*, decided in March 2019.[49]

The decision by the majority is grounded mainly on textual analysis that ultimately leads to an interpretation enlarging the scope of application of the power of detention, as it is argued by the statement of Justice Breyer's dissent according to whom

> [t]he language of the statute will not bear the broad interpretation the majority now adopts. Rather, the ordinary meaning of the statute's language, the statute's structure, and relevant canons of interpretation all argue convincingly to the contrary.

---

46 The plaintiffs sustained that the new policy was "arbitrary, capricious, an excess of statutory jurisdiction, and contrary to law, and [that] the agency was required to provide public notice of its policy change under 5 U.S.C. par. 552 (a) (1) (D)", from the March 15 summary judgement order, p. 54.

47 As indicated in the decision: "Courts are required to set aside agency actions that are "arbitrary, capricious, an abuse of discretion, or otherwise not in accordance with law [...] To determine whether a policy is arbitrary and capricious, courts consider whether the agency has relied on factors which Congress has not intended it to consider, entirely failed to consider an important aspect of the problem, offered an explanation for its decision that runs counter to the evidence before the agency, or is so implausible that it could not be ascribed to a difference in view or the product of agency expertise".

48 The same decision ruled as well on the *Khoury v. Asher case also from the Ninth Circuit.*

49 Alito, J., announced the judgment of the Court and delivered the opinion of the Court with respect to Parts I, III-A, III-B-1, and IV, in which Roberts, C. J., and Thomas, Gorsuch, and Kavanaugh, JJ., joined, and an opinion with respect to Parts II and III-B-2, in which Roberts, C. J., and Kavanaugh, J., joined. Kavanaugh, J., filed a concurring opinion. Thomas, J., filed an opinion concurring in part and concurring in the judgment, in which Gorsuch, J., joined. Breyer, J., filed a dissenting opinion, in which Ginsburg, Sotomayor and Kagan, JJ., joined.

Furthermore, because of the difference in interpretation – Justice Breyer argues

> [t]he issue may sound technical. But it is extremely important. That is because the Government's reading of the statute – namely, that paragraph (2) forbids bail hearings for all ABCD aliens regardless of whether they were detained "when … released" from criminal custody – would significantly expand the Secretary's authority to deny bail hearings.[50]

The ground of dissent involves reference (rather than indifference, as in the majority's opinions) to mainstream constitutionalism in the United States (as anticipated in the introductory remarks). Reference is quite explicit in a question and answer given in Breyer's dissent:

> Why would Congress have granted the Secretary such broad authority to deny bail hearings, especially when doing so would run contrary to basic American and common-law traditions? […] The answer is that Congress did not do so. Ordinary tools of statutory interpretation demonstrate that the authority Congress granted to the Secretary is far more limited.[51]

4.2.6 *Immigration Policy: The DACA Program*

The Obama Presidency had developed a policy known as the Deferred Action for Childhood Arrivals (DACA): the policy mandated a two-year period delaying the deportation of

50 *See Breyer's dissent, Nielsen, Secretary of Homeland Security, et al. v. Preap at al.*, p. 4.

51 *See* Breyer's dissent, *Nielsen, Secretary of Homeland Security, et al. v. Preap at al.*, pp. 4-5. The reasoning continues on more technical ground, eventually concluding: "To reiterate: The question before us is not 'narrow'. *Ante*, at 2 (Kavanaugh J., concurring). That is because we cannot interpret the words of this specific statute without also considering basic promises that America's legal system has long made to all persons. In deciphering the intent of the Congress that wrote this statute, we must decide – in the face of what is, at worst, linguistic ambiguity – whether Congress intended that persons who have long since paid their debt to society would be deprived of their liberty for months or years without the possibility of bail. We cannot decide that question without bearing in mind basic American legal values: the Government's duty not to deprive any 'person' of 'liberty' without 'due process of law', U. S. Const., Amdt. 5; the Nation's original commitment to protect the 'unalienable' right to 'Liberty'; and, less abstractly and more directly, the long-standing right of virtually all persons to receive a bail hearing". I would have thought that Congress meant to adhere to these values and did not intend to allow the Government to apprehend persons years after their release from prison and hold them indefinitely without a bail hearing. In my view, the Court should interpret the words of this statute to reflect Congress' likely intent, an intent that is consistent with our basic values. To speak more technically, I believe that aliens are subject to paragraph (2)'s bar on release only if they are detained "when … released" from criminal custody. To speak less technically, I fear that the Court's contrary interpretation will work serious harm to the principles for which American law has long stood."

minors who, although having entered the United States illegally, had a clean criminal record and met educational or military service requirements. Because of their positive personal features, such individuals deserved to be called 'dreamers'. This policy was discontinued by the Trump Administration, and in November 2018 the U.S. Court of Appeals for the Ninth Circuit affirmed a district court's preliminary injunction against the Department of Homeland Security.

The Solicitor General appealed against the Ninth Circuit Court and at the same time petitioned the Supreme Court, requesting the Court to give its judgment before the Court of Appeals' decision,[52] but the Supreme Court refused.[53]

4.3 Civil Rights

The second substantive area that has been experiencing strong judicial challenges to President Trump's political agenda concerns civil rights, an area whose most recent developments – concerning, in particular, the LGBTQ community – appears quite weak and vulnerable in a time when conservative and religiously-biased worldviews prevail.

4.3.1 *Civil Rights: The Transgender Ban in the Armed Forces*

The acceptance of transgender people within the U.S. Armed Forces has traditionally been a sensitive issue – subject to opposition, criticism and reluctance. President Obama lifted the ban on recruiting transgender people, starting July 2017. President Trump postponed that date to January 2018 but decided, soon after, to adopt his own policy, and the ban was re-established by the issuance of a Memorandum, which was judicially challenged.

Federal District Courts in Maryland, California, Washington and Washington, D.C. issued preliminary injunctions enjoining the Administration from enforcing or implementing policies and directives connected to the ban ordered in the Memorandum. A new 2018 Memorandum and an Implementation Plan were then adopted. However, transgender individuals who were regularly recruited after January 2018 and others started new judicial actions achieving suspension of the new regulations.[54]

52 *See* A. Howe, '*Trump Administration Asks Supreme Court to Intervene on DACA*', *SCOTUSblog*, 18 January 2018, 9:02 p.m., available at www.scotusblog.com/2018/01/trump-administration-asks-supreme-court-intervene-daca/.

53 *See* Proceedings and Order, No. 17-1003 listing the Court's decision (Petition for a writ of certiorari before judgment denied without prejudice). It is assumed that the Court of Appeals "will proceed expeditiously to decide this case", 26 February 2018) available at www.supremecourt.gov/docket/docketfiles/html/public/17-1003.html.

54 The order of the Maryland US District Court (*Brock Stone, et al. v. Donald J. Trump, et al.*) so describes the events: "The President made known his July 2017 decision by publishing a series of Tweets stating "[t]he

At this stage, the Administration asked the Supreme Court to intervene in order to prevent the continuation of lower courts' proceedings and the suspension of the enforcement of the ban to be in force. The Supreme Court did not accede entirely to the Presidential request: it simply terminated the suspension ordered by the lower courts, but it did grant certiorari before those lower courts would reach a decision of their own.[55]

The decision was taken by a strict 5-4 majority composed of the 'conservative' Justices, although such outcome does not necessarily affect a future ruling on the merits.[56]

4.3.2 *Civil Rights: Limiting Federal Funds for Family Planning*

In February 2019, the U.S. Department of Health and Human Services announced new rules that would limit federal funding for family planning. The District of Columbia and 21 states[57] filed lawsuits claiming that the new policy and its rules, named the Final Rule,

> would fundamentally alter the Title X family planning program – a federal grant program that currently provides over $286 million annually in vital family planning and preventive health services to low-income individuals. The

---

United States Government will not accept or allow … [t]ransgender individuals to serve in any capacity in the U.S. Military". Later (August 2017) he issued a Memorandum for the Secretary of Defense and the Secretary of Homeland Security formalizing the ban on transgender service members and requested the Secretary of Defense to develop a plan of implementation".

55 *See* A. Liptak, *Supreme Court Revives Transgender Ban for Military Service*, in NYT, January 22, 2019: "[i]n granting stays of injunctions issued by Federal District Court judges in California and Washington State, the justices in the majority may have been influenced by the complaint by the administration that lower courts have been able to frustrate its policies by the issuance of injunctions applying to the entire country. It is with great reluctance that we seek such emergency relief in this court," Solicitor General Noel J. Francisco wrote. "Unfortunately, this case is part of a growing trend in which federal district courts, at the behest of particular plaintiffs, have issued nationwide injunctions, typically on a preliminary basis, against major policy initiatives. Such injunctions previously were rare, but in recent years they have become routine. In less than two years, federal courts have issued 25 of them, blocking a wide range of significant policies involving national security, national defense, immigration and domestic issues."

56 *See* (January 22, 2019): Application (18A625) granted by the Court. The application for stay presented to Justice Kagan and by her referred to the Court is granted, and the District Court's December 11, 2017 order granting a preliminary injunction is stayed pending disposition of the Government's appeal in the United States Court of Appeals for the Ninth Circuit and disposition of the Government's petition for a writ of certiorari, if such writ is sought. If a writ of certiorari is sought and the Court denies the petition, this order shall terminate automatically. If the Court grants the petition for a writ of certiorari, this order shall terminate when the Court enters its judgment. Justice Ginsburg, Justice Breyer, Justice Sotomayor and Justice Kagan would deny the application, *Donald J. Trump, President of the United States, et al., Petitioners v. Ryan Karnoski, et al.*, available at www.supremecourt.gov/docket/docketfiles/html/public/18-676.html.

57 The other plaintiffs are the states of Oregon, New York, Colorado, Connecticut, Delaware, Hawaii, Illinois, Maryland, Commonwealth of Massachusetts, Michigan, Minnesota, Nevada, New Jersey, New Mexico, North Carolina, Commonwealth of Pennsylvania, Rhode Island, Vermont, Commonwealth of Virginia and Wisconsin.

> Final Rule would impose burdensome and unnecessary restrictions that would reduce access to care, interfere with the patient-provider relationship, and undermine Congress's intent in enacting Title X of the Public Health Service Act nearly five decades ago.[58]

There is no action before the Supreme Court at the present time.

4.4 FINAL REMARKS

The electoral campaign of Donald Trump was rough and promised to initiate a rough presidency. The pledge seems to have been substantially honoured, in both content and style.

In fact, the electoral political agenda has not been adapted to a more balanced approach, in order to somehow accommodate the necessary electoral partisanship with presidential policies that would try to aggregate a national consensus and be more representative of shared mainstream orientations. President Trump, in my opinion, clearly believes in a presidency that is a mere continuation of the electoral campaign by other means – as if he were inspired by Carl von Clausewitz's understanding of the relationship between war and politics.

It is therefore consequent – given such premises – that policies and programs that have qualified the campaign and raised voters' support find their faithful execution through the presidential agenda. Nevertheless, in a constitutional democracy, governmental action – however framed – inevitably causes corresponding reactions and widespread opposition.

Thus, the electoral campaign inevitably continues on both sides, politically – and the political clash has already determined a divided government since the 2018 mid-term elections – and judicially, as this short survey of litigation has described.

Two years since the President took office, some initial and partial elements of analysis of litigation over the presidential agenda do suggest that we are facing, on the one hand, a very active lower federal Judiciary – certainly an *activist* federal Judiciary in the Administration's perception – and, on the other hand, a Supreme Court that is likely to be unable to perform a balancing function because of its own internal cleavages between (more) liberal and (more) conservative Justices.

The lower federal Judiciary, of course, is under the pressure of a very reactive civil society that knows how to be as ideological as the President's provocative actions. It is also interesting to see how member states are willing to undertake the judicial track in order

58 From the text of the complaint (*Oregon v. Azar*), available at www.nj.gov/oag/newsreleases19/Oregon_v_Azar_Filed-Complaint.pdf.

to confront presidential policies that, among other things, cause reductions of transferred federal funds that negatively affect their performance in the field of social services that citizens (and voters) expect from their state and not from federal agencies or departments.

The Supreme Court may be seen as undertaking a course of decision-making that – while possibly having different *nuances* – tends to be closer to defending presidential claims to an exclusive power in the field of national security.

It remains to be seen how the majority of the Court will decide the crucial case concerning the proclamation of national security: it might be that the need to overcome the opposition by a bipartisan Congress will lead to staying on the path shown in the well-known precedent in *Youngstown Sheet & Tube Co. v. Sawyer.*[59]

The following are Justice Jackson's wise words in his concurring opinion,

> Presidential powers are not fixed but fluctuate depending upon their disjunction or conjunction with those of Congress [...] When the President acts pursuant to an express or implied authorization of Congress, his authority is at its maximum, for it includes all that he possesses in his own right plus all that Congress can delegate[60] [...] When the President acts in absence of either a congressional grant or denial of authority, he can only rely upon his own independent powers [...][61] [...] When the President takes measures incompatible with the expressed or implied will of Congress, his power is at its lowest ebb.[62] [...] Presidential claim to a power at once so conclusive and preclusive must be scrutinized with caution, for what is at stake is the equilibrium established by our constitutional system.

Another noteworthy element of the Trump's Administration conduct in court is the practice of requesting the Supreme Court to anticipate its opinion even without a formal

59 *Youngstown Sheet & Tube Co. v. Sawyer*, 343 U.S. 579 (1952).

60 And the text continues by saying: "In these circumstances, and in these only, may he be said (for what it may be worth) to personify the federal sovereignty. If his act is held unconstitutional under these circumstances, it usually means that the Federal Government, as an undivided whole, lacks power. A seizure executed by the President pursuant to an Act of Congress would be supported by the strongest of presumptions and the widest latitude of judicial interpretation, and the burden of persuasion would rest heavily upon any who might attack it."

61 Although J. Jackson's opinion recognizes that "there is a zone of twilight in which he and Congress may have concurrent authority, or in which its distribution is uncertain. Therefore, congressional inertia, indifference or quiescence may sometimes, at least, as a practical matter, enable, if not invite, measures on independent presidential responsibility. In this area, any actual test of power is likely to depend on the imperatives of events and contemporary imponderables, rather than on abstract theories of law".

62 And it is further stated that, in such a circumstance, "for then he can rely only upon his own constitutional powers minus any constitutional powers of Congress over the matter. Courts can sustain exclusive presidential control in such a case only by disabling the Congress from acting upon the subject".

previous decision of a Court of Appeals: such a practice implies a sort of permanent state of emergency – even without a formal proclamation – consequent to the political costs caused by lower federal courts' decisions. The practice is regulated by the Supreme Court's rules, which indicate that certiorari before judgment

> will be granted only upon a showing that the case is of such imperative public importance as to justify deviation from normal appellate practice and to require immediate determination in this Court.[63]

Once again, the pressure of President Trump's political agenda requires an adaptation of the rules of the game. The first challenge to the Supreme Court is then its ability to make use of its power to defend such rules before Trumpism accomplishes the reshaping of the federal Judiciary and the remodelling of the federal Constitution in his own image.

---

63 *See* K. Russell, '*Overview of Supreme Court's Cert. before Judgment Practice*', *SCOTUSblog*, 9 February 2011, available at www.scotusblog.com/2011/02/overview-of-supreme-court%e2%80%99s-cert-before-judgment-practice/.

5 President Trump and the American Governors: Two Years of a Conflictual Dialogue

Francesco Clementi[*]

5.1 Governorship in the American Political-Institutional System

The figure of the Governor represents a very relevant part of the historical overall evolution of the all-executive power in the American political-institutional system.[1]

Often, they are less considered, overshadowed by the President, but, nevertheless, within their States governors preside over the largest and most important political and economic territories of the American communities, which are sometimes roughly equivalent to nations.[2]

Governors have powers specifically granted by State Constitutions, but their political value derives largely out of the force of their personality. They are the states' strongest chief legislators,[3] working to encourage, first of all, business for their states; almost all governors appoint a cabinet to govern the state departments, propose their states' budgets and serve in at least informally as their parties' leaders.[4] The governors – obviously – set

---

* Associate Professor of Comparative Public Law, University of Perugia.

1 The title 'governor' is one of the few constants throughout American governmental history. In fact, since 1792, the title of 'governor' has been universally used in the States, except only for a brief period after the Revolutionary War when New Hampshire and Georgia began designating the executive head differently, by calling him 'President'. *See* J.E. Kallenbach, *The American Chief Executive: The Presidency and the Governorship*, Harper & Row, New York, 1966; M. Ferguson (Ed.), *The Executive Branch of State Government. People, Process, and Politics*, ABC CLIO, Santa Barbara, 2006; J. Dinan, *The American State Constitutional Tradition*, University Press of Kansas, Lawrence, 2009. More recently: S.M. Ambar, *How Governors Built the Modern American Presidency*, University of Pennsylvania Press, Philadelphia, 2012.

2 It is necessary to consider that, for instance, California's economy is mostly equivalent to Brazil's and the GDP of Texas is on a par with Canada's. This picture concerns even smaller and less populated States, considering that Nebraska's economy rivals that of Ecuador's and Vermont's is comparable to Paraguay's. *See* K.B. Smith (Ed.), *State and Local Government. 2018-2019*, CQ Press, Washington, DC, 2019.

3 Recently, *see* A. Rosenthal, *Engines of Democracy. Politics and Policymaking in State Legislatures*, CQ Press, Washington, DC, 2009, pp. 264-301. T. Beyle, (Ed.), *Governors and Hard Times*, CQ Press, Washington, DC, 1992.

4 *See amplius*: J.J. Scott, 'Elections, Gubernatorial', *in* L. Sabato & H.R. Ernst (Eds.), *Encyclopedia of American Political Parties and Elections*, Checkmark Books, New York, 2007, p. 123. *See also*, more recently, T. Kousser & J.H. Phillips, *The Power of American Governors*, Cambridge University Press, Cambridge, 2012.

the state's agenda, outline proposals and use their power to influence the states' legislatures to pass bills, linked to their political address.[5]

The powers and functions assigned to governors in the early State Constitutions were almost uniformly limited,[6] but gradually, over time, the governorship accrued more power and strong legitimacy with the expansion of the suffrage, emerging into a more prestigious office.[7]

Historically, the nation's governors first met in 1908, thanks to President Theodore Roosevelt, and formed the Governors' Conference (GC) in 1912; for some governors the GC had to be the hammer against Washington to foster and to promote the states' collective interests in national policies, but the future President of the United States, Woodrow Wilson – at that time Governor of New Jersey – persuaded the rest of the governors to use the GC to promote only state-specific issues such as administration, budgeting and uniformity of laws.[8]

It was only at the end of the late 1930s, after the federal New Deal programmes, that the governors began to concern themselves with federal issues (overcoming the bad reputation they had gained in the past, saying they were more interested in appearing in the newspaper's social pages, than leading government).[9]

---

5 *See* D.P. Redlawsk (ed.), *The American Governor*, London, Palgrave, 2005; L.A. van Assendelft, *Governors, Agenda Setting, and Divided Government*, University Press of America, Lanham, 1997; T. Beyle & M. Ferguson, 'Governors and the Executive Branch', *in* V. Gray & R.L. Hanson (Eds.), *Politics in the American States*, 9th edn, CQ Press, Washington, DC, 2008; A. Rosenthal, *The Best Job in Politics: Exploring How Governors Succeed as Policy Leaders*, CQ Press, Washington, DC, 2013.

6 *See* J.N. Rakove, *Original Meanings: Politics and Ideas in the Making of the Constitution*, New York, Alfred A. Knopf, 1996; G.A. Tarr, *Understanding State Constitutions*, Princeton University Press, Princeton, 1988.

7 For example, the Governor of New Jersey Woodrow Wilson claimed, "The whole country…is clamouring for leadership, and a new role, which to many persons seems little less than unconstitutional, is thrust upon our executives", as quoted in J.M. Matthews, 'The New Role of the Governor', *Am. Polit. Sci. Rev.*, No. 6, 1912, p. 224. In any case, with a history of decline and reversal, for a long time an element has determined the alternate fortunes of the governorship: the approval of the Sixteenth Amendment to the U.S. Constitution, ratified in 1913, which provided the federal government with the important tool of the income tax, a great instrument for effective monopolizing revenue sources, centralizing against the States' taxation. Therefore, only when it became clear that the Governors are among the country's best-known political figures, did the Governorate change the pattern, transforming its office and overcoming what seemed to be an announced decline. *See* S.M. Ambar, *How Governors Built the Modern American Presidency*, University of Pennsylvania Press, Philadelphia, 2012; L. Sabato, *Goodbye to Good-Time Charlie: The American Governorship Transformed*, 2nd edn, CQ Press, Washington, DC,1983.

8 *See* A. O'M. Bowman and R.C. Kearney, *State and Local Government*, 10th edn, Cengage Publisher, Washington, DC, 2018; V. Gray & P. Eisinger, *American States and Cities*, Longman, New York, 1997.

9 The bad reputation of the governors as politicians was certified by the popular use of sarcastic phrases to describe those political figures, for example, "flowery old courthouse politicians, political pipsqueaks or good-time Charlies". *See* L. Sabato, *Goodbye to Good-Time Charlie: The American Governorship Transformed*, 2nd edn, CQ Press, Washington, DC, 1983, p. 9. On the other hand, not by chance, Harold Laski marked the States' governors, substantially, as 'second rate politicians'. *See* H.J. Laski, *The American Democracy: A Commentary and an Interpretation*, Allen & Unvin, London, 1949, p. 146.

Therefore, with the ending of the Great Depression and World War II, the Governors found a new way, trying to access and to influence the federal political process, increasing their presence and power in Washington, definitely.[10]

For these reasons, the GC expanded its role to represent the interests of the governors and the states before the federal government, especially after the establishment of an office for federal-state relations in Washington in 1966, and also changing the name in the National Governors' Conference (NGC) (later, in 1977, in the National Governors' Association, NGA).

At the same time, in American history, serving as a state's governor has often enough been a great and favourable path to run for the presidency, and this evidence is confirmed by the fact that 17 presidents have previously served as governors, providing them with the experience to run a government bureaucracy, deal with the legislature and respond to the judiciary.[11]

Governors have become some of the leading political actors, even outside the United States (considering, e.g., the great political relations and connections between the Governor of Iowa and the Chinese President Xi Jinping, which have permitted Terry Branstad to recently become the new US ambassador to China[12]). And governors are the best popular

10 Historically, the influence and the power of Governors are stronger, broadly speaking, when the Republican Party wins a majority of seats in Congress, in keeping with the famous and old political theory that Republicans are less centralized than Democrats in the government's style and political address. *See* C.S. Weissert, *The National Governors' Association: 1908–1983*, in *State Government*, No. 2, 1983, pp. 44-52; and also: S. Matheson, 'Intergovernmental Relations and the New Federalism', *in* R.D. Behn (Ed.), *Governors on Governing*, University Press of America, Lanham, 1991.

11 Since 1787, the United States has had 45 presidents and over 2,400 governors. In particular, the governors who became President were: Thomas Jefferson (1801-1809, former Governor of Virginia); James Monroe (1817-1825, former Governor of Virginia); Martin Van Buren (1837-1841, former Governor of New York); John Tyler (1841-1845, former Governor of Virginia); James K. Polk (1845-1849, former Governor of Tennessee); Andrew Johnson (1865-1869, former Governor of Tennessee); Rutherford B. Hayes (1877-1881, former Governor of Ohio); Grover Cleveland (1885-1889 and 1893-1897, former Governor of New York); William McKinley (1897-1901, former Governor of Ohio); Theodore Roosevelt (1901-1909, former Governor of New York); Woodrow Wilson (1913-1921, former Governor of New Jersey); Calvin Coolidge (1923-1929, former Governor of Massachusetts); Franklin Roosevelt (1933-1945, former Governor of New York); Jimmy Carter (1977-1981, former Governor of Georgia); Ronald Reagan (1981-1989, former Governor of California); Bill Clinton (1993-2001, former Governor of Arkansas); George W. Bush (2001-2009, former Governor of Texas). Nine governors were elected while in office (Thomas Jefferson, James Monroe, Martin Van Buren, John Tyler, James K. Polk, Andrew Johnson, Grover Cleveland, Jimmy Carter, Ronald Reagan). Only one, William Howard Taft, served as a territorial governor. *See* J. Dinan, *The American State Constitutional Tradition*, University Press of Kansas, Lawrence, 2009. Between 1976 and 2004, Jimmy Carter, Ronald Reagan, Bill Clinton and George W. Bush, governors all, combined to win seven out of eight presidential elections. Since then, only one governor (Mitt Romney, of Massachusetts) has gotten as far as winning a major party nomination.

12 *See* R. Lardner, 'Senate Confirms Iowa Governor as Ambassador to China', available at www.pbs.org/newshour/world/senate-confirms-iowa-governor-ambassador-china.

expression of a political figure: responsible for implementing policies and accountable to the public for the policies' success or failure.

Consequently, the role of governors in Washington and, in general, in the federal system, has increased; therefore, today, the governors are really at the crossroads of the American political system and are a very relevant part of the American political discourse; and all these elements explain why the role of the governors is so relevant to study and to understand executive power in the American constitutional tradition, especially in the context of the American presidency.

5.2 Governorship and Presidency: An Old and Deep Relationship

In an institutional system based on a separation of powers and on a federal constitutional system, an understanding of the relationship between the Governors and the President is imperative to capture the deep sense and the political actions of the President and the presidency. This is even more true when one considers that states play a central role in defining America's political and institutional infrastructure and that, except for the President, as mentioned earlier, governors are the most important and powerful elected executives in the American political system.

There is an intimate relationship between the President and the Governors.

The rising political importance of governorship – within the main field of the modern executive branch of the United States and in the general American political-institutional system[13] – is reflected primarily by the fact that the gubernatorial elections are held on the same presidential election day in November, while not all states elect governors in the same year.

In particular, while nine states (Delaware, Indiana, Missouri, Montana, New Hampshire, North Carolina, North Dakota, Utah and Vermont) elect their governors during presidential election years, the other 34 States – the majority – elect them during the second year of the presidential term, the so-called mid-term. Still other states – Kentucky, Mississippi and Louisiana – elect their governors in the third year of the presidential term, while Virginia and New Jersey elect them in the year immediately following a presidential election.[14]

Inevitably, therefore, the coincidence of the mid-term elections with the elections of some governors also represents a general 'referendum' on the President's activity, elected just two years before: a sort of 'implicit vote of confidence', as some authors claim, along the lines of those of parliamentary forms of government. Indeed, not surprisingly, in the

13 *See* J.D. Aberbach & M A. Peterson, *The Executive Branch*, Oxford University Press, Oxford, 2005.

14 In particular, 48 States elect their governors for a four-year term, while only two, New Hampshire and Vermont, have two-year gubernatorial terms. Except the State of Virginia, which does not allow a governor to be re-elected, two-term limits – consecutive or not – are a very common practice among the States.

seminal work of 1888, which is *The American Commonwealth*, James Bryce – *Regius* professor of civil law at Oxford, then politician and future British ambassador in the United States – has emphasized that the mid-term elections offer to the American electorate the opportunity to judge, first of all, the actions of the president's government, basically allowing that

> the people within two years to express their approval or disapproval of his conduct by sending up another House of Representatives which may support or oppose the policy he has followed.[15]

In this sense also, the elections for the complete renewal of the 435 members of the House of Representatives are like a national 'second election', as this competition – in addition to the presidential one – is the only politically articulated electoral moment, even on small colleges, on everything in the national territory; an electoral moment capable of simultaneously involving, on the same day, the entire audience of voters. (In fact, the Senate is always a partial competition, because it renews only one third of its members every two years, involving only the specific electoral perimeter of each State, called upon to renew its representation from time to time.)[16]

Therefore, every election during the presidential mandate is strategic for the presidency, and the commitment of the President is a substantial and relevant part of a popular test on the presidency.[17]

---

15 *See* J. Bryce, 'The House of Representatives', in *The American Commonwealth*, Vol. 1, cap. XIII, p. 157.

16 To understand how distinctive campaign dynamics have had a collective national impact, more recently, on the local and national House and Senate campaigns in the 2016 election, *see* S.D. Foreman, M.L. Godwin (Eds.), *The Roads to Congress 2016: American Elections in a Divided Landscape*, Palgrave Macmillan, London, 2018. Also, *see* N.W. Polsby, A. Wildavsky, S.E. Schier, D.A. Hopkins, *Presidential Elections: Strategies and Structures of American Politics*, Lanham, Rowman & Littlefield, 2015.

17 States and Governors, at the end, are laboratories for the study of Executive Power and, in general, the Presidency, considering – according to Larry Sabato – that "Once maligned foes of the national and local governments, governors have become skilled negotiators and, importantly, often crucial coordinators at both of those levels. Once ill-prepared to govern and less prepared to lead, governors have welcomed into their ranks a new breed of vigorous, incisive, and thoroughly trained leaders" (in L. Sabato, *Goodbye to Good-Time Charlie: The American Governorship Transformed*, 2nd edn, CQ Press, Washington, DC, 1983, p. 2.). From an Italian perspective, regarding the most recent influences between the mid-term elections and the gubernatorial ones, *see also* F. Clementi, *Un'anatra non così zoppa (o delle elezioni di midterm del 6 novembre 2018), in Federalismi*, No. 21, 2018, available at www.federalismi.it/nv14/editoriale.cfm?eid=495 In general, regarding all the electoral process, *see* M.D. Brewer, & L.S. Maisel, *Parties and Elections in America: The Electoral Process*, Lanham, Rowman & Littlefield, 7th edn., 2015.

5.3 Donald Trump, the Republican Governors and the Electoral Race: A Forced and Inescapable Endorsement

Given their prominence and power also for the destiny of the presidency, the Governors play fundamental role in defining the federal political agenda through an intense dialogue with the President and the Congress.[18]

The political dialogue between the President and the Governors is realized, in general, both in formal meetings, such as the annual meeting, and in informal contacts.

However, the dialogue begins, in reality, with the commencement of the presidential electoral campaign, considering that the endorsement of a governor – besides his or her vote for the electoral college – keenly influences the electorate and the popular favour towards (or not) a candidate; moreover, it is able to shift the definitive results, as the recount dispute in Florida's 2000 presidential election demonstrates.[19]

At the beginning of the presidential race, during the presidential primaries, very few analysts and commentators considered Donald Trump a serious political force and presi-

18 *See* W. Anderson, *The Nation and the States, Rivals or Partners?*, University of Minnesota Press, Minneapolis, 1955; D.A. Leal, *Electing America's Governors: The Politics of Executive Elections*, Palgrave Macmillan, London, 2006; S.J. Kimberley, *Governing the American State: Congress and the New Federalism, 1877–1929*, Princeton University Press, Princeton, 2007; T. Carsey, *Campaign Dynamics: The Race for Governor*, University of Michigan Press, Ann Arbor, 1999; D. H. Haider, *When Governments come to Washington: Governors, Mayors and Intergovernmental Lobbying*, Free Press, New York, 1974.

19 On *Bush vs. Gore, see* J.M. Balkin, 'Bush V. Gore and the Boundary between Law and Politics', *Yale L. J.*, Vol. 110, 2001, pp. 1407; R.A. Posner, *Breaking the Deadlock: The 2000 Election, the Constitution, and the Courts*, Princeton University Press, Princeton, 2001; A.J. Jacobson & M. Rosenfeld (Eds.), *The Longest Night: Polemics and Perspectives on Election 2000*, University of California Press, Berkeley, 2002. The 2000 presidential election problems in Florida were very relevant, but it is not the first major vote-counting controversy in America's history. Recently, *see* E.B. Foley, *Ballot Battles: The History of Disputed Elections in the United States*, Oxford University Press, Oxford, 2016. At the same time, about the problem of voting in concrete in United States, *see* D.S. Tran, *Unrigging American Elections: Reform Past and Prologue*, Palgrave Macmillan, London, 2019.

dential candidate;[20] similarly, very few Governors – such as Chris Christie of New Jersey – were supporters of Donald Trump.[21]

Nevertheless, in a day-by-day race, while the Republican Party, especially at that time, was fractured between several and different factions as the Republican Study Committee, the Freedom Caucus, the Tea Party movement, the neoconservatives, the libertarians, traditional conservatives, the Christian right, and so on, progressively, the simplistic Trump's proposal has appeared increasingly more coherent for the American citizens and his political message grown up in an unpredictable way, grabbing every more the political consensus of the rest of the Republican candidates.[22]

Hence, while eroding the Republican claim of elite strategy 'Anyone-but-Trump', it is hardly surprising that, later, in order to correct this relevant political lack – the endorsement from State governors – Trump chose a governor as vice presidential running mate.

Therefore, at the end of the Republican presidential primaries, despite the opportunity to have the former House speaker Newt Gingrich or Governor Chris Christie, the candidate Donald Trump chose the 50th governor of Indiana from 2013 to 2017, Michael Pence, notwithstanding Pence's endorsement of Senator Ted Cruz of Texas in the 2016 Republican presidential primaries against Donald Trump.

Nevertheless, this choice was very astute, because Michael Pence, as several analysts and commentators explained later, was a very useful political figure to help connect the main old economic and political tissue of Republican Party billionaire donors with Trump,

---

20 Generally, the explanations for Donald Trump's presidential victory are based on a variety of factors: his celebrity status; the reopening of the investigation into Hillary Clinton's e-mails while she was Secretary of State thanks to James Comey's letter to Congress; the publishing of the hacked e-mails of the Democratic National Committee by WikiLeaks; and, moreover, the massive number of citizens, energized by the anti-establishment posture of Donald Trump, pumped also by his strong use of social media and fake news to influence his political narrative. The strongest factor was the supposed interference of Russian bogeymen in the democratic process of the United States. On this topic, in general, *see* P. Farhi, 'Trump's Bizarre Communications Strategy: Constantly Upstaging His Own Agenda', *Washington Post*, 28 July 2017; T.J. Coles, *Donald Trump, Inc. How Big Business and Neoliberalism Empower Populism and the Far-Right*, Clairview, West Sussex, 2017; S. Bordo, *The Destruction of Hillary Clinton*, Melville House Publishing, New York, 2017; E.T. May, *Fortress America: How We Embraced Fear and Abandoned Democracy*, Basic Books, New York, 2017; D. Frum, *Trumpocracy. The Corruption of the American Republic*, HarperCollins, New York, 2018.

21 Republican Party elites clearly regarded Donald Trump as an unappealing candidate who should be vetoed. In fact, no Republican official in the House, Senate or any governor's mansion substantially offered Trump support through the entire 'invisible primary' period. *See* A. Bycoffe, 'The Endorsement Primary', fivethirtyeight.com, 7 June 2016, available at https://projects.fivethirtyeight.com/2016-endorsement-primary/.

22 *See* M. Oliva & M. Shanahan, *The Trump Presidency: From Campaign Trail to World Stage*, Palgrave Macmillan, London, 2019; J. Green, *Devil's Bargain: Steve Bannon, Donald Trump, and the Storming of the Presidency*, Penguin Press, New York, 2017. B. Klaas, *The Despot's Apprentice: Donald Trump's Attack on Democracy*, Hurst & Co., London, 2017; M. Kranish, & M. Fisher, *Trump Revealed*, Washington Post Press, London, 2017. Also, *see* A. McMurry, 'Trumpolect: Donald Trump's Distinctive Discourse and Its Functions', *in* J. Kowalski (Ed.), *Reading Donald Trump. A Parallax View of the Campaign and Early Presidency*, Palgrave Macmillan, London, 2019, pp. 33-57.

who has generally been considered quite apart from those conservatives. At the same time, Pence – a typical political expression of the corporations of the American right wing – has given to Trump a strong link, especially with the Koch brothers, the most influential and powerful billionaire donors towards the extreme, radical and far right of the United States.[23]

After this choice, during the electoral and presidential campaign, in a steady succession – and in an inescapable and forced endorsement – a list of notable Republican individuals endorsed Donald Trump as the Republican Party's presidential nominee; and a relevant number of those were properly from the State and territorial governors.[24]

Hence, along racial, ethnic, religious, ideological, economic and geographic cleavages, the unprecedented alignment of many different divisions of U.S. electors has given to the Trump's candidature a great booster to break up the political and partisanship traditions; all those elements have supported, in a political polarization deeper than before, the great political discontent properly useful to Trump's campaign of advantaging disruption.[25]

With a few endorsements from the party's big names, without spending much of his own or anyone else's money, without a professionalized campaign apparatus, with a set of policy positions that challenged mainstream Republican principles, the Trump's outsider campaign – in reality, a regular feature of presidential election contests – has provided him with the opportunity to emphasize his distance from, and opposition to, a demonized politics-as-usual within the Washington Beltway.[26] And with this 'technique', through

---

23 *See* J. Mayer, *Dark Money: The Hidden History of the Billionaires Behind the Rise of the Radical Right*, Doubleday, New York, 2016.

24 The first ones were the New Jersey Governor Chris Christie in 2015 and Mike Pence, the Governor of Indiana, in 2016. Later, others endorsed the candidate Donald Trump, in particular the former Governors: Haley Barbour (Governor of Mississippi, 2004-12), Jan Brewer (Governor of Arizona, 2009-15), Donald DiFrancesco (Governor of New Jersey, 2001-02), Bob Ehrlich (Governor of Maryland, 2003-07), Jim Gilmore (Governor of Virginia, 1998-2002); Dave Heineman (Governor of Nebraska, 2005-15); Mike Huckabee (Governor of Arkansas, 1996-2007); Bobby Jindal (Governor of Louisiana, 2008-16); Frank Keating (Governor of Oklahoma, 1995-2003), Sarah Palin (Governor of Alaska, 2006-09); Sonny Perdue (Governor of Georgia, 2003-11); Rick Perry (Governor of Texas, 2000-15); Don Sundquist (Governor of TennesSee1995-2003); John H. Sununu (Governor of New Hampshire, 1983-89, and White House Chief of Staff, 1989-91). The Governors currently with President Trump are: Greg Abbott (Governor of Texas), Matt Bevin (Governor of Kentucky), Terry Branstad (Governor of Iowa), Sam Brownback (Governor of Kansas), Phil Bryant (Governor of Mississippi), Eddie Calvo (Governor of Guam), Chris Christie (Governor of New Jersey), Jack Dalrymple (Governor of North Dakota), Doug Ducey (Governor of Arizona), Mary Fallin (Governor of Oklahoma), Nikki Haley (Governor of South Carolina), Asa Hutchinson (Governor of Arkansas), Paul LePage (Governor of Maine), Pat McCrory (Governor of North Carolina), Matt Mead (Governor of Wyoming), Pete Ricketts (Governor of Nebraska), Rick Scott (Governor of Florida), Ralph Torres (Governor of the Northern Mariana Islands), Scott Walker (Governor of Wisconsin).

25 *See* A.I. Abramowitz, *The Great Alignment: Race, Party Transformation, and the Rise of Donald Trump*, Yale University Press, Yale, 2018; but also *see* the seminal volumes: G. Layman, *The Great Divide: Religious and Cultural Conflict in American Politics*, Columbia University Press, New York, 2001; J.K. White, *The Values Divide: American Politics and Culture in Transition*, CQ Press, Washington, DC, 2003.

26 *See* S.E. Schier & T.E. Eberly, *The Trump Presidency: Outsider in the Oval Office*, Rowman & Littlefield, Lanham, 2017.

different forms of disruption, refusing the normal conventions and classical Republican patterns of electoral politics, at the end, progressively, Trump has found the best way to become the 45th President of the United States; notwithstanding also the partnering between him and the Republican Governors – mainly, expression of the political establishment and structure of the Grand Old Party – has not so idyllic.

5.4 President Trump and the American Governors: Two Years of Conflicts, Especially on Immigration and Environment

The rejection of the classic conservative positions suggested has offered to President Trump a radically new policy agenda at the expense of conservative orthodoxy,[27] particularly regarding two major topics, which are very relevant, especially for the State governors: immigration and environment, both themes with relevant effects on labour and the economic dynamics.

Hence, these two themes mainly characterized the political confrontation between President Trump and the Governors during his first two years in office, marking also very several and relevant legal conflicts between States, Governors and President Trump.

Focused on immigration law and environment, in his two years in office President Trump has spent time transforming the presidency and modulating messaging and choices, even reinventing and revolutionizing the presidency.

In particular, continuing his presidential campaign, the immigration policies have been, in the middle of his tenure,[28] the real cornerstones of his political choices, especially around six themes: (a) the completion of the border wall with Mexico; (b) the deportation of immigrants who arrived in the United States as children, although they are currently protected under the Deferred Action for Childhood Arrivals programme (DACA); (c) the restriction of travel and work visas from eight countries; (d) the intensified screening of refugees while cutting the staff in organizations and support needed for the same; (e) the review of the H-1B visa programme; and (f) the curbing of legal immigration.

All these policies have been and are strongly interlaced with States and Governors, also determining – as we said – a long list of suits from the States to the President.

---

27 On the contrary, some scholars are against this interpretation, thinking that the main difference from the other past Republican Presidents is based only on a different style of presidency. *See* J. Herbert, T. McCrisken & A. Wroe, *The Ordinary Presidency of Donald J. Trump*, Palgrave, London, 2019. *See also* L. Bartels, '2016 Was an Ordinary Election, Not a Realignment', *Washington Post*, 10 November 2016.

28 *See* M. Gilmartin, P. Wood & C. O'Callaghan, *Borders, Mobility and Belonging in the Era of Brexit and Trump*, Policy Press, Bristol, 2018; M. Nelson, *Trump's First Year*, University of Virginia Press, Charlottesville and London, 2018.

The first political-legal conflict was on the Trump 'travel ban' –Executive Order n. 13769 'Protecting the Nation from Foreign Terrorist Entry into the United States' – signed by Donald Trump on 27 January 2017, and promptly sued from the States in the federal courts of the United States against the President; until now, after intense uncertainty, the main suit is still pending, although the intervention of the Federal Supreme Court in June 2018 has legitimated preliminarily the executive order because it respects the 'bona fide' test and the arguments presented by the Trump Administration were 'a sufficient national security justification', permitting to 'suspend entry of aliens into the United States', in particular, travellers from Syria, Iran, Libya, Yemen and Somalia.[29]

Then, after the Trump Administration released a list of immigration requests to Congress, especially a sum of $25 billion for a wall on the border with Mexico,[30] and also tried to cut federal funds from 'sanctuary' cities (the municipalities that did not want to cooperate with federal immigration agents), the Governors of the States in those cities strongly attacked President Trump and his administration for their immigration policies.

In regard to the DACA programme – launched by President Obama with an executive order in 2012, which offers a two-year deferral of deportation for eligible immigrants[31] – Trump tried to replace it by his immigration plan. However, the Federal District Court for the District of Columbia, on 24 April 2018, and a federal judge, on 4 August 2018, ruled that the Trump Administration must fully restore the programme. Hence, now the fight with the States and Governors against President Trump is until opened, because President Trump seeks to offer protection for the dreamers only for three years in exchange for border wall funding, while the Democrats have rejected it because it is not permanent.

The issues relating to immigration also involve the very well-known wall along the US-Mexico border, a symbol, or the most powerful political element of Trump's supporters, which President Trump wants to complete unreservedly.

To block this strategy, in 2017-2018, 16 States, in coordination with their Governors, filed a federal lawsuit challenging President Trump's national emergency declaration to pay for a wall along the US-Mexico border.

29 *See Trump v. Hawaii*, n. 17-965, 585 U.S. (2018).

30 President Trump promised to complete a wall on the 2,000-mile long US border with Mexico. The Secure Fence Act of 2006 built 650 miles of walls and fencing. Between 2007 and 2015, $2.4 billion was spent. Trump is using the defence funds to construct 100 miles of barrier fencing in protected wildlife refuges. He has also devoted funds to replace or enhance segments of the existing wall. The government uses the number of apprehensions to gauge immigration levels. In 2018, there were 403,479 such apprehensions, down from a record 1.67 million in 2000, because border security is better. Read, K. Amadeo, *Donald Trump on Immigration. Pros and Cons of Donald Trump's Immigration Policies*, in thebalance.com.

31 It is important to know that eligible people are those under 31, who were illegally brought to the United States as children. Since its launch, over 2 million persons 'dreamers!' have applied for and received work permits.

But recently, the Supreme Court, after a long debate, allowed Trump to use funds for the project.[32]

More recently, the California Governor, Gavin Newsom, with the Governors of Maine, Oregon and Pennsylvania, as well as the District of Columbia, sued the Trump Administration against the new rules blocking green cards for many immigrants, contesting the restriction of the legal immigration, especially regarding the indefinite detention for immigrant children.[33] Furthermore, 13 other States – including Colorado, Delaware, Illinois, Maryland, Massachusetts, Michigan, Minnesota, Nevada, New Jersey, New Mexico and Rhode Island – have sued the Trump Administration for the same reasons, considering that the new rules would add unlawful barriers to legal immigration in violation of the equal protection, guaranteed by the Fifth Amendment of the Constitution, and also interfering with States' rights.

In parallel, considering that Donald Trump's immigration policies follow economic nationalism and completely different ideas on environment, in June 2017 President Trump announced the withdrawal of the United States from the Paris Agreement on Climate Change, though the withdrawal cannot take place before 4 November 2020, the day after the 2020 presidential election. Promptly, after the presidential announcement, Governors of 13 states and Puerto Rico formed the United States Climate Alliance to adhere to the Paris accord and sued the Trump Administration against the replacement of Obama's Clean Power Plan.

Now, over 22 States, six cities and the District of Columbia,[34] have filed a lawsuit against the Trump Administration to block, repeal and replace the Obama-era policy environment plan that set emission-reduction targets, required states to restrict their use of coal-burning power plants and mandated a switch to renewable energy.[35]

Furthermore, three Governors have strongly fought with the Trump's Census programme, fearing that citizenship changes – included in the 2020 census – can reduce the

---

32 588 U.S. (2019), Supreme Court of the United States, n. 19A60, *Donald J. Trump, President of the United States, et al. V. Sierra Club, et al.*, on Application for Stay, July 26, 2019.

33 *See* D. Thompson, 'California Files Lawsuit over Trump Immigration Rule', available at www.nbcsandiego.com/news/local/Immigration-Public-Benefits-California-Lawsuit-Green-Cards-547450231.html. Read the text of the suit: www.courthousenews.com/wp-content/uploads/2019/08/CalifImmDetention-COMPLAINT.pdf. It's very interesting that, at the moment, this is the 56th lawsuit that the California State has filed against the Trump administration (the latest was the legal action to stymie federal officials' plans to change how the Endangered Species Act is implemented).

34 In particular, New York, State of California, State of Colorado, State of Connecticut, State of Delaware, State of Hawaii, State of Illinois, State of Maine, State of Maryland, Commonwealth of Massachusetts, People of the State of Michigan, State of Minnesota, State of New Jersey, State of New Mexico, State of North Carolina, State of Oregon, Commonwealth of Pennsylvania, State of Rhode Island, State of Vermont, Commonwealth of Virginia, State of Washington, State of Wisconsin, District of Columbia, City of Boulder (CO), City of Chicago, City of Los Angeles, City of New York, City of Philadelphia, and the City of South Miami.

35 Read the text of the suit: www.courthousenews.com/wp-content/uploads/2019/08/clean-power-suit.pdf.

number of voters and re-district them strategically, in a useful way to the Republican Party towards the next presidential elections of 2020.

What, then, is the significance of the legal battleground between the Governors and Trump before the courts?

Obviously, legal action by a state against the federal government in just two years is a rare, if not unprecedented, move.

Clearly, all the instruments of political connection between the President and the Governors have worked poorly. In fact, even the scheduled annual meetings,[36] as well as the informal dialogue, seem not to have allowed any real form of objective confrontation between the President and the States, even with non-Republicans.

We can add that the U.S. gubernatorial elections of 6 November 2018 in 36 States and three territories, during the mid-term elections, have presented a picture not so brilliant for President Trump, who must dialogue now with 27 Republicans and 23 Democrats, who have gained control of nine State and territorial governorships that had previously been held by Republicans and an independent (Kansas, Maine, Michigan, Nevada and New Mexico, in addition to defeating Republican incumbents in Illinois and Wisconsin, and the territory of Guam and the independent controlled territory of the U.S. Virgin Islands).

5.5 SOME FINAL REMARKS

In conclusion, two years of confrontation between President Trump and the Governors of the States have brought home to the President the crucial importance of liaising with the Governors the implementation of the President's legislative programme.

Furthermore, he has discovered how there can be adversaries – not only in a political sense but also through legal conflicts – namely the Governors against the President, resisting direct methods of persuasion concerning policies dear to their hearts that President Trump has organized.

Normally, even before taking office, the most modern US Presidents have been quick to attempt to share connections and best practices with Governors and to promote a non-partisan political debate when in charge.

36 Read the presidential remarks regarding the annual meeting with Governors of 2018 (www.whitehouse.gov/briefings-statements/remarks-president-trump-2018-white-house-business-session-governors/) and 2019 (www.whitehouse.gov/briefings-statements/remarks-president-trump-2019-white-house-business-session-nations-governors/).

In contrast, President Trump did not promote this, provoking even the Republican gubernatorial candidates to reconsider their support for him, in light of the major implications of such support for this divisive President for their personal electoral success.[37]

In his 2016 GOP convention acceptance speech, President Donald Trump said, "Nobody knows the system better than me, which is why I alone can fix it".

In these two years of presidency, the lesson should be very clear, mostly after the loss of the 2018 mid-term elections: President Trump has discovered how complex, articulate and different is the American political system, especially if you offer a unique perspective of a presidency like no other based on themes of populism and nativist nationalism,[38] instead of focusing the battle in depth on a range of key elements relevant for the presidency.

This substantially indifference and the disengagement of President Trump in front of the Governors and their political (and legal) vetoes demonstrates that it is not sufficient a great attitude towards the communication and a brutal approach in a political discourse to resolve the main political issues, especially if you face off to the larger and more complex liberal democracy of the world.

37 *See* A. Greenblatt, 'For or Against Trump? The Question Candidates for Governor Can't Escape', *Governing. The States and Localities*, 13 December 2017, available at www.governing.com/topics/politics/gov-trump-governor-elections-races-candidates.html.

38 *See* N. Gingrich, *Trump's America*, Center Street, New York, 2018.

6 Haunted by an Oppressive Ghost: The Trump Labour Agenda beyond the Dismantlement of Obama's Legacy

Davide Zecca[*]

6.1 The Trump Policies in the Area of Labour and Employment: What Was Expected

The election of Donald Trump has triggered many expectations related to the industrial and employment policy that the tycoon was willing to pursue during his term. His extensive expertise in running business and enterprises, together with the unavoidable, yet difficult to handle, interests as a current entrepreneur, have brought many commentators to forecast that the Trump presidency would have marked a major step backwards for the rights of workers and the prerogatives of trade unions within workplaces all over America. These fears were fed by the fact that the Obama social and labour agenda was perceived as very favourable to the workforce, sometimes at the expense of the interests of owners and the whole entrepreneurial sector.

In particular, there were specific issues within the broader labour and employment area that observers seemed especially concerned about during the transition from former President Obama to President Trump.[1] First, there was a dispute around the Department of Labor (DoL) authority to set the threshold above which workers must be considered 'white-collars', thereby no longer being entitled to the application of the overtime pay rule under the *Fair Labor Standards Act* (FLSA). The entry into force of the Final Rule adopted in the last year of Obama's second term was blocked just weeks after the presidential elections, and it was unclear whether the incoming administration was willing to set a threshold for the salary test and to appeal the decision of the District Court on the merits.

Second, employees' fears were focused on the so-called Persuader Rule enshrined in the *Labor-Management Reporting and Disclosure Act* (LMRDA), providing for reporting duties for entrepreneurs with reference to the hiring of consultants for bargaining with

* PhD Candidate, University of Pavia.

1 For an overall account of such expectations, *see* Holland & Knight, 'An Overview of What to Expect from the Trump Administration and the 115th Congress', 30 November 2016, p. 27, available at www.hklaw.com/files/Uploads/Documents/Events/113016TrumpAdminPPT.pdf.

employees. The interpretation of the rule by the DoL under the Obama administration received harsh criticism from employers and attorneys before a federal judge adopted an injunction holding that the purported construction exceeded the department authority under the LMRDA and that it also violated a bundle of rights arising out of the First Amendment, which included the client-attorney privilege.

Finally, the stability of several decisions adopted by the *National Labor Relations Board* (NLRB) during the Obama tenure were thought to be in danger as soon as President Trump was able to appoint new members to the agency, thereby reversing the political orientation of the college.

In the aftermath of Trump's first two years, in which he was supposed to be favoured by a solid majority in both branches of Congress, a first assessment may be carried out in regard to whether his labour agenda has translated into something successful. In this regard, I reckon it is useful to analyse the action of the Trump administration by distinguishing between the direct intervention through a limited number of deliberations by Congress, executive orders issued by the President himself and the regulations adopted by the DoL on one side, as opposed to the indirect effects arising out of President Trump's appointments to federal bodies vested with adjudicatory powers (the Supreme Court and the NLRB).

As the two ways of influencing the field of labour and employment are inherently different, it is worth dealing first with the actions taken directly by the administration, to address later the effects of the appointments to the nation's highest court and to the above agency. Finally, a few considerations relating to the attitude of the current administration and federal institutions with regard to the relationship between employers, managers and employees within workplaces will be offered for discussion.

6.2 THE AMENDMENT OF THE NORMATIVE FRAMEWORK

6.2.1 *The Congress*

The contribution of Congress to the implementation of Trump's labour agenda has been modest thus far, limited mainly to counteracting rules issued by the competent agencies during the two terms of President Obama. The single piece of legislation with meaningful effects on labour law is included in a far wider spending bill allocating resources for the fiscal year 2018, the so-called *Consolidated Appropriations Act 2018*:[2] namely, what matter the most for the purpose of this analysis are two amendments to the *FLSA* of 1938.[3]

---

2 H.R.1625 – 115th Congress (2017-2018), later become Public Law No: 115-141.

3 29 U.S.C. 201 *et seq.*

First, the bill integrated §7 of the Act by introducing a provision that excludes, when a major disaster takes place, the applicability of the whole §7 for a two-year interval to any employee cumulatively tasked with adjusting or evaluating claims arising from the disaster by an employer not engaged anyhow in activities related to insurance policies or contracts, receiving not less than $591/week for the period he is employed in the above task and assigned duties such as interviewing injured individuals and witnesses, investigating damages for the purpose of preparing estimates, recommending how to deal with coverage or compensability of claims or liability, negotiating settlements and giving recommendations regarding litigation.[4] Major disasters are defined as those declared and designated as such by State or Federal agencies or departments. The practical consequence of the newly enacted provisions is that those employees not working for insurance companies and involved in the evaluation of claims following the occurrence of a major disaster will not be bound by the limits concerning the maximum amount of weekly workload of workers (calculated in hours), above which they would be entitled to a wage worth one and a half times their regular pay.

Second, the bill amends §2 of the Act by providing that in case an employee receives tips, the employer is not allowed to keep the latter, not even to ensure the participation of managers or supervisors to the distribution of such money and notwithstanding the existence of a tip credit; the violation of the provision subjects the employer to liability to the employees concerned and to a civil penalty.[5] The provision affects, in addition, the Final Rules previously issued by the DoL,[6] providing that employers paying employees the minimum wage in accordance with the Act may also allow workers who usually do not receive tips, because they do not have direct contacts with customers (*i.e.* cooks and dishwashers), to take part in tip pools.[7] This implies that waiters and other categories of workers who used to be the only beneficiaries of tip pooling will have to share a portion of those revenues they were able to keep for themselves beforehand.[8]

While the foregoing is the only piece of legislation affecting labour law directly passed by the 115th Congress, the latter also approved four joint resolutions aimed at nullifying the effects of rules issued by the DoL mostly during the last few months of Barack Obama's second term. Before illustrating the content of the resolutions, it is interesting to explain the nature of these instruments of law. The Constitution of the United States of America

4 Sec. 109, Public Law No: 115-141.

5 Sec. 1201, Public Law No: 115-141.

6 Wage and Hour Division, Department of Labor, 'Updating Regulations Issued under the Fair Labor Standards Act', Final Rule, 5 April 2011, 76 Fed. Reg. 18832.

7 Wage and Hour Division, Department of Labor, 'Field Assistance Bulletin no. 2018-3', 6 April 2018, available at www.dol.gov/whd/FieldBulletins/fab2018_3.pdf.

8 For a synthetic reference to the discussion concerning pool tipping in the hospitality industry, *see* L. Badoux, 'The Consolidated Appropriations Act: Tipping in the Hospitality Industry', 19 April 2018, available at www.buchalter.com/publication/consolidated-appropriations-act-tipping-hospitality-industry/.

provides that "[e]very Bill which shall have passed the House of Representatives and the Senate, shall, before it become a Law, be presented to the President of the United States":[9] this is known as the Presentment clause, implying that the President of the Federation shall sign all laws after they are passed by both branches of Congress. The provision is relevant to discuss Congress power to disapprove rules or regulations issued by departments of the federal administration or administrative agencies. Notably, in 1983 the Supreme Court struck down as unconstitutional the congressional veto provision enshrined in §244(c)(2) of the Immigration and Nationality Act by holding that Congress was not empowered to pass a law allowing it to exercise a form of legislative power in derogation of the bicameralism principle and the Presentment clause.[10] What had happened was that the decision of the Attorney General (AG) not to deport a foreign citizen was disapproved by one House only, and the resolution was not presented to the President for signature. Given that the power had previously been delegated to the AG through a legislative deliberation, the Court found that "Congress must abide by its delegation of authority until that delegation is legislatively altered or revoked", which means that it can do so only by passing a bill that falls within the definition of the exercise of legislative power, and it implies the approval of a uniform text in both Houses and the signature into law of the President.[11]

The issue was later tackled by the Congress in 1996, when the *Congressional Review Act* (CRA) was passed:[12] the bill introduced a 'fast track' for Congress to paralyze the entry into force of rules promulgated by agencies, by requiring that they were timely submitted to Congress for approval and that Congress could prevent them from entering into force by approving a joint resolution of disapproval signed by the President; moreover, agencies cannot reinstate similar rules unless authorized to do so by Congress.[13] Therefore, from then on, joint resolutions of the two Houses signed by the President, which are normative tools usually resorted to in exceptional (*e.g.* creation of temporary commissions or exceptions to existing law) or limited circumstances (*e.g.* declaration of war, termination of national emergency), are the only instrument Congress may resort to in order to disapprove rules issued either by a governmental department or a federal agency.

What is indeed interesting is the unprecedented recourse that the 115th Congress and President Trump have made to the instruments mentioned: while no such set of rules had been nullified during Clinton's tenure and only one and five were, respectively, disapproved

---

9 Art. I, §7, cl. 2.

10 *INS v. Chadha*, 462 U.S. 919.

11 *INS v. Chadha*, 462 U.S. 954-955.

12 Subtitle E, *Contract with America Advancement Act* of 1996, Public Law 104-121.

13 For a summary of the issues addressed by this piece of legislation, *see, e.g.*, Congressional Research Service, 'The Congressional Review Act (CRA)', *Focus*, 18 December 2018, available at https://fas.org/sgp/crs/misc/IF10023.pdf.

under G.W. Bush and Obama (who, in any case, vetoed all joint resolutions), under the Trump administration 15 similar rules have already been the object of a joint resolution of disapproval by the Congress, amounting to nearly ¾ of the overall amount since the bill entered into force. The relevant number of joint resolutions approved in the above Congress would already be enough to label the activism of the Trump administration and the 115th Congress as historic in this regard. Nonetheless, what is notable is the extent to which the reliance on the CRA has expanded: by construing the statute as meaning that the 60-day term to approve the joint resolution of disapproval begins running only from the moment the rule is submitted to Congress, the administration has managed not only to invalidate rules promulgated by agencies or departments in the sunset of the Obama era, but also to affect regulations that dated back much earlier. This has been possible since those rules had never been submitted to Congress for approval by the Department or Agency that had issued them.

While still extraordinary, the effort of the Trump administration and of Congress in this field is far from over, but following a very intense rhythm in the first months of the presidency, the activity has apparently slowed down significantly, both to allow Congress to pursue other goals of the President's agenda and in consideration of the increasing difficulty for Republicans to hold on to the Senate majority, which was already limited on the inauguration day (*52 Republicans v. 48 Democrats*).[14] The outcome of the mid-term elections of November 2018 has imposed a temporary interruption to the practice of disapproving agencies' and departments' rules, especially since the Democratic party is currently majoritarian in the House of Representatives and has no intention of backing similar proposals by the administration.

It is worth mentioning the rules promulgated by the DoL that the joint resolution passed in the initial months of the Trump presidency nullified: those are the "Federal-State Unemployment Compensation Program; Middle Class Tax Relief and Job Creation Act of 2012 Provision on Establishing Appropriate Occupations for Drug Testing of Unemployment Compensation Applicants" rule;[15] the "Clarification of Employer's Continuing Obligation to Make and Maintain an Accurate Record of Each Recordable Injury and Illness" rule;[16] the "Savings Arrangements Established by Qualified State Political Subdivisions

14 P.J. Jr. Larkin, 'The Trump Administration and the Congressional Review Act', *Geo. J.L. & Pub. Pol'y*, Vol. 16, No. 2, 2018, p. 505.

15 1 August 2016, 81 Fed. Reg. 50298; the rule was disapproved by H.J. Res. 42, 31 March 2017, Public Law 115-17.

16 19 December 2016, 81 Fed. Reg. 91792; the rule was disapproved by H.J. Res. 83, 3 April 2017, Public Law 115-21.

for Non-Governmental Employees" rule[17] and the "Savings Arrangements Established by States for Non-Governmental Employees" rule.[18]

6.2.2 The President

For what concerns the activity directly carried out by the President himself, four executive orders affecting the field of labour law have been issued by Trump in these first two years (evenly split between 2017 and 2018). First in line, the Presidential Executive Order on the *Revocation of Federal Contracting Executive Orders*[19] is essentially an instrument aimed at revoking an executive order entitled *Fair Pay and Safe Workplaces* (and its subsequent amendments) signed by President Obama during his second term.[20] The Order had been passed to make up for the deficiencies in terms of compliance with labour law by federal contractors: for solicitations related to contracts over $500,000, offerors should comply with specific duties of transparency; the document also provided for potential remedies where recommendations to correct incompliant conducts were not followed. It is worth noting that the Order had been passed together with an analogous instrument of law aimed at prohibiting governmental contractors from discriminating employees on the basis of sexual orientation or gender identity.[21]

The revocation of the order means that it has never had any effect, as its application was enjoined just days before it was set to enter into force, at the end of October 2016.[22] Nonetheless, from the simultaneity of the signature of the two preceding orders above it may be inferred that the more serious reporting duties weighing on the shoulders of federal contractors had been designed, at least to some extent, to ensure an adequate enforcement of the prohibition of discrimination on sexual orientation and gender identity imposed by the above executive order. The decision to revoke the whole instrument of law will therefore likely limit the intensity of governmental oversight over the conduct of federal contractors, potentially affecting the protection of LGBTQ rights within workplaces.

17 20 December 2016, 81 Fed. Reg. 92639; the rule was disapproved by H.J. Res. 67, 13 April 2017, Public Law 115-24.

18 30 August 2016, 81 Fed. Reg. 59464; the rule was disapproved by H.J. Res. 66, 17 May 2017, Public Law 115-35.

19 Executive Order 13782, 27 March 2017, available at www.federalregister.gov/documents/2017/03/30/2017-06382/revocation-of-federal-contracting-executive-orders.

20 Executive Order 13673, 31 July 2014; §3, Executive Order 13683, 11 December 2014; Executive Order 13738, 23 August 2016.

21 Executive Order 13672, 21 July 2014, available at www.federalregister.gov/documents/2014/07/23/2014-17522/further-amendments-to-executive-order-11478-equal-employment-opportunity-in-the-federal-government.

22 *Associated Builders and Contractors of Southeast Texas v. Anne Rung*, United States District Court for the Eastern District of Texas, Case 1:16-CV-425, 24 October 2016, available at www.crowell.com/files/20161024-ABC-Southeast-Texas-v-Rung.pdf.

However, it was correctly argued that the attempt to intervene to make up for wage gender gap, denial of increased pay for hours worked overtime and further violations of labour law via an executive order (which is the instrument lame duck Presidents usually resort to where Congress does not show willingness to implement their agenda) proves ineffective as it enacts a very weak and fragile normative framework, which can easily be rolled back by the following Commander-in-Chief; thus, it is appropriate to support the argument that the matter would effectively be tackled only upon adequate congressional or judicial input.[23]

Next, the gunsight of Trump's rifle aimed for the removal of yet another heritage of the Obama administration, the National Council on Federal Labor-Management Relations and the correlated forums: the institution had been created during the first year of the first term of the former President and it ideally served the purpose of establishing "a cooperative and productive form of labor-management relations throughout the executive branch".[24] The improvement of the labour-management relations in the public sector had been a goal long pursued by US administrations to foster the productivity of government-run activities; nonetheless, usually more conservative Presidents have rolled back progressive openings to the normalization of the relationship between managers and workers (*e.g.* G.W. Bush revocation of Clinton's Executive Order 12871, creating the National Partnership Council).[25] The story repeated two years ago, as the assessment of President Trump has been that the Council had failed to fulfil its goal and had therefore been a waste of resources that could have been otherwise invested: therefore, he proceeded to sign the order that revoked the institution.[26]

The executive orders signed in 2017 belong, therefore, to the attempt to dismantle certain policies enacted under the previous administration; conversely, the executive orders promulgated in 2018 adopt a more propositional approach, by detailing already existing normative frameworks and establishing advisory bodies. In the first place, President Trump signed an Executive Order to ensure that federal employees spend the prevailing part of their work-hours performing the duties they are assigned: the aim of the instrument of law was to avoid the practice of federal workers being paid for performing activities related to the collective representation of employees' interests, unless it is so provided by the law.[27] Therefore, the effect of the order is to restrict the freedom of association of federal workers,

23 B. Canales, 'Closing the Federal Gender Pay Gap Through Wage Transparency', *Hous. L. Rev.*, Vol. 55, No. 4, 2018, p. 969.

24 Executive Order 13522, 9 December 2009, later extended by Executive Order 13708, 30 September 2015.

25 R.M. Tobias, 'Future of Federal-Sector Labor-Management Relations', *Conflict Resolution Quarterly*, Vol. 33, Supplement 1, Winter 2015, S101.

26 Executive Order 13812, 29 September 2017, available at www.federalregister.gov/documents/2017/10/04/2017-21559/revocation-of-executive-order-creating-labor--management-forums.

27 Executive Order 13837, 25 May 2018, available at www.federalregister.gov/documents/2018/06/01/2018-11916/ensuring-transparency-accountability-and-efficiency-in-taxpayer-funded-union-time-use.

as those employees who previously performed representative tasks during work-hours will no longer be authorized to do so, if not to a limited extent and subject to the threat of disciplinary sanction in case of incompliance.

Finally, Trump decided to set up a National Council for the American Worker chaired by the secretaries of Commerce and Labor together with the Assistant to the President for Domestic Policy and the Advisor to the President overseeing the Office of Economic Initiative, while simultaneously encompassing a number of other members of the administration at high levels.[28] The Council has mere advisory powers, as it is tasked with providing recommendations to the President on the policies and strategies to adopt with reference to American workers. The Council should be able to avail of the assistance of a wider ad hoc Advisory Board, set up for the two years following the entry into force of the order. The creation of the body has no direct effect on the rights and prerogatives of workers and its success could be assessed only after some time.

6.2.3 *The DoL*

The third and final branch of direct intervention into the field of labour and employment law is made up of the administrative and regulatory activity carried out by the DoL, which has enjoyed a greater stability at its apex compared with other departments of the Federal administration under President Trump[29]. The first issue to be addressed is the determination of the overtime rule: it is the provision that determines the threshold above which employees should not be recognized the right to a higher wage for overtime hours worked, as provided by the *FLSA*. More specifically, the statute provides that minimum wage and overtime requirements do not apply to employees employed in a bona fide executive, administrative or professional capacity and for outside sales and computer employees;[30] for the scope of its application, this is also known as the 'white-collars' exemption, as it applies to non-manual workers, as opposed to 'blue-collars' (manual workers). The regulation issued in this regard by the DoL details the professional characteristics that qualify a member of each of these categories of workers as exempt, while also setting specific salary requirements:[31] regulations have historically required workers to meet a threefold cumulative test, aimed at verifying whether they were paid a predetermined and fixed salary (salary basis test) matching a minimum amount (salary level test), and their tasks primarily

28 Executive Order 13845, 19 July 2018, available at www.federalregister.gov/documents/2018/07/24/2018-15955/establishing-the-presidents-national-council-for-the-american-worker.

29 This was the case at least until July 2019, when Secretary Alexander Acosta was forced to resign.

30 *Fair Labor Standards Act*, §13(a)(1), 29 U.S.C. 213.

31 29 Code of Federal Regulation – Part 541 – Defining and delimiting the exemptions for executive, administrative, professional, computer and outside sales employees.

involved executive, administrative or professional duties as defined by each regulation (duties test).[32]

Already modified seven times from the entry into force of the Act, the salary level had last been amended in 2004, before President Obama directed the Department to update it in 2014: the Final Rule adopted in 2016 by the DoL set the standard to $913/weekly ($47,476/year), thereby requiring businesses to pay overtime wages to an estimated 4.2 million employees.[33] Set to enter into force on 1 December 2016, the rule was put on hold by the nationwide preliminary injunction granted by a District Court from Texas in late November 2016.[34] After President Trump took office, the DoL published a request for information regarding the matter (26 July 2017); soon thereafter, the Federal court before which the recourse against the overtime rule was pending granted a summary judgment in favour of the plaintiffs and against the DoL, declaring that the agency did not have authority to adopt the salary test as the only marker for the exemption of 'white-collar' workers, in consideration of Congress' unambiguous delegation of powers.[35] The judgment was later appealed by the Department of Justice (on behalf of the DoL) under the Trump administration: the underlying reason was that the DoL was willing to have its authority to set a predetermined salary to serve as the basis for the salary level test recognized, in order to elaborate a new, lower threshold in this regard.[36] Nonetheless, while the nationwide injunction to the entry into force of the rule is still in force, the DoL has circulated a notice of proposed rule-making that would set the aforementioned threshold at $679/week ($35,308/year).[37]

The second labour regulation that has been heavily tackled by the Trump administration is the so-called Persuader Rule: a Final Rule was issued in the last year of President Obama's term as well to impose more serious reporting duties for employers in regard to the hiring of consultants for the purpose of addressing the organization of union representation and

32 Wage and Hour Division of the Department of Labor, 'Defining and Delimiting the Exemptions for Executive, Administrative, Professional, Outside Sales and Computer Employees', Final Rule, 23 May 2016, I. Executive Summary, available at www.federalregister.gov/documents/2016/05/23/2016-11754/defining-and-delimiting-the-exemptions-for-executive-administrative-professional-outside-sales-and.

33 United States Department of Labor, 'Overtime for White Collar Workers. Overview and Summary of Final Rule', available at www.dol.gov/sites/default/files/overtime-overview.pdf.

34 *Nevada v. US Department of Labor*, United States District Court for the Eastern District of Texas, Case 4:16-cv-00731-ALM, 22 November 2016.

35 *Nevada v. US Department of Labor*, United States District Court for the Eastern District of Texas, 31 August 2017.

36 K. Tornone, 'DOL Abandons Overtime Rule, Asks Court to OK Salary Threshold Concept', *HR Dive*, 30 June 2017, available at www.hrdive.com/news/dol-abandons-overtime-rule-asks-court-to-ok-salary-threshold-concept/446257/.

37 Wage and Hour Division, Department of Labor, 'Notice of Proposed Rulemaking: Overtime Update', available at www.dol.gov/whd/overtime2019/index.htm.

collective bargaining.[38] More specifically, while under the previous regulatory framework owners were due to report to workers' representatives only when the hired consultants interacted directly with employees, the rule made it compulsory for employers to also report the hiring of any consultant for the above purposes, even when the professional did not enter into contact with the employees. As it happened for the overtime rule, yet again a Federal district judge before which a motion for summary judgment was filed granted a nationwide injunction to the application of the rule just days before it was set to enter into force.[39] On 16 November 2016, the summary judgment of the District Court permanently blocked the entry into force of the Persuader Rule; while the DoL appealed the decision just weeks before President Trump was sworn in, the rule's fate was doomed. Eventually, in the midst of the 2017 summer, the DoL rescinded the regulation, specifying that the previous legal framework was still applicable and arguing in favour of the rights of citizens to exchange views with and receive advice from their lawyers without mandatory disclosure to the government.[40]

6.3 The Indirect Influence on Adjudicatory Bodies

6.3.1 *The Supreme Court*

The effects of the election of Donald Trump to the US presidency extend well beyond the actions taken by himself, his administration or the 115th Republican-majoritarian Congress directly: indeed, the US Constitution grants the President influential powers over several institutions tasked with adjudicatory powers, as the White House appoints federal judges and, especially, the Justices sitting at the Supreme Court, subject to the advice and consent of the Senate, while also shaping the composition of the NLRB.

With reference to the first instance, it is not an overstatement to identify the filling of the seat previously occupied by Antonin Scalia as one of the political actions that will

38 Labor-Management Standards Office, 'Interpretation of the "Advice" Exemption in Section 203(c) of the Labor-Management Reporting and Disclosure Act', Final Rule, 24 March 2016, available at www.federalregister.gov/documents/2016/03/24/2016-06296/interpretation-of-the-advice-exemption-in-section-203c-of-the-labor-management-reporting-and.

39 *National Federation of Independent Business v. Perez*, U.S. District Court for the Northern District of Texas, Case 5:16-cv-00066-C, 27 June 2016, available at www.chamberlitigation.com/sites/default/files/cases/files/16161616/Order%20Granting%20Preliminary%20Injunction%20--%20NFIB%20v.%20Perez%20%28U.S.%20District%20Court%20-%20Northern%20District%20of%20Texas%29.pdf.

40 E.M. Hutchinson & R. Meisburg, 'DOL Repeals Obama-Era "Persuader Rule"', *Hunton Employment & Labor Perspectives*, 26 July 2018, available at www.huntonlaborblog.com/2018/07/articles/labor-unions/dol-repeals-obama-era-persuader-rule/.

contribute the most to determining the legacy of Trump's presidency (at least thus far). As a matter of fact, the death of the strongly conservative Italian-American Justice had offered to Barack Obama an outstanding chance to move the political orientation of the highest court of the nation towards positions that had not been seen since the Burger Court decades ago. The inflexible and resolute stance taken by then Senate Majority Leader Mitch McConnell not to consider any nominee from President Obama, then in the last year of his second term, allowed Trump to begin his tenure by nominating Neil Gorsuch to the Supreme Court. The nomination, which is already yielding results favourable to the conservative base of the Republican party, is set to be even more important after the resignation of Justice Anthony Kennedy and the nomination of Brett Kavanaugh. Notably, Gorsuch was in the 5-4 majority split on ideological lines that decided in the 2017 term the landmark case *Janus v. AFSCME.*[41]

The dispute arose from a complaint filed by a public-sector worker, Mark Janus, who originally joined a suit previously filed by then newly elected Illinois' Governor: the issue at stake was whether the State law allowing the imposition of agency fees to non-unionized workers was compatible with the freedom of speech recognized under the First Amendment to the Federal Constitution.[42] Illinois law allows governmental employees to unionize and provides that if a union receives a majority of the votes within a bargaining unit, it is the sole subject authorized to bargain with the employer on behalf of all the members of the unit, regardless of their decision to join the union or not.[43] While employees not willing to join the union are exempted from the payment of the full membership dues, they are nonetheless compelled to pay a so-called agency fee, which amounts to a certain percentage of the membership dues. This fraction is calculated by determining which of the union activities pertain to the collective bargaining process and which are, instead, connected with the political commitment of the union: only the first (so-called chargeable expenditures) may be imposed on non-unionized workers, while the second (non-chargeable expenditures) cannot.[44] The agency fee is established on a yearly basis, and notified to non-unionized employees, while it is directly deducted from the employees' wages by the

41 138 Sup.Ct. 2448.

42 Interestingly, the validity of the basic assumption of both *Abood* and *Janus*, namely that requiring an individual to pay money to fund a cause he does not support implies an infringement of his freedom of speech, has been questioned as well, *see* W. Baude & E. Volokh, 'Compelled Subsidies and the First Amendment', *Harv. L. Rev.*, Vol. 132, No. 1, 2018, p. 171; someone has developed the reasoning even further, arguing that agency fees are money only fictitiously belonging to employees, while in reality it is money paid by employers to unions and should, as a result, be treated as unions' rather than employees' property, *see* B.I. Sachs, 'Agency Fees and the First Amendment', *Harv. L. Rev.*, Vol. 131, No. 4, 2018, p. 1046.

43 Illinois Public Labor Relations Act (IPLRA), available at www.ilga.gov/legislation/ilcs/ilcs3.asp?ActID=108&ChapterID=2.

44 *Abood v. Detroit Board of Education*, 431 U.S. 209 (1977).

employer. It is worth noting that agency fees are not allowed at the federal level, while some States had already forbidden them even before the judgment at stake was delivered.

The Supreme Court first went through the arguments supporting the decision in the relevant precedent in this regard (*Abood v. Detroit Bd. of Ed.*)[45]: while it acknowledged the nature of labour peace as a compelling State interest, it criticized the inference that the designation of a single union as the lone representative of all employees in a unit implies the imposition of agency fees on non-members, providing data concerning union membership in the federal sector; moreover, it refused to accept the willingness to avoid freeriding of the benefits of the union activities from non-members as a compelling State interest, holding that, on the contrary, the workers forced to fund the union are not hidden beneficiaries of the mechanism but rather individuals compelled to pay against their own willingness.

The other argument supporting the legitimacy of agency fees was the reference to another precedent where the issue of governmental employees' freedom of speech was at stake: in *Pickering v. Board of Education* the Supreme Court had held that "it cannot be [denied] that the State has interests as an employer in regulating the speech of its employees that differ significantly from those it possesses in connection with regulation of the speech of the citizenry in general", while adding that a balance needs to be struck between the interest of the individual employee to comment on matters of public interest as a citizen and that of the State in promoting the efficiency of the public service.[46] However, the Court distinguished *Janus* from *Pickering* as one involved the compulsory subsidization of speech employees may not share, while the other concerned the impact of an employee's speech on his public responsibilities; moreover, it recognized that the union speech at stake was of substantial interest, but it concluded that this did not justify the heavy burden imposed with agency fees. The last hurdle to overcome was the status of precedent of *Abood v. Detroit Bo. of Ed.*: Justice Alito, writing the majority opinion, argued that the doctrine of *stare decisis* did not play a decisive role in the case at stake, as the reasoning of the precedent was flawed by a misinterpretation of two previous decisions, the case did not provide an adequately workable standard, it had remained an exceptional circumstance in the First Amendment case law and contracts stipulated with that normative framework in mind would soon expire and be up for renegotiation.[47] The Court then held that agency fees may be collected only by unions from non-unionized workers when employees explicitly consent to it.

45 For references to the Supreme Court case law between *Abood* and *Janus* and the signals that pointed to a finding of the Court in this direction, *see* D.F. Forte, 'To Speak Or Not to Speak, That Is Your Right: *Janus v. AFSCME*', *2017 Cato Sup. Ct. Rev.*, 2017-2018, p. 171.

46 *Pickering v. Board of Education*, 391 U.S. 563, 568 (1968).

47 *Janus v. ACSFME*, 138 Sup.Ct. 2448 (2018), Alito, J., VI, 33-47, Slip op.

The most likely immediate consequences of the Court holding in *Janus* are a decrease in funds available for public-sector unions, which may affect their efficiency and their organization, and a likely reduction of the percentage of unionized workers, as now all workers benefit from the union activity even without paying any fee to the union. Whether the foregoing may undermine labour peace in State public administrations is yet to be seen, although the evidence presented by the appellants before the Supreme Court provides for a different empirical finding.

6.3.2 The NLRB

For what concerns the other adjudicatory body whose decisions have had and will have a great impact upon labour law, some background information may be useful to introduce it. Part of the legacy of Roosevelt's New Deal legislation, the NLRB is an agency composed of five members appointed by the President with the advice and consent of the Senate for a five-year term (except when nominated to fill a mid-term vacancy). A chairman of the agency is designed by the President as well;[48] Board members are irremovable, except for negligence and misbehaviour in office, and may be re-elected. Its main tasks are to oversee elections to form or decertify unions of private-sector employees and investigate and prosecute alleged violations of workers' rights enshrined in the *National Labor Relations Act* (NLRA); hence, the Board may exercise both adjudicatory and regulatory powers (*e.g.* by issuing rules).

While many federal agencies' statutes encompass partisan balance requirements (*i.e.* statutory provision prescribing that appointees of a given ideology or political orientation may not overcome the simple majority of members),[49] the bills creating or amending the NLRB do not; however, history shows how, after an initial short period when non-partisanship was deemed a necessary feature to be appointed to serve on the Board, from the Eisenhower administration onwards partisans of either employers or employees have been extensively nominated to the NLRB.[50] While the Chairman has usually been nominated among academics or government officials (even inside the NLRB itself), this has failed to prevent the agency from being perceived as an excessively politicized body and, thereby, it undermined the trust and compliance with its decisions.[51] That notwithstanding, the nominations to the NLRB have always complied, at least this far, with a sort of informal

48 *National Labor Relations Act* of 1938 (so-called *Wagner Act*), 29 U.S.C. §§ 151-169.

49 For references *see* B.D. Feinstein & D.J. Hemel, 'Partisan Balance with Bite', *Columbia Law Review*, Vol. 118, No. 1, 2018, pp. 9-82.

50 For an extensive account of the appointments to the NLRB *see* J. Flynn, 'A Quiet Revolution at the Labor Board: The Transformation of the NLRB 1935-2000', *Ohio St. L. J.*, Vol. 61, No. 4, 2000, p. 1361.

51 J.J. Brudney, 'Isolated and Politicized: The NLRB's Uncertain Future', *Comp. Lab. L. & Pol'y. J.*, Vol. 26, No. 2, 2005, p. 221.

partisan balance requirement, as may be ascertained by going through the composition of the Board over the last few decades. This tacit rule did not imply that nominations to the NLRB have not been challenged all through these years, as occurred during the second term of President Obama.[52]

The day Donald Trump was sworn in as the 45th US President, only three out of the five seats of the Board were occupied, with a two-to-one Democratic majority (Mark Gaston Pearce and Lauren McFerran, Democratic; Philip Andrew Miscimarra, Republican). Trump soon nominated Miscimarra, already exercising the duties of Acting Chairman, as the full Chairman of the Board; however, it took Trump until the end of the 2017 summer to re-establish a Republican majority with the nomination of Marvin Elliot Kaplan (2 August 2017; sworn in on 8 August) and William Emanuel (25 September 2017; sworn in on 26 September).

The shift in the majority was promptly noticed in the 2017 autumn, when the agency began to target a number of decisions issued during the Obama Presidency in order to reinstate a more employers-friendly normative framework. The first issue to be tackled was the liability towards employees of companies and subcontractors in the case of indirect control: in *Browning-Ferris Industries of California* the NLRB had revisited the then current standard for the assessment of the existence of a joint employment to determine whether the company at stake was obliged to bargain with a union representing employees that were only indirectly employed by the company, concluding that joint employment could exist even in case the employer does not exercise any actual control over the employees of the other employer (subcontractor).[53] The NLRB has since rolled back on the decision, holding in *Hy-Brand Industrial Contractors* that the decision in *Browning-Ferries* was not rooted in the common law and would threaten the stability of labour-management relations.[54] It is noteworthy that the finding in *Hy-Brand* has been vacated by the Board after only three months, following the discovery that one NLRB member was as well a shareholder of one of the law firms assisting one of the parties to the case.[55] Finally, at the end of 2018, the Court of Appeals for the DC Circuit, on petition of review of the NLRB's Order in *Browning-Ferries,* upheld the agency's construction of the joint-employer standard as encompassing both direct and indirect control of employees' terms and conditions of employment; however, it underlined the failure of the Board to draw the borders of indirect control over essential terms and conditions of employment (that implies the existence of joint employment) and indirect control considered intrinsic to ordinary third-party con-

52 *National Labor Relations Board v. Noel Canning*, 134 Sup.Ct. 2550 (2014).

53 *Browning-Ferris Indus. of Cal.*, 362 N.L.R.B. No. 186, 27 August 2015.

54 *Hy-Brand Industrial Contractors, Ltd.*, 365 N.L.R.B. No. 156, 14 December 2017.

55 *Hy-Brand Industrial Contractors, Ltd.*, 366 N.L.R.B. No. 26, 26 February 2018.

tracting relationships.[56] The decision of the DC Court of Appeals to remand the case to the Board for further elaboration on the distinction over indirect control over terms of employment and influence over ordinary or routine matters may not be the final word on the joint-employer criterion, as the Board itself is committed to exercise its rule-making power in this regard, in order to develop a uniform standard not dependent on case-by-case adjudication.[57]

Moving to the field of unions' organization, the issue of the determination of bargaining units for the purposes of unions' elections had been addressed by the NLRB in *Specialty Healthcare*,[58] when it was held that the traditional community of interest test shall apply to draw the boundaries of bargaining units and that when an employer contended that a proposed bargaining unit was inappropriate as it excluded certain employees, the burden of proof to demonstrate that the excluded employees shared an overwhelming community of interest with the concerned unit was on him. However, the re-established Republican majority within the Board overruled the 2011 Order, finding that it was excessively deferential to petitioned-for units and that it betrayed the intent of the legislature by requiring that an overwhelming (rather than merely substantial) interest shared by workers existed in order to determine the appropriateness of a bargaining unit and to ensure that employees enjoy the fullest freedom in the exercise of the rights granted under the NLRA.[59] Thus, the current orientation of the NLRB in this regard is to adhere to the traditional community of interest standard in its pre-*Specialty Healthcare* construction.

For what concerns the obligations of employers with reference to changes in terms and conditions of employment, the agency had recently found that it is unlawful for employers to implement unilateral amendments of the above lacking prior negotiation of a collective bargaining agreement, even when those changes reflected a past practice previously in force between the parties.[60] One more time, the change of pattern has been short-lived, as the decision has been overruled on the ground that it distorted the meaning of the word 'changes' and that it was unfit to the Board's task to foster stable bargaining relationships: the Board holds that the application of contractual conditions that had already been implemented in the past does not amount to a change and that, in any case, employers unilaterally altering the content of the terms of employment are nonetheless bound by the bargaining duties stemming from a union request.[61]

56 US Court of Appeals for the District of Columbia, *Browning-Ferris Indus. of Cal. v. NLRB*, No. 16-1028, 28 December 2018.
57 Seyfarth Shaw, 'D.C. Circuit Invalidates NLRB's Browning-Ferris Joint Employer Test', 31 December 2018, available at www.seyfarth.com/publications/OMM123118-LE.
58 *Specialty Healthcare & Rehabilitation Center of Mobile*, 357 NLRB No. 934, 26 August 2011.
59 *PCC Structurals, Inc.*, 365 NLRB No. 156, 15 December 2017.
60 *E.I. Du Pont de Nemours*, 364 NLRB No. 113, 26 August 2016.
61 *Raytheon Co.*, 365 NLRB No. 161, 15 December 2017.

With reference to the adjudicatory activity, it is eventually worth mentioning another rollback of the NLRB, affecting the content of so-called 'employer-rules'. During the last year of Obama's second term, the NLRB had found unlawful some provisions of a Hospital's Code of Conduct, aimed at fostering the creation of a harmonious workplace for employees, for they impinged on the rights of employees under §7 NLRA;[62] in doing so, the Board had applied a standard that dated back to the 2004 *Lutheran Heritage Village-Livonia* precedent.[63] The shift in the majority has led to a further change in the NLRB approach, as the *Lutheran Heritage* rule, which led to the invalidation of several such rules on the assumption that employees would reasonably construe them to restrict the activities protected under §7 NLRA, has currently been abandoned for its failure to take account of potential justifications of the rules, for requiring employers to avoid any possible interference with §7 NLRA, for penalizing rules for their mere ambiguity, for excessively limiting NLRB's discretion and for making the result of any challenge to such rules extremely uncertain.[64] Thus, the Board elaborated a new standard, requiring the evaluation of the nature and the extent of the potential impact of the rules upon NLRA protected rights together with the existence of legitimate justifications associated with the rules. Therefore, employer-rules may now be qualified as: lawful, because, when reasonably interpreted, they do not prohibit or interfere with the exercise of NLRA's rights or such adverse impact is outweighed by the connected justifications; subject to particularly strict and individualized scrutiny in accordance with the above standard; unlawful, for limiting NLRA's protected rights while failing to be accompanied by appropriate justifications.

Meanwhile, President Trump has managed to affect the activity of the Board even further by nominating Peter Robb as General Counsel of the NLRB (8 November 2017; sworn in on 17 November 2017): the office, lasting for a term of four years, is particularly relevant as it is its incumbent that determines the cases to prosecute for unfair labour practices, while also overseeing the NLRB regional bureaux.

After the expiration of Miscimarra's term, the Board was split 2-2 for almost four months, before a fifth member, Republican-leaning lawyer John Francis Ring, was appointed and nominated Chairman of the NLRB (respectively, 11 and 12 April 2018; sworn in on 16 April 2018).

It is finally appropriate to refer to representation case rules, which have been targeted by the NLRB Republican majority since it regained control of the Board. In April 2015, NLRB representation case rules eased the process to unionize and made it faster to organize elections within a bargaining unit, together with several other changes favourable to

62 *William Beaumont Hospital*, 363 NLRB No. 162, 13 April 2016.

63 343 NLRB 646, 19 November 2004.

64 *Boeing Co.*, 365 NLRB No. 154, 14 December 2017.

workers.[65] The NLRB has requested comments from the public on the appropriateness of amending these rules, thereby testifying a commitment to intervene in this regard, although the process has not yet come to a conclusion.

The second year of Trump's presidency has seen the NLRB deliver less relevant decisions in the exercise of its adjudicatory power. The Board is currently composed of only four members, after Mark Pearce's term expired in August 2018; Donald Trump, in compliance with the implicit partisan balance rule and to the surprise of many, renominated Pearce to the Board, but the Senate took no action on the nomination, which has therefore expired as a new Senate is now in session. It remains to be seen whether Trump will reiterate its previous appointment or will pick another candidate; it will also be interesting to verify whether the NLRB will resume its intense activity of the end of 2017 or fail to exploit the Republican majority and whether it will be as inconclusive as it was in 2018.

6.4 Trends and Emerging Issues

The attempt to summarize the policies implemented by the Trump administration in the labour and employment area allows some preliminary considerations from different perspectives, although with the necessary *caveat* that it will be only at the end of Trump's term(s) that a more reasoned analysis might be offered.

First, it looks like the Trump agenda in this particular field has seldom followed a predetermined and consistent path, while often being led by the aim of dismantling policies (recently) implemented by the previous administration; this has happened especially, but not exclusively, by passing joint resolutions of disapproval in Congress (the highest number ever since the CRA entered into force), by ordering the DoL to rescind departments' rules and by shaping the NLRB so as to favour the rollback of decisions on a number of issues addressed during Obama's tenure. This wandering itinerary provides the opportunity to briefly discuss a symptom of the crisis that traditional lawmaking processes seem to be facing overseas. More specifically, the extensive resort to acts issued by the President himself (*e.g.* executive orders) or rules adopted by branches of the government or agencies makes it far easier for an incoming administration to invalidate much of the normative framework developed under the tenure of the previous administration. This would be more difficult to undertake via legislative means, first because the President may not hold a majority in both Houses of Congress, second because passing bills or resolutions (usually) takes more time and a more consistent effort than the signature of executive orders or the adoption of rules by departments. Moreover, not only do the President and Congress act promptly in rescinding agencies' rules whenever they are given the possibility to do so,

65 A full account may be available at www.govinfo.gov/content/pkg/FR-2014-12-15/pdf/2014-28777.pdf.

but the analysis of the field of labour law has shown that courts and district judges are increasingly availing of the tool of nationwide injunctions to prevent unwelcome administrative regulations from entering into force and being applied.[66] Thus, a presidency whose legacy is composed mainly of rules elaborated by agencies or introduced by the President and encompasses only to a limited extent bills passed by Congress is an administration whose traces are not likely to last long.[67]

Moreover, Trump's presidency appears rather bothered when forced to bargain with unions, especially in the public sector, as may be inferred by the decision to limit the time governmental employees may spend fulfilling representation activities adopted through an ad hoc 2018 Executive Order. On top of that, the Supreme Court decision in *Janus*, favoured by the nomination of Gorsuch and one of Trump's most tangible trophies to display before his electorate towards the 2020 presidential campaign, emphasizes the relevance put upon negative freedom of association and speech in federal workplaces by the current administration.

Eventually, a progressive and generalized attempt to find ways for employers to avoid the tight obligations provided by the NLRA, whose clearest example is the effort to limit the instances when overtime pay is due to employees (*e.g.* by maintaining a large white-collars exemption) should not go unnoticed when providing a comprehensive picture of the labour environment in the Trump era.

66 This three-pronged attack on the regulatory power of agencies is discussed by G. Romeo & N. Palazzo, 'Who Fears the Big Government? A Coordinated Attempt to Downsize Federal Agencies' Power in the United States', *Global Jurist*, Vol. 18, No. 2, 2018.

67 The topic is addressed by S. Thrower, 'Policy Disruption through Regulatory Delay in the Trump Administration', *Pres. Stud. Q.*, Vol. 48, No. 3, 2018, pp. 517-536.

7 The Fiscal Policy

*Giancarlo Rando**

7.1 Framework of the Tax Cuts and Jobs Act

On 22 December 2017, President Donald Trump signed the tax reform commonly known in the debate as the Tax Cuts and Jobs Act (TCJA), a piece of legislation that has profoundly innovated the US tax system. In fact, it has been the most important tax reform in the last 30 years and involved both individuals and corporations.[1] It was, somehow, the realization of one of President Trump's electoral promises, and the goal was to improve the performance of the American economy through two means: increase the competitiveness of the American market for companies and workers, and bring home trillions of dollars held by offshore companies for tax reasons.

The law was approved with the opposition of the Democrats: they were convinced that the new legislation would benefit only the interests of the richest corporations and individuals.

The reform occasioned a significant number of innovations. The most significant of them concerned, first of all, a permanent reduction of the federal tax on companies from 35% to 21%. Other important changes were: the introduction of new rules on US multinationals; innovations also on the side of individuals, with a reduction and simplification of taxes, an increase in tax credit for children, as well as on basic deductions and family benefits; the abolition of personal exemptions and deductions.

Until the approval of the TCJA, the United States had the highest level of corporate taxation among the Organisation for Economic Cooperation and Development (OECD) countries. Up to a certain point this did not represent a problem for American companies, which managed to reduce the amount of taxes in different ways: location of the headquarters of companies in jurisdictions with lower taxation, transfer pricing manipulation and foreign tax credit schemes. Thanks to these fiscal stratagems, the big American multinationals, despite the years of economic crisis experienced worldwide, have managed not to pay many taxes thanks to the location of their activities in low-tax countries.

---

* Giancarlo Rando is Researcher in Comparative Public Law, Giustino Fortunato University.

1 For an overview of this historic reform and the possible impact on EU fiscal policy *see* H. Niesten, 'Unravelling the Recent US Tax Reform: A Paradigm Shift in the International and EU Tax Landscape', *European Taxation*, Vol. 58, No. 10, 2018.

The reform has lowered the corporation tax rate to 21%, which represents the lowest percentage in 80 years and, unlike the taxation of individuals, the reduction should be permanent. In this way, the reform also wanted to reduce the incentive of American companies to the so-called tax base erosion and profits shifting (BEPS) outside US borders. The reduced percentage of 21% now positions the United States within the OECD range, which fluctuates between 20% and 30%. Furthermore, the new legislation removes the complex mechanism represented by the Alternative Minimum Tax (AMT) and replaces it with other anti-base erosion measures such as the new base erosion and anti-abuse tax (BEAT).

One of the most significant changes in the new discipline is that from a worldwide tax system to a territorial system. The system of territorial taxation is directed to reduce the incentive to keep profits outside the US territory through a total exemption when these profits are repatriated to the United States.

Before the TCJA the American multinationals paid taxes with a worldwide taxation system. Contrary to the approach adopted by the majority of countries in the world, the United States taxed the profits of its companies when they were repatriated to the United States. The momentous change towards a territorial system contains limitations to ensure that US-headed multinational companies are taxed at least once somewhere. These 'anti-avoidance' provisions are intended to counteract the base erosion and international profit shifting, especially in the context of a digital economy and technology companies.

Perhaps the most important measure of this transition from a worldwide taxation system to one that has been defined as *quasi-territorial* is the 100% exemption for the portion of foreign-source dividends received from US shareholders from what the law defines as 'specified 10% foreign corporation'.[2] Furthermore, foreign companies are subject to taxation on their US source income. Therefore, foreign dividends are subject to a system of territorial taxation, but the dividends must not be income from subpart F[3] or income subject to the minimum tax rule. Since the new tax regime continues to tax some foreign income under the F subpart and still taxes the income of the domestic corporations' foreign branches, it is more accurately described as a quasi-territorial system. This choice towards a partial territorial tax system with reference to corporations follows the example of many other developed economies. The purpose is to significantly reduce the levy on dividends.

In the transition from a worldwide taxation system to a territorial system, the TCJA stated that US multinationals operating abroad must pay a one-off limited tax for the profits they bring back to the United States. Profits earned before 2018 are subject to a

2 The IRC, Sec. 245A defines "specified 10% foreign corporation" as any foreign corporation with respect to which any domestic corporation owns at least 10%.

3 Under the F subpart of the IRC, certain types of income and investments from foreign corporations controlled by US shareholders (Controlled Foreign Corporations, CFCs) are considered to be distributed to US shareholders and subject to US current taxation.

15.5% tax on offshore cash equivalents and 8% on other assets, such as illiquid assets. The multinationals, to mitigate the effect of this measure, can pay by spreading it over eight years.

Before the introduction of the TCJA a large number of US multinationals postponed the payment of the high taxes of 35% in the United States, accumulating them abroad. It is suggestive that four among the biggest American companies (Apple, Microsoft, Pfizer and General Electric) held *one quarter* of their entire profits outside of the United States.

The objective of the reform, from this point of view, has been reached: the big companies that had displaced their profits in tax havens or in more favourable jurisdictions from the fiscal point of view have brought trillions of dollars into the United States.

To compensate for these measures, the TCJA implemented the *OECD BEPS action 4*, through the introduction of a limitation of the deductibility of business interests. Net interests are now deductible only to the extent of 30% of the 'adjustable taxable income'.[4] The adjustable taxable income excludes items (such as income, gains and deductions) that are not attributable to trade or business, net operating loss deduction, business interest or business interest income (EBIT) and, for fiscal years starting in 2018 and ending before 1 January 2022, also deductions for depreciation, amortization and depletion (EBITDA).

The TCJA also includes anti-avoidance measures to contrast the base erosion and international profit shifting. There are *outbound* transaction measures: a new category of controlled foreign company (CFC) income called global intangible low-taxed income (GILTI) and an incentive for companies to repatriate their intangibles through the foreign-derived intangible income (FDII) at a preferential 13.125% rate. There are also *inbound* transaction measures: a new AMT focused on deductible payments made by US persons to related foreign persons (the base erosion and anti-abuse tax, BEAT).

7.1.1 Outbound Transaction Measures (GILTI, FDII)

Both GILTI and FDII are measures directed to outbound transactions, *i.e.* foreign income earned by domestic companies and their foreign subsidiaries.[5]

7.1.1.1 Global Intangible Low-Taxed Income

The GILTI is an anti-erosion measure that subjects US owners of a CFC to US taxation at a rate of 10.5% for that part of the CFC's net income that exceeds a 10% return on foreign tangible assets.

4 IRC, Sec. 163 (j).

5 For more details *see* C. Pérez Gautrin, 'United States – US Tax Cuts and Jobs Act: Part 1 – Global Intangible Low-Taxed Income (GILTI)', *Bull. Int. Tax.*, Vol. 73, No. 1, 2019.

This tax applies if US shareholder owned 10% of the CFC at any time of the year when the foreign company was a CFC and owned any interest in the CFC on the last day of the CFC's fiscal year. The US shareholder must include his share of the CFC's GILTI in his income. For these purposes, the non-subpart F net income of CFCs in excess of a 10% return on depreciable tangible assets must be considered GILTI. A deduction of up to 50% is generally allowed (until 2026, then 37.5%), which can reduce the effective tax rate on GILTI to 10.5%. Before the enactment of the new legislation, no portion of a CFC's active profit would be taxed if it was not distributed to US shareholders.

This measure was elaborated to limit the incentives for American taxpayers to move abroad, particularly to low-tax jurisdictions. The shift to a (quasi) territorial tax system may exaggerate the base erosion incentives, so the inclusion of GILTI in the US shareholder income means reducing these incentives by ensuring that CFC gains exceeding a deemed return on tangible assets are subject to some extent to US taxation.

7.1.1.2 Foreign-Derived Intangible Income

The other side of the GILTI is a measure that allows a US corporation to deduct up to 37.5% of the FDII plus 50% of the GILTI included in the gross income of the domestic corporation.[6] The FDII discourages US companies from keeping intangible fixed assets outside the United States. In this way, US companies are encouraged to sell goods and provide services to foreign customers and are indirectly encouraged to build intangible fixed assets *in the United States*. The income deriving from these export activities will be taxed at a reduced rate of approximately 13% (16.4% from 2026). This measure should stimulate the shifting of intangible profits into the United States. However, the question that has arisen is whether this measure could be considered an illegal export subsidy and a violation of WTO obligations of the United States.[7]

7.1.2 Inbound Transaction Measures (BEAT, Pass-through Benefits)

The so-called BEAT (which stands for base erosion and anti-abuse tax) addresses inbound transactions, *i.e.* expenses by domestic companies with regard to payments to foreign persons.[8] The BEAT is directed to intercompany payments that subtract income from US taxes due to their deductibility. In essence, the BEAT is a minimum tax of 10% applied to all payments made by US and foreign multinational companies to related foreign companies. The tax applies only when the gross US receipts are over a threshold of 500 million dollars

6 IRC, Sec. 951A.

7 *Cf.* Niesten, 2018, para. 3.5.1.2.

8 *See* C. Pérez Gautrin, 'United States – US Tax Cuts and Jobs Act: Part 2 – The Base Erosion and Anti-Abuse Tax (BEAT)', *Bull. Int. Tax.*, Vol. 73, No. 3, 2019.

and therefore has a limited application for multinational groups without a significant presence in the United States. However, the tax base is calculated by disallowing deductions with respect to deductible payments made by domestic corporations to related foreign persons. Furthermore, tax credits cannot be used to reduce the liability of the taxpayer with reference to the BEAT. As a result, domestic corporations that make significant payments deductible to foreign affiliates or that rely on tax credits to reduce their regular contribution to the US tax system may well feel the effect of BEAT. Furthermore, the cost of goods sold (COGS) is generally excluded from the definition of base erosion payments. A US business that imports products to manufacture them or resells is less affected than a company that pays for services. For example, if multinationals like Apple, Starbucks, Google or Microsoft were to bring their brand and expertise into a low-tax country, the United States could tax the profits made there. Or at least the royalties to that country would be subject to American taxation.

The BEAT will have major consequences for companies operating on international markets. Non-US companies need to control accurately the effects of the BEAT, so, on the one hand, the BEAT encourages US companies to keep the money in the United States, but, on the other hand, it can hit foreign companies that have US subsidiaries. The BEAT may create conflicts with US tax treaties. Many tax treaties provide for anti-discrimination provisions that guarantee that interests, rights and other payments made by a US resident to the treaty partner resident will be deductible under the same conditions as they are for a US resident company. These provisions generally include an exception for national laws that enforces the arm's length standard. It is unlikely that the BEAT can be covered by this exception, because its application does not depend on compliance with the arm's length standard. There is the risk, in short, that there will be an increase in double taxation.

Another feature of the TCJA is that it aims to reduce the tax burden on individuals who conduct their business through the so-called pass-through entities. Historically, owners (often US individuals) of pass-through entities paid taxes on company profits equal to the rate they paid individually (up to 39.6%). From 1 January 2018 the TCJA allowed a deduction of up to 20% of qualified domestic business income, which allowed lowering the maximum rate for pass-through to 29.6%. This deduction is only possible for the owners of specific service businesses that have an annual income below $157,500. This norm is available only for domestic income and is not available for pass-through business generating foreign-source income. This provision will also expire after eight years. The US companies that have significant US operations benefit from this deduction for pass-through entities. This is a significant measure because pass-through companies represent around 80% of US business and 35% of US business income.

7.1.3 Changes in Tax Rates for Individuals and Families

For 2018 most of the tax rates for individuals have been reduced. The rates for 2018 are: 10% (before 10%), 12% (before 15%), 22% (before 25%), 24% (before 28%), 32% (before 33%), 35% (before 35%) and 37% (before 39.6%).[9] Furthermore, for 2018, tax rates and brackets for the unearned income of children have changed and are no longer influenced by the parents' tax situation. The new rates applicable to a child's unearned income of more than $2,550 are 24%, 35% and 37%. Other important legislative changes for individuals and families concern the increasing of standard deductions, the suspension of personal exemptions, increasing of the child tax credit and the limitation or discontinuation of certain deductions.

In the period 2018-2025, the TCJA suspends personal exemptions but more or less doubles the standard deduction to $12,000 for singles, $18,000 for heads of households and $24,000 for those making a joint declaration. For some taxpayers, the increased standard deduction could offset the elimination of exemptions and perhaps even give some additional tax savings. However, for those who have many dependents these changes can result in increased taxation, and this depends in part on how much they can benefit from the family tax credits.[10]

Beginning in 2018, the TCJA doubled the tax credit for children to $2,000 for each child under the age of 17. The TCJA also made the child tax credit available to more families than in the past. The limit to benefit from the tax credit is now $400,000 for married couples and $200,000 for other taxpayers, compared with the 2017 threshold of $110,000 and $75,000, respectively. It should, however, be noted that these provisions expire in 2025.

The TCJA has limited or suspended many itemized deductions. Itemizing saves tax only if the itemized deductions exceed the standard deduction. Since the TCJA almost doubled the standard deduction for 2018 and generally reduced itemized deductions, many taxpayers that typically itemized may no longer benefit from this practice.

The elimination of the deduction of state and local taxes had been proposed. The idea did not pass but the amount of deductions was greatly diminished. For the period 2018-2025 the taxpayer can request a deduction of no more than $10,000 for the aggregate of state and local property taxes and either income or sales taxes.

The TCJA restricts the limits on deductions for home mortgage interest. For the period 2018-2025 the deduction limit is $750,000. However, the limit remains at $1 million for mortgage debts incurred before 15 December 2017, which will significantly reduce the number of taxpayers affected.

---

9 *See* IRS, 'Tax Reform, Basic for Individuals and Families', publication 5307, Tax Year 2018, available at www.irs.gov/tax-reform.

10 For the possible ways of reforming the regime of personal exemptions, *see* R. McClelland, 'Fixing the TCJA: Restore the Personal Exemptions', 21 March 2019, available at www.taxpolicycenter.org.

The qualified medical expenses are deductible only if they exceed the AGI (adjusted gross income) threshold. The TCJA reduces the threshold from 10% of the AGI to 7.5% for all taxpayers for both regular and AMT purposes in 2017 and 2018.

The AMT is a separate taxation system that limits certain deductions, disallows others and treats certain incomes differently from normal taxation. The top AMT rate of 28% is lower than the top regular income tax rate but typically applies to a higher taxable income base. If the AMT liability exceeds the regular tax liability, you have to pay the AMT. The TCJA temporarily reduces the number of taxpayers who will have to pay AMT with a change in the exemption thresholds. However, like nearly all the dispositions on individual taxation, the AMT reduction will end after 2025, and millions of taxpayers will have to comply again with the AMT's rules.

The modern AMT was developed in 1979 with the original intent to ensure that the highest-income households pay some taxes. The original intent, however, was lost. By 2017 less than 1/5 of the households with income greater than $1 million paid the tax, while nearly 80% of AMT taxpayers had income under $500,000. By raising the exemption amount and the income level at which the exemption operates, the TCJA strongly reduced the number of taxpayers subject to the AMT from about 5 million to about 200,000 in 2018, according to some estimates of the Tax Policy Center. These changes came at a cost for the federal budget: the Joint Committee on Taxation estimates that they will reduce federal revenue by $637 billion in ten years.[11]

A popular technique for reducing the tax burden is to transfer investments or other income-producing assets to family members with low-tax brackets. The so-called 'kiddie tax' aims to combat this practice.

Before the TCJA, when the kiddie tax was applied, all but a small part of the child's unearned income was taxed at the marginal rate of the parents (if higher). The kiddie tax generally applies to 18-year-olds or younger or full-time students from 19 to 23 years old. The TCJA makes the kiddie tax higher by taxing a child's unearned income according to the brackets used for trusts and estates, which are taxed at the highest marginal rate (37% for 2018) once 2018 taxable income reaches $12,500. For a married couple filing a tax return jointly, the highest tax rate has no effect until their 2018 taxable income is over $600,000. In other words, in many cases children's unearned income will be taxed at higher rates than their parents' income.

Another, profound, innovation of the TCJA is the elimination, starting from 2019, of the so-called individual mandate under the Affordable Care Act, which required taxpayers not covered by a qualifying health plan to pay a penalty.

11 For these considerations and for some proposals to amend the AMT's provisions in the TCJA, *see* R. McClelland, 'Fixing the TCJA: How Should Congress Treat the Alternative Minimum Tax?', 19 March 2019, available at www.taxpolicycenter.org.

7.2 Implications of the TCJA for the States

The TCJA has had important consequences for state budgets. Many states link their tax law to federal tax rules, through a practice called 'coupling' or 'conforming' to the federal tax code. There are different ways of doing this. One is to calculate the state income tax through the federal definition of the income, called AGI.[12] Then states apply deductions, exemptions and other adjustments, state rates and, finally, any additional credits. Other states conform to federal law even more, adopting the federal deduction and exemption amounts and thus imitating the federal calculation up to the determination of taxable income. Other states calculate their own AGI but use federal definitions for the amounts included therein.

Beyond the details of how the single states conform to the federal tax code, there is certainly a common factor in all states: the tax cuts made by the TCJA brought the consequence, for all states, of a reduction of the federal funding for education, healthcare, infrastructure and other important issues. While it appears that some states may realize some revenue gains by coupling to changes in the TCJA, many provisions of the TCJA can reduce states' revenues to an unknown extent, depending on how states will interpret their laws' interaction with the federal tax laws. It should be noted that most of the personal income tax provisions expire after 2025, so even if some states will see a gain in revenues, these gains will be temporary and small in comparison with states' funding needs.

The TCJA doubles the federal standard deduction, to which about nine states and the District of Columbia are coupled. This change would reduce taxes in general for everyone because it reduces the amount of income subject to tax, but the effect is not equal in all states. Each state also currently couples to some extent to federal itemized deductions, and so it is necessary to calculate the interaction between standard and itemized deductions.

With regard to itemized deductions, the TCJA increases the medical expenses deduction, eliminates some miscellaneous deductions and puts a cap on the federal deduction for state and local taxes (the so-called SALT deduction) at $10,000. The majority of states (31 states and the District of Columbia) follow the federal deduction policy to some extent. Most of these states do not couple to the federal deduction for state income taxes paid but allow a deduction for property taxes. The result of the coupling with the new federal norms would be a reduction of the income tax base. In fact, few people pay $10,000 in property taxes alone, so states with low property taxes will see even less of an increase of the income tax base, while states that allow a deduction for state income taxes would see an expansion of the income tax base.

---

12 D. Grundman, 'What the Tax Cuts and Jobs Act Means for States – A Guide to Impact and Options', 26 January 2018, available at https://itep.org.

The TCJA increases inequalities. One effect of the act is the elimination of limits for itemized deductions for very high-income taxpayers. These taxpayers previously had their total deduction amount limited but can now fully deduct their charitable contributions and allowable mortgage interests on their federal taxes, and in states that couple to the TCJA, also on their state taxes. In many states, the highest-income families will experience not only a federal tax cut but also a state tax cut, as a result of federal changes on deductions.

On the other hand, in states that do not couple to the federal standard deductions but require residents to take the state standard deduction if they opt for the federal standard, many people who will now take the new higher federal deduction will be forced to take the state standard deduction even if it is less convenient for them. This, on the one hand, will raise revenue in these states, while, on the other hand, affecting, in particular, middle or upper-middle-income taxpayers who previously used itemized deductions at the federal level.

The TCJA eliminates the federal personal and dependent exemptions. Many states are potentially affected by this change because some states fully couple to the number and dollar amount of federal exemptions; in others the amounts of the exemptions are independent of federal law, while the number of exemptions is based on allowable federal exemptions. The elimination of these exemptions raises revenue for the states because it increases the amount subject to tax. For this reason, for the states it could be convenient to couple to the federal legislation on exemptions. The problem is that the exemption is a flat amount, so the effect is regressive, and the increase in revenue is a tax increase that burdens low- or middle-income taxpayers much more than those with higher income.

The new 20% deduction for 'pass-through' businesses would affect those states that couple to federal taxable income. Even if there are few states that are affected by default by this measure, the tax cut is relevant at the federal and state levels, but the tax cuts are concentrated on the highest-income 5% of the residents.

In some states[13] there is a deduction for federal income taxes paid. Since the TCJA operates a big reduction of taxes, the consequence is a reduction in the amount that taxpayers can deduct in the states that allow the deduction, so, in particular, the states that allow an uncapped deduction will experience an increase in the revenue. This revenue gain is, however, temporary and could change dramatically in the opposite direction if the Congress decides to change the norms in the future.

13 Alabama, Iowa, Louisiana, Missouri, Montana, Oregon.

7.3 Is It a Regressive Reform?

There are two major criticisms of the TCJA. The first is related to its cost. Last year the Congressional Budget Office (CBO) estimated that the TCJA would reduce revenue by 1.9 trillion in a decade.[14] The second is that most tax cuts went to the wealthiest taxpayers.[15] So the TCJA would essentially be a regressive reform. The Institute of Taxation and Economic Policy (ITEP) has estimated that the TCJA has provided about half of its tax benefits to the richest 5% in America in fiscal year 2018. About a quarter of the benefits would have gone to the richest 1% of the households.

Here are some measures that have been deemed regressive (and therefore to be changed) by some scholars.

The TCJA includes a 20% deduction for income from pass-through businesses, subject to personal income tax instead of the corporate income tax. Sometimes, these enterprises are really 'small businesses', but in other cases they include many enormous companies. Most pass-through income flows to the richest 1% of Americans.

The vague definitions on the kinds of business that can or cannot receive this tax break appear designed to encourage taxpayers to devise schemes to use this tax break in ways that lawmakers did not contemplate.

Itemized deductions are typically used by well-off taxpayers, whereas low- and middle-income households claim the standard deduction. The benefit of deductions is bigger the more income the taxpayer has.

The TCJA does not solve this problem of equality but limits one itemized deduction, the deduction for SALT, with a cap of $10,000. This provision targets residents of higher-taxed states more than others. However, simply repealing the cap on SALT deductions would end in an expansion of TCJA's tax cut for rich people.

One solution proposed is to replace the SALT deduction cap with new limits that would apply to all itemized deductions.[16]

Before the TCJA, individuals could leave more than $5 million to their heirs without paying taxes (a married couple could leave twice this amount).

Most wealthy people could leave much more than that thanks to some tax breaks with merit (like deduction for charitable donations) and some loopholes with no merit (*i.e.* schemes to hide assets in trusts).

14 C. Davis, 'Fact-Checking on Trump Law Need a Fact Check', 13 February 2019, available at https://itep.org.

15 R. Phillips, 'Five Things to Know on the One-Year Anniversary of the Tax Cuts and Jobs Act', 17 December 2018, available at https://itep.org.

16 An example by ITEP would cap the total households' itemized deductions at $50,000 for married couples, 30,000 for singles and 40,000 for heads of households and would be annually adjusted for inflation (*see* S. Wamhoff & M. Gardner, 'Progressive Revenue-Raising Options', February 2019, p. 3).

Instead of closing these loopholes that weaken the estate tax, the TCJA further weakened it by doubling the exemptions. Now an individual can leave at least $11.2 million, a married couple $22.4 million without paying the estate tax.

By increasing significantly the exemption level of the estate, gift and generation skipping tax, the TCJA has cut the number of taxpayers affected by the tax by 2/3 and will reduce the revenue by $83 billion over the next decade.[17]

7.4 CONSEQUENCES OF THE TCJA ON US ECONOMY

More than a year since the entry into force of the TCJA we have a full year of data relating to the American economy. In summary, we can clearly identify a trend for the year 2018, which was certainly positive. According to the latest government statements, the growth rate of the adjusted economy for the American economy was 2.9%, the highest growth since 2015 and just 0.1% less than the growth promised by President Trump, who had assumed 3%.

If the trend is certainly positive, the economy began to show signs of slowing down at the end of 2018. In the last quarter of 2018, annualized growth was 2.6% (from 4.2% in April-June and from 3.4% in July-September). However, in the first quarter of 2019 the GDP grew by 3.2% and went beyond the forecasts of the financial analysts, which were around 2.5%.[18]

The positive changes for the American economy, however, cannot, according to scholars, be attributed solely to the approval of the TCJA. The stimulus certainly represented by the TCJA was accompanied by an increase in federal and state spending on defence-related and non-defence programmes.[19]

Certainly, companies have benefited greatly from the TCJA, which, as we have seen, has provided for them a very important change in the corporate tax rate and some incentives to repatriate capitals. However, the significant tax savings that American companies achieved in 2018 were translated into repurchases of shares and distribution of dividends, rather than into investments in new productive infrastructure. However, in this regard, the labour market has experienced extremely important growth in 2018, with an increase of 223,000 jobs per month. Although this fact should therefore be emphasized and linked

17 For these estimates and a proposal for setting the estate tax's exemption levels to the previous ones, *see* R. *McClelland, 'Fixing the TCJA: Restoring The Estate Tax's Exemption Levels'*, 20 March 2019, available at www.taxpolicycenter.org.

18 *Cf.* News Release (and related materials), 'Gross Domestic Product, First Quarter 2019 (Advance Estimate)', available at www.bea.gov.

19 H. Gleckman & A. Boddupalli, 'What 2018's Economic Data Tell Us about the TCJA', 4 March 2019, available at www.taxpolicycenter.org.

to the Keynesian effect of the TCJA, it must be said that the average growth in jobs in previous years was, nevertheless, important, being 186,000 in 2016 and 175,000 in 2017.

Unfortunately, although the United States is in a situation of full employment, wages have not followed economic growth. Wages, after inflation, grew by 1.9%, with growth concentrated in the last quarter of the year. Supporters of the TCJA claim that there will be an increase in business investment that will also generate an increase in workers' productivity and wage growth, but at present there is no evidence that this will happen.

There is concern about the effect that the significant tax cut made by the TCJA and the increase in federal spending have certainly generated: an increase in the federal budget deficit and debt. The numbers are very significant: for the 2018 fiscal year the increase was $113 billion.

The CBO[20] affirmed that the TCJA will increase the deficit by nearly $1.9 trillion between 2018 and 2028. The $1.9 trillion estimate already includes an estimate of the TCJA's growth effect, which the CBO says would reduce the impact on the deficit from $2.3 trillion to $1.9 trillion from 2018 to 2028.

Some recent analysis noted that at no other time in modern US history has the economy been so strong, while the deficit has been so large. Usually, deficits reach important size when the US is in a recession, but the continual passage of tax cuts seems to have pushed the country into an era of endless deficits.

20 *See* www.cbo.gov/system/files/115-th-congress-2017-2018/reports/53651-outlook.pdf.

8 'Back to Basics': Waste Management Policy and the Trump Administration

Marina Petri[*]

8.1 Introduction

Waste management policy is important for developing a sustainable economic model, while providing citizens with an effective service that ensures both economic efficiency and public health and safety in a multilevel setting. Indeed, the rationales for public waste management policy are both economic and environmental,[1] implying the necessity of developing an articulated policy response to the challenges presented by this sector, which is crucial for households and market operators alike.

In the US, both the Federal Government and the member States are in charge, to varying degrees, of the design and implementation of waste management policy. In this context, a flexible approach to regulation, implying different and asymmetrical tools, is paramount to the development of an effective policy framework, which must be coupled with a cohesive set of monitoring and tracking provisions.

In all evidence, regulating the generation and disposal of waste is crucial to the achievement of environmental goals,[2] as waste management policy is to be studied as part of the broader environmental policy strategy. In this regard, this short chapter will focus on waste management law and policy from a comprehensive perspective, while wider environmental policy tools have been thoroughly considered elsewhere in this volume.

In particular, in order to present the main tenets of President Donald Trump's waste management policy, the key elements characterizing sector regulation in the US will be

---

* Bocconi University.

1 The economic rationales for public intervention in the waste sector are linked to both economies of scale in the management of landfills and the nature of the (negative) public good of waste. Public actors intervening with ad hoc policy measures can tackle these issues by creating an efficient market model that allows for an optimal allocation of this good, which can thus be made 'excludable'. Moreover, the improper and unregulated management of waste generates negative externalities. *See* M.K. Macauley & M.A. Walls, 'Solid Waste Policy', *in* P.R. Portney & R.N. Stavins (Eds.), *Public Policies for Environmental Protection*, Resources for the Future, Washington, DC, 2000, pp. 268-281 and I. Brisson, 'Packaging Waste and the Environment: Economics and Policy', *Resources, Conservation and Recycling*, Vol. 8, No. 3, 1993, pp. 183-292.

2 For instance, the crucial links between President Donald Trump's waste management policy and climate change have been observed by J.E. Aldy, 'Real World Headwinds for Trump Climate Change Policy', *Bull. At. Sci.*, Vol. 73, No. 6 (*Special Issue: A Year of Trump. The Existential Risk Scorecard*), 2017, pp. 376-381.

first presented (para. 2). Then the strategic and enforcement dynamics qualifying the Trump administration's approach to waste management policies will be underlined (para. 3).

8.2 Waste Management Policy at a Glance

As anticipated, waste management is a complex policy area, at the crossroads of environmental, economic and sociolegal concerns. Developing a coherent waste management strategy in a federal legal order such as the US requires a cohesive set of policy tools and incentivizing mechanisms providing a multifaceted answer to the variegated issues characterizing this sector, while giving the appropriate inputs to the wide array of stakeholders involved, including citizens and the industry, as well as public agencies and research institutions.[3]

In the US context,[4] a pivotal role is played by the Environmental Protection Agency (EPA), which regulates solid waste permits, authorizations and incentives, under the 1976 Resource Conservation and Recovery Act (RCRA), establishing the paramount legal framework for solid waste handling operations, from gathering to final disposal. More precisely, the RCRA covers a broad range of hard (laws and regulations) and soft law (policy and guidance) instruments, allowing EPA to set minimum national technical standards for the design and operation of disposal facilities, while States issue permits to ensure compliance with EPA and State regulations.[5]

The notion of solid waste, constituting the key structural element of the RCRA, is broad and multifaceted, as it includes a wide variety of discarded materials of solid, semi-solid, liquid or containerized gaseous nature, requiring different management techniques and policy tools. Notably, solid waste is classified according to its damaging potential in relation

3 Within this scenario, a crucial role is played by the Supreme Court, which arguably shaped US waste management law with a series of rulings, overturning the attempts of States to limit interstate waste trade (*see* A. Johnson, 'The Development of Waste Management Law', available at www.iswa.org/uploads/tx_iswaknowledgebase/538338_Paper.pdf).

4 For a general overview of waste management in the US, a comprehensive analysis of which would go beyond the scope of this paper, *see* N. Kollikkathara, H. Feng & E. Stern, 'A Purview of Waste Management Evolution: Special Emphasis on USA', *Waste Manag.*, Vol. 29, No. 2, 2009, pp. 974-985, where special emphasis is laid on municipal waste management strategies from a diachronic perspective. *Cf.* the less recent contribution by T. Eighmya & D.S. Kosson, 'U.S.A. National Overview on Waste Management', *Waste Manag.*, Vol. 16, No. 5-6, 1996, pp. 361-366.

5 *See* the explanatory memorandum on EPA website, available at www.epa.gov/rcra/resource-conservation-and-recovery-act-rcra-overview#how%20does%20rcra%20work.

to the health and safety of individuals and the environment, following the rigid divide between hazardous (RCRA, Subtitle D) and non-hazardous waste (RCRA, Subtitle C).[6]

Non-hazardous waste, which includes municipal (solid) waste, industrial waste and agricultural and animal waste (as well as food waste),[7] is regulated through the implementation of State programmes complying with federal requirements, which ban open dumping while setting design, location, finance and clean-up actions for waste landfills. In all evidence, the role played by States is crucial, while federal policies have a more systematic role, preventing contamination as well as providing monitoring systems for groundwater contamination and landfill gases. Similarly, hazardous waste[8] regulation at the federal level is fundamentally composed of a general, comprehensive, programme following the 'cradle-to-grave' approach (disciplining hazardous waste from its origin to its transport, treatment, storage and disposal). Notably, however, the primary enforcement role of hazardous waste requirements is played by EPA, which may authorize States to implement the programme autonomously on an ad hoc basis.[9]

As far as disposal techniques are concerned, it is paramount to note that landfills and, only secondarily, waste-to-energy[10] treatment (through combustion or incineration) represent the key distinguishing figures of the US context, which is accordingly character-

6 It is interesting to note that the paramount divide is between hazardous and non-hazardous waste, marking a qualifying difference with regard to the legal orders, such as several continental European contexts, where the regulatory categorization of waste is based on market structure (regulated market for municipal waste/liberalized market for industrial waste) and the hazardous nature of waste has a more transversal, additional, character.

7 Municipal waste is referred to as garbage, and it covers both items of a commercial, institutional and domestic origin, and packaging materials, including refuse. Industrial waste is composed mainly of four different subcategories: construction and demolition waste (C&D), medical waste (specifically regulated under the 1988 Medical Waste Tracking Act), treatment waste (sludge, by-products – requiring an autonomous process to be reused – and co-products, which are directly reusable) and 'special waste', composed of six groups of special products requiring specific management techniques, such as uranium waste or fossil fuel combustion waste. Sewage is not included in the notion of industrial waste and is therefore not covered by solid waste management policy. Finally, the category of agricultural and animal waste covers the waste generated from farming to wholesaling food, including decomposed materials.

8 Hazardous waste can either be domestic (hazardous household waste) or industrial in nature (four categories are qualified as hazardous industrial waste: listed waste, universal waste, characteristic waste, mixed waste).

9 *See* the explanatory memorandum on EPA website, available at www.epa.gov/rcra/resource-conservation-and-recovery-act-rcra-overview#how%20does%20rcra%20work.

10 Indeed, it has been suggested that the usage and exploitation of waste (and non-hazardous waste in particular) as a source of semi-clean energy could represent a plausible way out of several energy conundrums in the American context, underlining the potential impact that a development of waste-to-energy treatment plants could have on the combined waste and energy markets. *See* B. Glover & J. Mattingly, 'Reconsidering Municipal Solid Waste as a Renewable Energy Feedstock', *Environmental Energy and Study Institute (EESI) Issue Brief*, 2009, pp. 1-8.

ized by a relatively[11] limited percentage of recycled waste. Figures 1 and 2[12] show the structure of the waste sector, regarding waste management and disposal, as well as the trends diachronically characterizing the municipal waste segment, according to the implementation of a policy approach that is more in line with the principle of 'waste hierarchy',[13] starting from the 1980s. Notably, it should be underlined that, notwithstanding the increasing percentage of recycled and composted municipal solid waste (peaking after the 1980s), the tons of waste being landfilled have remained stable within the US. Indeed, while the generation of municipal waste has increased,[14] the excess waste production has been absorbed by recycling and waste-to-energy disposal, while the actual amount of landfilled waste has not decreased, creating potential environmental and economic concerns over the structure of the waste sector industry in the country.

11 The suggested comparison relates to the European context. A telling measure of EU recycling practice and standards is included in the 2018 'Circular Economy Action Plan', especially in the Framework Directive 2018/851 (Directive (EU) 2018/851 of the European Parliament and of the Council of 30 May 2018 *amending Directive 2008/98/EC on waste*) and in the Landfills Directive (Directive (EU) 2018/850 of the European Parliament and of the Council of 30 May 2018 *amending Directive 1999/31/EC on the landfill of waste*), setting a 65% recycled waste target by 2035, while imposing a ceiling of 10% municipal waste to be landfilled by the same date.

12 The data used is the most recent official data on waste management in the US available to date, and it refers to the year 2015. EPA's methodology for collecting and elaborating it is available at www.epa.gov/facts-and-figures-about-materials-waste-and-recycling/methodology-epas-facts-and-figures-materials. Unfortunately, no official data is available marking the effects of the Trump presidency on waste policy.

13 The notion of waste hierarchy is used both in the US and in the EU context, and it focuses on the different priority to be assigned to different policy aims and tools within waste management. In particular, EPA's integrated waste management hierarchy includes five pathways, rigidly ordered as follows in terms of preferability: waste prevention, recycling, composting, energy-to-waste recovery, landfilling.

14 The correlation between (municipal) waste generation and economic growth is a key tenet of economic growth theories, supported by overwhelming evidence throughout the world (*See, inter alia*, R.C. D'Arge & K.C. Kogiku, 'Economic Growth and the Environment', *Rev. Econ. Stud.*, Vol. 40, No. 1, 1973, pp. 61-77). Subverting this trend is one of the paramount elements to be enshrined in a coherent implementation of the waste hierarchy principle. For an analysis of the first data supporting the decoupling of municipal waste generation and economic growth in the European Union, *see* M. Mazzanti, 'Is Waste Generation De-linking from Economic Growth? Empirical Evidence for Europe', *Appl. Econ. Lett.*, Vol. 15, No. 4, 2008, pp. 287-291.

Figure 1 Waste management in the US (year 2015).

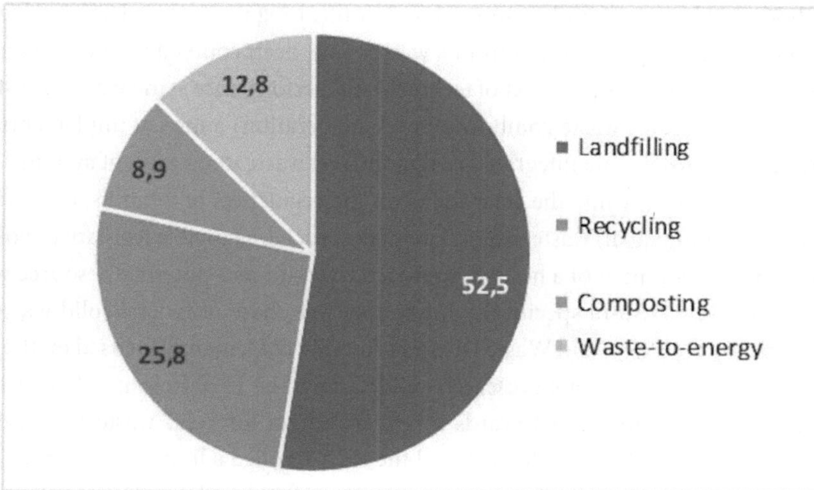

Figure 2 Municipal solid waste management in the US (tons per year 1960-2015).

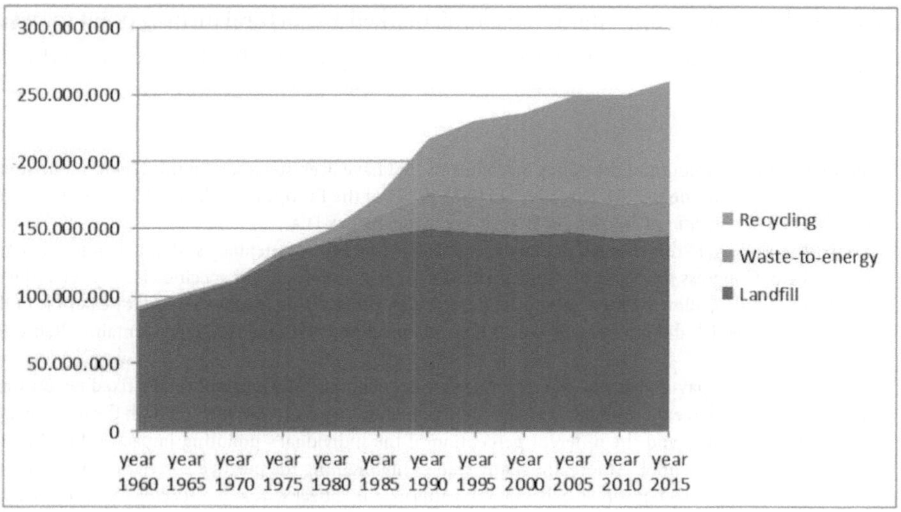

A wide array of policy tools, which are not substantially different from those employed as long-term policy measures to foster the hierarchy of waste generation (and, thus, generation prevention) in the European context,[15] have been used, to varying degrees, in the US legal order. In particular, both economic incentives[16] (such as pay-as-you-throw tariffs in the case of household waste[17]) and command-and-control regulatory mechanisms (such as the permits regime in place for hazardous waste) have been coupled with the definition, at the federal level, of a composite set of technical and performance standards (for instance, emissions regulation for waste combustion and incineration) aimed at implementing an environmentally sustainable integrated and multilevel waste management system.

As a matter of fact, while the clear focus on the regulation of landfills, as a primary mechanism for (municipal) waste disposal, remains crucial, a tangible legislative evolution has led to the development of a holistic approach to waste, as a potential resource within the economic cycle.[18] More specifically, while the first phase of federal solid waste law, characterized by the 1965 Solid Waste Disposal Act (SWDA), mainly focused on the regulation of landfills and the related research and training, the 1970 Resource Recovery Act (RRA) determined a first shift towards a new paradigm for solid waste management. Interestingly, however, both the SWDA and the RRA implied a limited role for the State, which did not actively regulate the sector; rather, these first legislative initiatives aimed at emphasizing good practices (such as reuse and a rudimental form of recycling), in a regulatory setting that was substantially dominated by the relevant market players.

As anticipated, the 1976 RCRA, envisaging an active engagement of the State in waste regulation while making open dumping illegal, marked a structural turning point for waste management law in the US, further developed through the 1984 Hazardous and Solid

15 For an incomplete account of the policy mechanisms that have been suggested in this regard at the supranational level within the EU, *Cf.* Directive (EU) 2018/851 of the European Parliament and of the Council of 30 May 2018 *amending Directive 2008/98/EC on waste*, Annex IVa.

16 It is worth recalling, in this context, that in order to achieve an environmentally sustainable waste management system, Congress proposed the implementation of deposit refunds for specific plastic goods (the so-called 'bottle-bills'), allowing for a composite tax/subsidy incentivizing mechanism. A key example of this policy attempt, which did not become law, is the 1994 proposed National Beverage Container Reuse and Recycling Act.

17 The link between a pay-as-you-throw tariff model, more economically efficient than a fixed tax on waste generation imposed over households, and the reduction of waste generation rests on both the incentivizing nature of the measure and the different perception of the individual's polluting impact induced by the implementation of this tool. Among the many studies highlighting the positive correlation between pay-as-you-throw tariffs and positive behavioural patterns for citizens, *see* A. Bucciol, N. Montinari & M. Piovesan, 'Do Not Trash the Incentive! Monetary Incentives and Waste Sorting', *Scand. J. Econ.*, Vol. 117, No. 4, 2015, pp. 1204-1229.

18 Notably, the key elements of the Resource Conservation Challenge (RCC) launched by EPA in 2002 include pollution prevention (through reuse and recycling) as well as energy and material conservation. The recycling target included in RCC amounted to 35% of municipal waste. The RCC has been defined as a 'forum of leadership' within EPA's solid waste office, aiming at enacting the 2020 Vision and Pollution Prevention programmes enshrined in RCRA (*see* National Service Center for Environmental Publications (NSCEP), 'Resource Conservation Challenge: Strategic Plan; What Can You Save Tomorrow?', available at https://nepis.epa.gov).

Waste Amendments (HSWA), promoting waste prevention rather than waste disposal.[19] This approach was complemented by the 1980 Comprehensive Environmental Response, Compensation and Liability Act (CERCLA), usually referred to as 'Superfund', providing an ad hoc discipline for abandoned and historical dumping sites, often contaminated,[20] which are not covered by the RCRA. Superfund plays a crucial role in waste management policy, as the regulation applicable to historical sites has tangible consequences for the sustainability of the sector, in a context so strongly characterized by the centrality of landfills.[21] Moreover, it is worth underlining that Superfund has been amended only once to date, with the 1986 Superfund Amendments and Reauthorisation Act (SARA), introducing stronger State participation and incentivizing a bottom-up approach to regulation, given the key role assigned to citizens' empowerment.

In all evidence, the brief account that has just been presented can by no means be considered exhaustive, as a complex corpus of sector-specific regulation contributes to giving a cohesive discipline to waste management, with particular regard to hazardous waste.[22] What is more, international trade plays a crucial role in this context, as no storage or treatment requirements for solid waste exports are included within the RCRA: limited regulation is provided regarding waste transportation outside the US territory, prompting waste operators to frequently export hazardous and non-hazardous waste overseas.[23] It is clear that international trade dynamics can thus decidedly shape internal waste management policy, as underlined by the recent halt on waste purchases declared by China on environ-

19 RCRA has been amended two more times since HSWA became law: with the 1992 Federal Facility Compliance Act (focusing on federal enforcement) and with the 1996 Land Disposal Program Flexibility Act.

20 Arguably, the development of Superfund is connected to a series of environmental accidents in contaminated and hazardous dumping sites, widely covered by American media between 1978 and 1979, the infamous of which is the so-called 'Love Canal tragedy' of 1979 (*see* E.C. Beck, 'The Love Canal Tragedy', *EPA J.*, January 1979, available at https://archive.epa.gov/epa/aboutepa/love-canal-tragedy.html).

21 *See* G. Valaoras, 'Waste Management Policies in the United States of America', *in* P. Nicolopoulou-Stamati, L. Hens & C.V. Howard (Eds.), *Health Impacts of Waste Management Policies*, Springer, Dordrecht, 2007, pp. 121-131.

22 For instance, *see*, *inter alia*, the 1988 Medical Waste Tracking Act, which has been mentioned earlier, and the 2003 Used Oil Management Standards.

23 *See* H. Wu, 'Legal Development in Sustainable Solid Waste Management Law and Policy in Taiwan: Lessons from Comparative Analysis Between EU and U.S.', *Nat'l Taiwan Univ. L. Rev.*, Vol. 6, No. 2, 2011, pp. 461-494. On the specific issues relating to hazardous waste, *see* T. Waugh, 'Where Do We Go from Here: Legal Controls and Future Strategies for Addressing the Transportation of Hazardous Wastes across International Borders', *Fordham Environ. Law J.*, Vol. 11, 2000, pp. 477, 483, 490-91. The different approach chosen in the US, as opposed to the EU model, is particularly striking in this context, and its main structural characteristics, albeit enshrined in a differentiated setting, have relevant consequences for the shape and evolution of waste management techniques in the two legal orders. *See* K. Dreher & S. Pulver, 'Environment as "High Politics"? Explaining Divergence in US and EU Hazardous Waste Export Policies', *Rev. European Commun. & Int'l Environ. Law*, Vol. 17, No. 3, 2008, pp. 306-318.

mental grounds,[24] modifying the market structure and rates for recycled waste, as the US faces an increase in domestic waste vis-à-vis a lack of internal treatment facilities.[25]

8.3 The Trump Factor: 'Back to Basics'?

In the previous paragraph, a few distinguishing traits of the US waste policy have been put forward. In particular, the paradigmatic policy shift from waste disposal to waste prevention and recycling has been underlined. Notably, it has been argued that the key normative and programmatic tools enacting the principle hierarchy of waste management, while developing the idea of waste as a resource, are enshrined in the 1976 RCRA, while the so-called 'Superfund' focuses on the recovery of historical and contaminated sites and landfills. Indeed, both these instruments call for a crucial design and implementation role to be played by EPA, which is also attributed to relevant criminal and civil enforcement competences.

In this regard, it is not surprising that President Donald Trump's early 2019 controversial[26] appointment of Mr Adam Wheeler as Acting Administrator of EPA, following Mr

24 Starting from January 2018, China banned the import of a wide range of waste products following President Xi Jinping's approach to global pollution (the so-called National Sword policy), thus introducing a relevant shift in the international context, where China used to represent the top destination for foreign scraps. This element has sparked a heated debate in international media (*see*, for instance, Y. Nee Lee, 'The World Is Scrambling Now that China Is Refusing to Be a Trash Dumping Ground', *CNBC Investing*, 16 April 2018, available at www.cnbc.com/2018/04/16/climate-change-china-bans-import-of-foreign-waste-to-stop-pollution.html and H. Zhao, 'The Tipping Point: How China's Waste Ban Made the World Rethink Its Rubbish', *OECD Forum Online*, 26 May 2018, available at www.oecd-forum.org/users/78382-zhao-hui/posts/33611-the-tipping-point-how-china-s-waste-ban-made-the-world-rethink-its-rubbish).

25 According to the Institute of Scrap Recycling Industries' '2018 Factsheet', available at www.isri.org/docs/default-source/commodities/overall-industry-fact-sheet_2018.pdf?sfvrsn=18, around 5.6 billion of metric tons of scrap were exported from the US to China in 2017. The key role of the Chinese market for the US waste sector is also in line with the 2018 report (*see* Institute of Scrap Recycling Industries (ISRI), '2018 Recycling Industry Report', available at www.scrap2.org/yearbook/, p. 63 ff.), underlining the unpreparedness of the US waste sector with regard to China's policy shift while triggering wider policy developments in the recycling sector (*see inter alia* C. Katz, 'Piling Up: How China's Ban on Importing Waste Has Stalled Global Recycling', *Yale Environment*, 7 March 2019, available at https://e360.yale.edu/features/piling-up-how-chinas-ban-on-importing-waste-has-stalled-global-recycling and N. Javorsky, 'How American Recycling Is Changing after China's National Sword', *CityLab online*, 1 April 2019, available at www.citylab.com/environment/2019/04/recycling-waste-management-us-china-national-sword-change/584665/).

26 *See* L. Lambert, 'Trump Nominates Acting EPA Head, an Ex-coal Lobbyist, to Run Agency', *Reuters*, 9 January 2019, available at www.reuters.com/article/us-usa-trump-epa/trump-nominates-acting-epa-head-an-ex-coal-lobbyist-to-run-agency-idUSKCN1P324H and B. Kimmel, 'EPA Nominee Andrew Wheeler Is Even Worse than Scott Pruitt', *CNN*, 15 January 2019, available at https://edition.cnn.com/2019/01/15/opinions/andrew-wheeler-bad-choice-epa-kimmell/index.html.

Scott Pruitt's 2018 departure,[27] has determined the way forward for waste policy in a substantive way. The wider approach chosen in environmental matters by EPA since 2017 is discussed elsewhere in the present volume. Accordingly, this section will suggest a narrower focus on waste matters, so as to highlight the structural elements of convergence and divergence from the key tenets of the most recent waste policy dynamics in the US.

In this regard, and at the very outset of this overview, it is worth observing the general market dynamics of the waste sector in the Trump era. Notably, a recent analysis of EPA's 2018 Year Review[28] by the Environmental Data and Governance Initiative[29] is quite telling in evaluating the reduced pollution and treated hazardous waste trends relating to the years 2017 and 2018. More specifically, the study points out that 2018 marks the second lowest amount of reduced or treated and disposed hazardous waste in a decade (the lowest *ratio* pertaining to 2017, the first year of the Trump administration). Albeit incomplete, the data shows that the generation of hazardous waste has not decreased, jeopardizing the implementation of the hierarchy of waste management.

Interestingly, it is worth underlining that a correlation could be inferred between the low reduction in treated and disposed hazardous waste and the tangible budget cuts operated by the Trump administration.[30] As a matter of fact, it is crucial to stress that issuing a relevant reduction in public expenses represents one of the founding pillars of President Trump's wider environmental and energy policy agenda.[31]

What is more, according to EPA's annual review,[32] a striking $2 billion have been saved during the Trump administration, as a consequence of steady deregulation.[33] The effects

27 Scott Pruitt was Head of EPA from February 2017 to July 2018, after being nominated by President Trump amid criticism over Mr Pruitt's strong rejection of scientific consensus over man-generated climate change. Mr Pruitt's premature resignation from office is due to a series of ethical investigations regarding serious misconducts when acting as Head of EPA. *See, ex multis,* C. Davenport, L. Friedman & M. Haberman, 'E.P.A. Chief Scott Pruitt Resigns under a Cloud of Ethics Scandals', *The New York Times*, 5 July 2018, available at www.nytimes.com/2018/07/05/climate/scott-pruitt-epa-trump.html?module=inline.

28 The annual review published by EPA summarizes the main regulatory and strategic outcomes of the relevant fiscal year, focusing on the steps pursued in environmental matters. EPA year in review 2018 (hereinafter: EPA year in review), published in early 2019, is available at www.epa.gov/sites/production/files/2019-01/documents/epa_2018_yearinreview_0128-4.pdf.

29 L. Fredrickson *et al.*, 'A Sheep in the Closet. The Erosion of Enforcement at EPA', 20 November 2018, available at https://envirodatagov.org/wp-content/uploads/2018/11/Sheep-in-the-Closet.pdf. Hereinafter, 'EDGI report'.

30 In line with this trend, President Donald Trump's 2020 budget 'A Budget for a Better America' (available at www.whitehouse.gov/wp-content/uploads/2019/03/budget-fy2020.pdf) issues a 31% budget cut for EPA.

31 Notably, a deregulating approach to environmental policy, coupled with severe budget cuts, constitutes one of the qualifying assets of the 'America First Energy Plan', which has been duly taken into account elsewhere in this volume.

32 EPA year in review 2018, p. 5.

33 In the case of waste policy, in 2018 EPA removed several products (such as copper filter cakes) from the list of hazardous waste, it reviewed the technical rules on coal ash waste from power plants and suspended (through a 90-day stay) the application of the Obama administration's regulation of landfill emissions.

of relevant budget cuts are thus coupled with consistent deregulation, defining a minimal role for EPA in the implementation of substantive environmental regulation, embraced by both Mr Pruitt and Mr Wheeler during their leadership of the Agency.[34] President Donald Trump's focus on the imperative to proceed with sector-specific deregulation, while cutting public expenditure, is indeed in line with the approach taken in an array of policy areas.

Presenting a systematic analysis of this phenomenon would go beyond the scope of this contribution. Rather, it is relevant in this context to point out how this policy approach has shaped waste management law in the first two years of the Trump administration. Former EPA Acting Administrator Scott Pruitt's legacy is famously linked to the launch of his 'back-to-basics' agenda on air quality,[35] prompting EPA to concentrate on its core mission ('environment, economy, engagement'). While this 'back-to-basics' perspective did not explicitly encompass a specific focus on waste management, it is possible to affirm that President Donald Trump's EPA has pursued a limited list of high-profile objectives in its waste policy, which are arguably linked to the very structural functions of the Agency.

The most tangible example of these dynamics is the implementation of Superfund. As anticipated, Superfund regulates closed and abandoned hazardous waste sites, while providing for liability for those responsible for the release of in-site hazardous waste and establishing a trust fund for clean-up where no responsible subjects can be identified. In this regard, both short-term removals and long-term remedial response actions are envisaged by law, reducing in a stable and permanent way the threats associated with the release of hazardous substances.[36] Notably, EPA is responsible[37] for defining a National Priorities List (NPL), updated annually,[38] spelling out the sites where long-term clean-up activities can be carried out. In 2017, Mr Scott Pruitt launched the 'Superfund task force',[39] defining a key role for the implementation of Superfund as a way to "protect [...] human health and the environment, at the core of EPA's mission",[40] and in December 2017 an

According to EPA's year in review, 33 major deregulatory initiatives were finalized during the Trump administration (*see* p. 2).

34 On this issue, it has been convincingly argued that, in light of the trends characterizing enforcement data in 2017 and 2018, "the switch in EPA leadership from Pruitt to Wheeler has turned out to be more superficial than substantive. It has not so much halted as sustained the pro-industry, antiregulatory remaking of EPA begun under Pruitt" (*see* EDGI report, p. 9).

35 *See* S. Pruitt, 'Memorandum – Back-to-Basics Process for Reviewing National Ambient Air Quality Standards', 9 May 2018, available at www.epa.gov/sites/production/files/2018-05/documents/image2018-05-09-173219.pdf.

36 *See* EPA, 'Superfund: CERCLA Overview', available at www.epa.gov/superfund/superfund-cercla-overview.

37 The site assessment leading to an NPL listing is a multiphase process guided by Hazard Ranking System (HRS) criteria, which also focus on potential remedial actions to be undertaken.

38 As of May 2019, there were 1337 NPL sites on the US territory, 157 of which had a federal nature. EPA data, available at www.epa.gov/superfund/superfund-national-priorities-list-npl.

39 *See* EPA, 'Superfund Task Force', available at www.epa.gov/superfund/superfund-task-force.

40 *Ibidem.*

Administrator's Emphasis List was developed (and dynamically updated), identifying the sites to be prioritized.

Accordingly, the remediation and demolition of NPL Superfund sites has represented the key waste policy achievement of Trump administration's EPA, resulting in the deletion of 22 NPL sites in 2018 alone.[41] Following a 'back-to-basics' approach, the success of the Superfund programme has been welcomed as a tangible implementation of the paramount principles guiding EPA's regulatory action.[42] It is worth noting that the remediation of key NPL sites is coherent with a global strategy aiming at focusing on high-profile programmes, in spite of a consistent decline in EPA's performance of other enforcement actions in the (hazardous) waste sector.[43] What is more, even Superfund administrative orders for cost recovery, addressed to responsible companies in order for them to reimburse the Agency for clean-up costs, are registering a steady decline.[44]

In line with the aforementioned overall approach to waste regulation, envisaging the launch and implementation of high-profile programmes, the Trump administration has managed to define a wide-ranging programme to tackle food waste,[45] as well as the negotiation of the US-Mexico-Canada (USMCA) Environmental Cooperation Agreement, which includes a few provisions dealing with the reduction and management of marine litter.[46] While both initiatives, albeit different, have been praised for their transformative

41 EPA Year in Review 2018, p. 11.

42 *See, ex multis*, J. Hopkins, 'Trump Is Eliminating Superfund Sites at Faster Pace than Obama', *The Daily Caller*, 10 October 2018, available at https://dailycaller.com/2018/10/10/epa-deleting-superfund-sites/.

43 According to the EDGI report (p. 25), the RCRA hazardous waste programme showed a 17% decline in case initiations and a 23% decline in case conclusions during 2018, suggesting a tangible decline in EPA's enforcement effectiveness. *See* L. Peterson, 'Enforcement of Environmental Laws Drops under Trump Administration', *Project on Government Oversight*, 20 February 2018, available at www.pogo.org/analysis/2018/02/enforcement-of-environmental-laws-drops-under-trump-administration and A. Rosenberg, 'EPA Can't Stop Polluters When the Trump Administration Cuts Enforcement Staff', *Union of Concerned Scientists*, 13 September 2018, available at https://blog.ucsusa.org/andrew-rosenberg/the-epa-cant-stop-polluters-when-the-trump-administration-cuts-enforcement-staf.

44 EDGI report, p. 27.

45 EPA launched the 'Winning on Reducing Food Waste' initiative in late 2018, in partnership with the U.S. Department of Agriculture (USDA) and the Food and Drug Administration (FDA). According to EPA's review 2018, the programme aims to "improve coordination and communication across federal agencies as we work to better educate Americans on the impacts and importance of reducing food loss and waste" (*see* EPA year in review, p. 14).

46 The agreement, signed by Mr Wheeler on 11 December 2018, is a trilateral trade agreement including a rather limited set of provisions on marine litter, namely Art. 24.12, which is substantially programmatic in nature, as it does not set any specific obligations for the State Parties. Indeed, "Recognizing that the Parties are taking action to address marine litter in other fora, consistent with Art. 24.25 (Environmental Cooperation), the Parties shall cooperate to address matters of mutual interest with respect to combatting marine litter, such as addressing land and sea-based pollution, promoting waste management infrastructure, and advancing efforts related to abandoned, lost, or otherwise discarded fishing gear" (para. 3). Indeed, this international agreement is not isolated, as it follows President Trump's signature of the bipartisan bill against ocean pollution in October 2018 (Save Our Seas Act of 2018, S. 3508).

potential,[47] it could be argued that they lack the internal coherence[48] and strength[49] necessary to influence waste management policy through a better implementation of its key principles.

Similar considerations could be developed with regard to EPA's federal policy initiatives on recycling, which lack the long-term vision and, more importantly, the resources to define a new paradigm for the waste industry. Notably, in 2018 EPA held its first Recycling Summit,[50] which set up a forum for discussion providing a wide array of stakeholders (including NGOs, market operators and investment funds) with a common cooperative platform for a unified response to the challenges of the circular economy.

The four areas of intervention identified in the Summit, however, seem potentially unfit to address the challenges of the paramount transition the American waste sector must undergo in order to increase its share of recycled waste. More precisely, they cover outreach and education strategies to incentivize the usage of recycled goods (area 1), the modernization of the relevant infrastructure through new private investments (area 2), the definition of cross-sector communication and collaboration (area 3) and the identification of shared standards for recycled waste measurements and tracking (area 4).[51] It is paramount to note that these policy inputs do not set any explicit goal for recycling ratios, while focusing mainly on communication strategies. What is more, these measures do not cater to citizens, as they do not include any specific indication on economic incentives and relevant tariff methods, while remaining in line with a minimalistic approach to the role of the regulator.

---

47 *See, inter alia*, on the Save our Seas Act, B. Kahn, 'Trump Signs Actually Good Bill to Clean Up Ocean Garbage', *Earther*, 12 October 2018, available at https://earther.gizmodo.com/trump-signs-actually-good-bill-to-clean-up-ocean-garbag-1829711006, and on the 'Reducing Food Waste Initiative', C. Rosengren, 'Trump Administration Wants to Make Food Waste Great Again', *Wastedive*, 19 October 2018, available at www.wastedive.com/news/trump-administration-wants-to-make-food-waste-great-again/540087/.

48 Notably, as underlined in EPA's year in review, the rationale of both waste-related initiatives is linked to strengthening the economic competitiveness of American companies, rather than pursuing a cohesive and coherent environmental sustainability of the waste management system.

49 Particularly with regard to food waste, EPA proposed, in 2015, a 50% target for the reduction of food waste by 2030. The new food waste initiative does not seem equipped to effectively achieve this goal, which remains a voluntary commitment with no financial obligations. *See* C. Rosengren, 'Where the US Stands on Federal Food Waste Policy', *Wastedive*, 27 June 2018, available at www.wastedive.com/news/US-federal-food-waste-policy/526586/.

50 The symbolic echo of the Summit was amplified by President Trump's message on America Recycles Day (which is indeed the day in which the Summit was held). In his message, Mr Trump underlined the link between waste and resources as a way to further the leadership of American businesses in retail. *See* White House Statements and Releases, 'Presidential Message on America Recycles Day', 15 November 2018, available at www.whitehouse.gov/briefings-statements/presidential-message-america-recycles-day/.

51 EPA Year in Review 2018, pp. 13-14.

8.4 Conclusions

This chapter has dealt with the main features of waste policy in the US, with a paramount focus on the ways in which the Trump administration has shaped waste regulation and enforcement in the first two years of Mr Donald Trump's presidency. In this regard, the paramount role played by EPA has been highlighted, while focusing on its enforcement priorities and market design initiatives in relation to the waste sector.

In all evidence, the main feature characterizing the regulatory dynamics in this policy area is the deregulatory approach pursued by the Tump administration, which has been coupled with the significant cuts operated to EPA's budget. Notably, this paradigm has implied a strong prioritization of high-profile areas of intervention in the waste sector, such as Superfund, notwithstanding a relevant decline in civil and criminal enforcement actions of the Environmental Protection Agency.

In this context, the Trump administration has failed to address the main challenge facing the US waste sector, implying a decisive market shift from landfill disposal to recycling. Indeed, recycling still represents a marginal solution for waste management, as more than 50% of the waste generated and treated in the US is landfilled. The areas of intervention proposed by EPA lack any reform potential in this regard, and they are in line with the wider approach to environmental matters pursued by the Trump administration.

9 The Healthcare Reform

Guerino D'Ignazio[*]

9.1 The ACA as a Landmark Statute of the Obama Presidency

The Affordable Care Act (ACA or 'Obamacare') was the most important healthcare legislation enacted in the United States since the creation of Medicare and Medicaid in 1965.[1] The law was one of the major reforms approved during the eight years of Obama's presidency and the one with the most immediate impacts on American citizens. To some extent, the health reform earned a special status over the last few years and, surely, it should be considered a landmark statute[2] of the entire Obama presidency. The health system, reformed by the ACA, had a specific gap to fill as its main goal: the US health spending, including public and private funds, was one of the highest among Western countries in relation to GDP but, nevertheless, the average life of American citizens was lower and infantile mortality greater in comparison with those in other Western countries. Approximately 46 million Americans did not have any health insurance, and this inevitably caused a care deficit.[3] The ACA's achievement was historic: it extended health insurance coverage to all citizens, thus overcoming the limitations of previous legal protection of social rights in the United States. In fact, in the absence of constitutional protection, social rights have always been based on the principle of individual responsibility and, thus, the freedom of

* Full Professor of Comparative Public Law, University of Calabria, Italy.

1 A whole century after Theodore Roosevelt's presidential campaign in 1912, a comprehensive national system of care finally became a reality in the United States. More than half of the states, 31 states and the District of Columbia, most of them with Republican governors, had enlarged Medicaid as of January 2017. The ACA had increased Medicaid enrolment by about 10 million people. *Cf.* F.J. Thompson, M.K. Gusmano & S. Shinohara, 'Trump and the Affordable Care Act: Congressional Repeal Efforts, Executive Federalism, and Program Durability', *Publius*, Vol. 48, No. 3, 2018, p. 399. An overview of the conventional arguments in favour of a national solution for health reform is provided by N. Bagley, 'Federalism and the End of Obamacare', *Yale L. J.*, Vol. 127, 2018.

2 According to A. R. Gluck & N. Huberfeld ('What Is Federalism in Healthcare For', in *Stan. L. Rev.*, Vol. 70, 2018, pp. 1746 *et seq.*), ACA implementation is very peculiar because it is a story of states exerting power that checked federal authority from within the statute, not from outside it. Consequently, the goal of the statute is not only to improve the quality of care, but also to maintain a balance of power between the states and the federal government in the healthcare policy arena. Furthermore, this dynamic has resulted in extensive policy variation and experimentation within the ACA's national framework.

3 *Cf.* C. Bologna, 'Dall'approvazione della riforma sanitaria alla decisione della Corte suprema: la parabola (inconclusa) dell'Obamacare', *Forum di Quaderni Costituzionali Rassegna*, Vol. 11, 2012, p. 6.

choice about the actual signing (or not) of health insurance.[4] At the heart of the ACA was the principle that any single federal law attempts to solve the three major problems of American health policy: inequitable access to health insurance, waste and ineffectiveness in the delivery of healthcare services and poor population health.[5]

In consideration of the centrality of the health system, which influences the quality of life of American citizens, disputes and conflicts are inevitable for any policy reform affecting these issues, and the ACA could not be an exception. Although the ACA has proven surprisingly resilient, litigations are emblematic of the 'ideological' dispute about what sorts of healthcare services can or must be covered, under what conditions and at whose expense.[6]

9.2 The New President and the Slogan 'Repeal and Replace'

During the presidential election campaign in 2016, there was a confrontation between the Republican Donald Trump, a staunch opponent of Obamacare, and Hillary Clinton, a staunch defender of the reform. The Republican candidate vigorously criticized the economic policies of the outgoing President, particularly the ACA, by openly declaring his willingness to repeal this reform. His campaign promise to dismantle Obamacare featured the slogan 'repeal and replace'. Provocative phrases such as 'socialized medicine' and 'death panels'[7] were often used by representatives of the Republican Party, as a 'slogan' for their political contraposition, with the aim to stress that their hostility was beyond the content of the reform.

In October 2016, during a rally in Sanford, Florida, President Trump promised, "My first day in office, I am going to ask Congress to put a bill on my desk getting rid of this disastrous law and replacing it with reforms that expand choice, freedom, affordability."[8]

Immediately after his election as 45th President of the United States,[9] Trump began his personal battle against the ACA, moving in the opposite direction of the Obama administration.

4 On the constitutional protection of the social rights *Cf.* G. Bognetti, *Lo spirito del costituzionalismo americano*, Vol. II, pp. 140-149.

5 *Cf.* W.M. Sage, 'Legal and Constitutional Influences on the Implementation of U.S. Health Care Reform', 15 April 2013, p. 2, available at https://papers.ssrn.com/sol3/papers.cfm?abstract_id=2265640.

6 *Cf.* J.H. Adler, 'The Future of Health Care Reform Remains in Federal Court', *in* A. Malani & M.H. Schill (Eds.), *The Future of Health Care Reform in the United States*, University of Chicago Press, Chicago, 2015, p. 54.

7 *Cf.* M. Stopa, 'The Reality of Death Panels', *Boston.com*, 22 January 2011.

8 *Cf.* R. Fretwell Wilson, R. Graver & L. Sobal, 'Trumpcare Expect the Phoenix to Rise from the Ashes', *Ill. L. Rev.*, 29 April 2017.

9 Donald Trump received 306 electoral votes and 62,985,106 popular votes, while the figures for Hillary Clinton were 232 and 65,853,625, respectively.

During the first two years of Trump's presidency, the ACA represented the battleground between the Republicans and the Democrats and, above all, between the President and Congress, in which the majorities of the House of Representatives and of the Senate were reversed after the mid-term elections of November 2018.

The President issued, immediately after taking office, an executive order to the Department of Health and Human Services and other agencies involved in administering the ACA, prescribing that regulations be interpreted as loosely as possible[10] and encouraging the development of a free and open market in interstate commerce for the offering of healthcare services and health insurance, with the goal of achieving and preserving the maximum range of options for patients and consumers.[11]

In his first speech, before Congress, Trump said: "Action is not a choice. It is a necessity. So I am calling on all Democrats and Republicans in Congress to work with us to save Americans from this imploding Obamacare disaster."[12]

During the first two years of the presidency, Trump has repeatedly attempted to repeal the Obamacare without full success, but there is no doubt that he will continue in his attempts to cancel the health reform from the US legal system. The new President acted both through the legislation and through his administrative powers.

There have been several attempts by Congress to implement Trump's strong appeal to 'repeal and replace' the ACA. The initial intent was to provide an organic reform in order to repeal and replace the ACA at the same time.

The House of Representatives, on March 2017, voted successfully in favour of the bill named American Health Care Act (AHCA), also known as 'Trumpcare', which is a provision of law that had to reform the health system by replacing the ACA. The AHCA was passed by a handful of votes, 217 to 213, and the result could not be met because the battle was going to be difficult in the Senate. In fact, the decisive game was played right in the Senate, where the bill was rejected twice, although the Republicans enjoyed the majority. The Republican party could not afford a defeat of this magnitude, since the abolition of Obamacare is one of the pillars of Trump's policy, so senators Graham and Cassidy elaborated a new bill that called for a strong devolution that was able to assign to the states the financial resources that the federal government would have otherwise spent for the expansion of the Medicaid. However, some states would have received less financial resources than if no changes had been made to the ACA.[13]

---

10 *Cf.* A. Inserro, '5 Ways Trump Is Changing Health Care', *AJMC*, 30 November 2018, available at www.ajmc.com/newsroom/5-ways-the-trump-administration-is-changing-healthcare.

11 *Cf.* T. Jost, 'Trump Executive Order on ACA: What It Won't Do, What It Might Do and When', *Health Affairs*, 21 January 2017, available at www.healthaffairs.org/do/10.1377/hblog20170121.058405/full/.

12 *Cf.* A. Kodjak, 'Trump's Address to Joint Session of Congress, Annotated', *NPR*, 28 February 2017.

13 *Cf.* Thompson *et al.*, 2018, p. 402.

The ACA indeed offers a window into the American federalism in action, and any reform of the healthcare system will have significant consequences for the federal system. The ACA's federalism is featured not through a separation between the states and the federal government, but rather through a national system that invites states for implementation, thus generating new state-federal arrangements.

> States move back and forth between different structural models vis-à-vis the federal government; internal state politics produce different state choices; states copy, compete and cooperate with each other, and negotiation with federal counterparts is a near constant.[14]

Since these national and state-level solutions promoted experimentation and variation, a new reform could have reset all these experiments.

However, the bill was opposed not only by the Democrats but also by three Republican senators. Senator McCain surprised the Congress by breaking with his party and presented a proposal emphasizing his hopes for a bipartisan healthcare plan, crafting a bill that increases competition, lowers costs and improves care for the American people. He said: "I encourage my colleagues on both sides of the aisle to trust each other, stop the political gamesmanship, and put the healthcare needs of the American people first."[15]

Republicans could afford only two defections, so the senator's vote represented a defeat for the bill. One of the Republican senators, Collins, explained her position by highlighting that it was a consequence of the Congressional Budget Office (CBO) report, which made clear that such a reform would undoubtedly reduce the deficit of $834 billion, according to the estimate between 2017 and 2026, but that it would also cause a loss of health coverage for 14 million people in 2026.[16] Trump attacked the objectivity of the non-partisan CBO, whose periodic assessments of the Republican legislation forecast that it would greatly increase the number of uninsured. These reports received extensive media coverage and fuelled widespread negative assessments of the Republican bills.[17]

However, far from giving up his position, in December 2017 Trump managed to get the Congress to approve another pillar of his financial reform policy, the Tax Cuts and Jobs Act. This reform had significant consequences for the ACA. Mainly, it abolished the tax penalty for individuals failing to comply with the 'individual mandate' for the purpose of obtaining health insurance. In fact, one of the pillars of the ACA was precisely the

---

14 *Cf.* Gluck & Huberfeld, 2018, p. 1689.

15 L. Ramsey, 'How John McCain Became the Pivotal Vote That Sent the GOP's Healthcare Efforts into Disarray', *Business Insider*, 28 July 2017.

16 *Cf.* Congressional Budget Office, *American Health Care Act*, Washington, DC, 24 May 2017.

17 *Cf.* A. Lotven, 'NAIC Pushes Slew of Reg Changes to Stabilize Market, Affirm State Authority', *Inside Health Policy*, 22 August 2017.

'individual mandate', and the Supreme Court supported its constitutionality in the case *National Federation of Independent Business v. Sebelius (NFIB)*,[18] because it interpreted the mandate as a tax and inferred that the Congress had the power to tax and to spend.

The penalty was necessary in the ACA in order to encourage healthy individuals to buy insurance rather than being free-riders. The lack of this penalty implies a potential malfunctioning of the system owing to the growth in costs because of the disproportionate increase in the premium on the exchanges of less healthy people, with greater need for care. The increase in costs would imply a radical reform of the law in order to meet the necessary ACA sustainability. In this way, states with larger Medicaid programmes should probably increase the tax burden to support the programme and to compensate for spending on these programmes.

In December 2018, a federal judge in Texas ruled that the repeal of the 'essential' part of the statute meant the unconstitutionality of ACA as a whole, because of the amendment by the Tax Cuts and Jobs Act. Indeed, following the abolition of the penalty for those who do not purchase the insurance policy, a Texas judge declared the unconstitutionality of the individual mandate, holding that since the individual mandate cannot be separated from the rest of the law, the entire ACA would amount to being unconstitutional. The case at issue, *Texas v. United States*,[19] is an attempt by 20 state attorneys general, alongside two individual Texas residents, to revisit the Supreme Court's holding in *National Federation of Independent Businesses v. Sebelius* in the wake of the recent amendments to the ACA. Judge Reed O'Connor held that the statute's individual mandate is unconstitutional because it exceeded congressional power to tax. Moreover, the U.S. District Court for the Northern District of Texas found that the remaining provisions of the ACA were not severable from the individual mandate, so the entire statute was unconstitutional.

Reactions from the legal and political community were immediate and heated. President Donald Trump tweeted his approval of the decision, stating that it was 'Great news for America',[20] and argued that the case would open the way to something better.[21] Political supporters of the ACA decried the decision; Senator Chuck Schumer described it as 'devastating'.[22] The case is being appealed in the United States Court of Appeals for the Fifth

18 132 S.Ct. 2566 (2012). The other important decision of the Supreme Court on the ACA was *King v. Burwell* (576 U.S., 2015). The challengers, in *King v. Burwell*, argued that the statute provides for tax credits only for those who purchase insurance from a state-established exchange. The Supreme Court ruled on 25 June 2015, declaring subsidies legal.

19 *Texas v. United States*, 340 F. Supp. 3d 579 (N.D. Tex. 2018).

20 *Cf.* A.W. Meek, '*Is Texas v. United States* "Great News for America" or Yet Another Procedural Skirmish in the Battle for "Obamacare?"', *Kentucky L. J.*, 18 January 2019.

21 *Cf.* N. Cordes, 'Wall Street, Congress React to Federal Judge Ruling Obamacare Unconstitutional', *CBS News*, 17 December 2018.

22 *Cf.* Meek, 2019.

Circuit[23] and will presumably be appealed in the Supreme Court of the United States. The ACA, however, still remains in place,[24] and it is possible that the Court will decide one of the most controversial cases during the presidential election year of 2020.

The majority of the judges in the Supreme Court are conservative, following the nominations adopted by Trump, but the differences between President Trump and the President of the Supreme Court have been strong recently.

However, the differences with the President of the Supreme Court, John G. Roberts Jr., on the independence of the judiciary may lead to a serious institutional crisis between President Trump and the Supreme Court. The accusations made against federal judge Jon Tigar ('Obama judge') and the entire San Francisco district court for blocking the executive order of the President, through which the right to seek asylum was suspended for migrants who illegally cross the border with the United States, has marked a turning point in the relations between President Trump and the President of the Supreme Court, who, so far, has adopted a measure of moderate self-restraint against attacks from the White House. President Roberts defended the independence and integrity of the judiciary and reiterated that there are no 'politicized' judges, of Obama, Trump, Bush or Clinton, but only an 'extraordinary group' of independent judges, who should be appreciated for their daily commitment.[25] Already during the 2016 presidential election campaign, the candidate Trump strongly criticized President Roberts for his decisive vote that had 'rescued' the Obamacare, and there had been no reactions. In this case, however, the Chief Justice's strong reaction is justified because the attack was directed against the role of the judiciary itself.

9.3 Mid-Term Election of 2018

In the mid-term elections, in November 2018, Obamacare was at the centre of the debate, and many investigations and studies pointed out that the defence of this law had been

23 No. 19-10011 (5th Cir.). The Department of Justice already told the 5th Circuit Court of Appeals it does not plan to defend the ACA, but Republicans, generally, "worry that if Trump wins, Congress won't be able to pass anything to replace ObamaCare – and they'll pay for it at the ballot box". They realize that to get rid of ACA, "while Democrats control the House, would leave a vacuum in place of protections for people with pre-existing medical conditions, insurance subsidies and expanded Medicaid". *Cf.* A. Bolton & P. Sullivan, 'GOP Lawmakers Root against Trump in Court on ObamaCare', *The Hill*, 4 January 2019. In this case, as Obama declared, this would be a disservice to the American people, after some years of 'transition period'. *Cf.* J. Glenza, 'Obama Says Repealing Healthcare Law Is "Disservice to American People"', *Guardian*, 6 January 2017.

24 *Cf.* K. Keith, 'Federal Judge Strikes Down Entire ACA; Law Remains in Effect', *Health Affairs*, 15 December 2018.

25 *Cf.* A. Liptak, 'Chief Justice Defends Judicial Independence after Trump Attacks "Obama Judge"', *New York Times*, 21 November 2018.

decisive for the victory of the Democratic party in the House of Representatives and to limit the loss of the majority of the Democratic party in the Senate. Now that more people have better access to individual health insurance, they want to keep it.[26]

The mid-term elections, in general, were almost always unfavourable for the President-in-Office's party; however, the vote against the candidates of the Republican party or the Democratic party had particular significance in the last elections, since the whole electoral campaign turned into a referendum on President Trump. From this perspective, the electoral competition, as a referendum in favour of or against Trump, had the consequence that such a personalized electoral campaign transformed the election of single candidates into an indication of a substantially direct vote towards the President.

Also, this time the prevailing rule in the previous mid-term elections was confirmed, namely the penalty for the President's party, with the result that the Republican party lost its majority in the House of Representatives, the 'popular branch', where they were held as the 'true' national election of this round. Overall, the results of the election were a true 'Blue Wave' for the Democrats, and (also thanks to the strong mobilization) they won the popular vote by more than seven percentage points in the House of Representatives.

In the electoral campaign, the President focused on very divisive issues such as immigration, but also healthcare reform. The results of the mid-term elections highlight the profound division and polarization that persist in US politics, society and institutions. This division is reflected not only within the parties but, now, also at an institutional level, with a Republican Senate and a House of representatives displaying a strong democratic majority. If it is true that the divided government makes the President 'a lame duck', he will have greater difficulties in implementing his legislative agenda, and it will be difficult for the President to reach his goal of repealing the ACA, at least through legislation.

The Republican party is firmly in the hands of President Trump, who has managed to put aside some of his authoritative opponents, while a new generation of candidates has emerged in the Democratic party, chiefly women, who are able to interpret the needs of some segments of American society, which have had little representation in the Congress so far and who will certainly fight to reject all attempts by President Trump to repeal and reform the ACA.

The election results project uncertainties over the next two years, at least until the presidential elections of 2020, and the second two-year term of Trump's presidency could turn into a long electoral campaign. This is not the first time that a president has been governing without a majority in both houses of Congress, but Trump is a singular and unpredictable president, and the outcome of the mid-term elections could have unprecedented consequences in domestic politics.

---

26 *Cf.* A.S. Edwards, 'Forget "Repeal and Replace." The One Issue Unifying Americans Is Affordable Health Care', *Time*, 1 November 2018.

Moreover, it is important to highlight that people in the four 'red states' – Montana, Idaho, Nebraska and Utah – also voted in November to expand access to Medicaid.

9.4 CONCLUSION

In conclusion, the subsistence of US health reform will not be easy. Until now Obamacare has not been repealed. This determined the temporary defeat of Trumpian policies. Republican opposition to Obamacare was focused more on promises to erase the law than on implementation of policy changes.[27] However, it is likely that further implications will emerge in the near future.

The ACA is stuck in purgatory,[28] but the politics of healthcare have fundamentally changed. The cost of coverage in the individual market for people who lack subsidies has grown substantially, mainly because of the instability created by the administration and congressional repeal efforts. The number of uninsured continues to remain stable but is well below the 2013 levels.[29] Most of the goals implemented by the ACA are still in place; however, if Congress fails to take action to consolidate the achieved gains and if administration policies continue to undermine insurance markets, those gains may soon erode.

The debate about healthcare reform will be worth following politically as well as legally in the next future, in order to determine whether the ACA will continue functioning or will be cancelled.

27 *Cf.* J. Oberlander, 'The Republican War on Obamacare – What Has It Achieved?', *New Eng J Med.*, 23 August 2018, available at www.nejm.org/doi/full/10.1056/NEJMp1806798.

28 Id., p. 2.

29 Jost, 2018.

10 Pharmaceutical Policies after the First Two Years of President Trump

*Anna Ciammariconi**

10.1 Introduction

Even though pharmaceutical policies intersect with healthcare and health policy, fiscal policy and trade policy, this article focuses on the pharmaceutical policy of the first two-year period of the Trump Administration. In any case, it is useful to remember that among the strong suits of Trump's electoral campaign, the will to repeal and replace Obamacare stands out. In a nutshell, it is considered worthwhile to remember that the failed attempt to reform the Affordable Care Act (ACA-Obamacare) is founded on some main points that answer the need of wider liberalization: e.g. no more obligation for everyone to sign insurance (and therefore no penalty) and no more obligation for companies (with more than 50 employees) to pay the health insurance for its employees, in the name of some basic American principles like personal responsibility and free-market competition.[1] On the one hand, supporters of the will to overcome Obamacare argue that the abrogation of the duty to have a health insurance policy would encourage competition among the insurance companies and, consequently, reduce the prices; on the other hand, critics of the attempt to reform argue that it would diminish the number of people who decide not to subscribe to health insurance; consequently, the companies could increase insurance prices to gain profits.

Surely, the process to repeal the ACA has divided the same members of the Republicans (although in the context of a general criticism of Obamacare); on the one hand, supporters of the radical libertarian position want a complete replacement of Obamacare and reintroduction of private logic in the health sector; on the other, the Republicans' moderate wing favours changes to Obamacare but not its complete repeal.

* Lecturer in Comparative Public Law – University of Teramo.

1 Among the papers on this topic, *see* C. Bologna, *Dall'approvazione della riforma sanitaria alla decisione della Corte suprema: la parabola (inconclusa) dell'Obamacare*, Quad. cost., 1 ss., A. Pierini, *Il progetto di riforma sanitaria dell'Amministrazione Trump all'esame del Congresso: verso il superamento dell'Obamacare*, www.dpceonline.it; G. D'Ignazio, *The Health Care Reform*, article available in this book.

10.2 Some Data

The importance of the dimension of the pharmaceutical market in the United States can be best appreciated by examining some data. In a recent study published by the Organisation of Economic Cooperation and Development (OECD),[2] the United States had the highest level of per capita expenditure on drugs, at $792 (purchasing power parity; PPP), and Mexico the lowest, at $144 (PPP), only 18% of the level recorded by the US. All of the top 15 firms in terms of global pharmaceutical sales are headquartered in OECD countries, about half of them in the United States and the remaining half in Europe (France, Germany, Switzerland and the United Kingdom). Production and R&D activities are undertaken in many countries, not only in the country where the firm is headquartered. The United States accounts for 39% of global pharmaceutical production, slightly more than Europe's share of 36%. The United States, with a 45% global share, is the world's largest pharmaceutical market, followed by Japan, with 9% of global sales, France (6%), Germany (5%), the United Kingdom (4%) and Italy (4%).[3] The latest data of the OECD (e.g. in the category Health Resources, which includes many categories of employers in the health sector like doctors, nurses and pharmacists) shows that the US has the highest value anyway (with 305 510 pharmacists in 2017); however, there is a counter trend: the number of hospitals is 5,564 and – as in many other countries – in the US the number of hospitals shows a decrease during the years of the financial crisis. Unfortunately, the OECD does not provide data on the 'pharmaceutical market' (and indicators such as pharmaceutical consumption, pharmaceutical sales and generic market) in the US, although such data have been provided for other countries. Nevertheless, in recent years, the pharmaceutical industry has experienced deep transformation: e.g. for several drugs (including 'blockbuster drugs' – popular drugs), the term covered by intellectual property rights has expired; at the same time, there is a wider diffusion of generic drugs and, simultaneously, the pharmaceutical industry has addressed R&D on very expensive special drugs. Moreover, there is a relocation of industries, with production moving to third countries like South Korea, India, Singapore, Malaysia and Mexico, while management and research continue to reside in the US.

---

2 *See* www.oecd-ilibrary.org/social-issues-migration-health/pharmaceutical-pricing-policies-in-a-global-market 9789264044159-en.

3 A recent article of *University of Southern California* (about the *The Global Burden of Medical Innovation*) reveals that US consumers spend roughly three times as much on drugs as their European counterparts. *See* D. Goldman & D. Lakdawalla, *The Global Burden of Medical Innovation*, Leonard D. Schaeffer Center for Health Policy & Economics, 2018, p. 2. The article updates a previous study: G.F. Anderson, U.E. Reinhardt, P.S. Hussey, V. Petrosuan, 'It's the Prices, Stupid: Why the United States Is so Different from Other Countries', *Health Aff.*, Vol. 22, No. 3, 2003, p. 89.

10.3 THE 'GOAL' TO LOW DRUG PRICES DURING THE 2016 PRESIDENTIAL ELECTION CAMPAIGN AND THE PHARMACEUTICAL POLICY IN THE FIRST TWO YEARS OF TRUMP'S MANDATE

As already mentioned in the introduction, during the 2016 presidential election campaign, Donald Trump underlined the need *to repeal and replace* Obamacare and emphasized as a priority the need to reduce drug prices.[4] When in the White House, during a *Listening Session With Pharmaceutical Industry Leaders*, on 31 January 2017, the President underlined the need to lower drug prices for Medicare and Medicaid[5] and also highlighted the commitment of his administration to reducing the time for approval of new drugs and simplifying the regulation in order to streamlining practices in FDA. In other words, Trump's political ideas on pharmaceutical policy are founded on two main points: lowering prices and streamlining the process to put a drug on the market without waiting for many years. The second element determines the risk of reducing the controls on drugs before distributing them. The day after the Trump speech, the Nasdaq Biotechnology Index fell 3,4% points on the New York Stock Exchange (NYSE), and the representatives of Big Pharma underlined that this political orientation would have encouraged the production of low-technology drugs or equivalent drugs. On many other occasions too, President Trump has

4 *See, e.g.*, Trump remarks at Plymouth State University, N.H., 7 February 2016 or in Manchester, N.H., 8 February 2016 or during the interview on MSNBC, 17 February (reining in the cost of prescription drugs has become a major issue in the 2016 presidential campaign).

5 It is worth remembering that Medicare and Medicaid are two health government-run programmes. Medicare is a health insurance programme for people who are 65 years or older, for those who are younger but have certain disabilities and for people with end-stage renal disease (that requires dialysis or transplant). The programme is divided into four parts: (A) *hospital insurance* that is *premium free* and provides hospitalization coverage to individuals who are 65 years or older, regardless of income, as long as they or their spouses worked and paid Medicare taxes for at least ten years. (B) *medical insurance*, which helps to cover the expenses related to services provided by doctors and other health personnel, outpatient care, home health care, durable medical equipment (DME), some preventive services; for this program a monthly premium is required to be paid. Those eligible for Medicare Part A also qualify for Part B. (C) *medical advantage*, which includes all the benefits and services covered in Part A and Part B programmes; it is operated by private insurance companies approved by Medicare. Enrolling in Part C may reduce the costs of purchasing services separately, but individuals should carefully evaluate their medical needs because Part C participants generally pay out-of-pocket for the associated services. (D) *prescription drug coverage*, which helps to cover prescription drug costs; it is based on Medicare-approved private insurance companies and can help reduce prescription drug costs and protect against possible cost increases. Participants pay for Part D plans out of pocket and must pay monthly premiums and co-payments for certain prescriptions. Those enrolled in Medicare Part C are typically eligible for Part D. Every year people can switch plans, from 15 October to 7 December (during the Annual Election/Open Enrollment Period), and from 1 January to 31 March (during the Medicare Advantage Open Enrollment Period). *Medicaid* is a programme that provides health insurance to low-income families and individuals. Unlike Medicare, it is financed by both federal and state governments; Medicaid works differently in each State, even if there are federal guidelines to be applied. Patients usually pay no part of costs for covered medical expenses, while small co-payment is sometimes required.

reiterated his avowed objective of lowering drug prices and streamlining the FDA process to put a drug on the market. One such occasion was during a meeting with congressman E. Cumming (D-MD), when Trump confirmed the need to ensure more affordable prescription drug prices for all Americans, especially those who need life-saving prescription medications.[6] In this way, reforming the FDA and reducing the regulatory burdens on drug manufacturers so as to enhance competition will help accomplish those goals.[7] At various other forums, both the President and the Health and Human Services (HHS) Secretary, Alex Azar, stated that they had significantly expedited the FDA approval process, and during 2017 the FDA approved more than 1,000 low-cost generics, the highest in its history. In keeping with this address, the President, on 10 October 2018, signed two bills to lower the cost of prescription drugs – *Know the Lowest Price Act* (S. 2553) and *Patient Right to Know Act* (S. 2554) – a bipartisan legislation authored by Senators Collins and McCaskill to prohibit pharmacy 'gag clauses',[8] which restrict pharmacists from telling consumers when there are cheaper prescription drug alternatives available.[9] In particular, the *Know the Lowest Price Act of 2018* amended the *Social Security Act,* introducing new prohibitions on limiting certain information on drug prices, since a PDP sponsor and a Medicare Advantage organization offering a prescription drug plan or an MA-PD plan shall ensure the absence of restrictions for pharmacies from informing enrollees in such a plan of any differential between the negotiated price of a drug or of a lower price the enrollee would pay for the drug or biological without using any health insurance coverage.[10] The *Patient Right to Know Act* prohibits health insurers from restricting or penalizing the disclosure of certain drug pricing information to enrollees, and to require the filling of settlements between biosimilar product developers.[11]

10.4 THE BLUEPRINT PROGRAM

An apparent turning point in the pharmaceutical policy coincides with the adoption, in May 2018, of the document called 'American Patient First – The Trump Administration Blueprint to Lower Drug Prices and Reduce Out-of-Pocket Costs' (or 'Trump Administra-

6 In the same way, *see* President Trump's speech, 25 October 2018, available at www.whitehouse.gov/briefings-statements/remarks-president-trump-prescription-drug-prices/.

7 *See* in this regard the meeting between President Donald Trump and Congressman Elijah Cummings (D-MD) of 8 March 2017, available at www.whitehouse.gov/briefings-statements/readout-president-donald-j-trumps-meeting-congressman-elijah-cummings/.

8 It is opportune to point out that many states approved their versions of the gag clause ban.

9 *See* https://nashp.org/wp-content/uploads/2019/01/RxTracker-final-3.19.2019.pdf.

10 *See* 'Know the Lowest Price Act of 2018', available at www.congress.gov/bill/115th-congress/senate-bill/2553?q=% 7B%22 search%22%3A%5B%22know+the+lowest+price+act%22%5D%7D&r=1.

11 *See* 'Patient Right to Know Drug Prices Act', available at www.congress.gov/bill/115th-congress/senate-bill/2554/text.

tion Blueprint'/'Blueprint Program').[12] This plan is based on four strategies: *increasing competition, better negotiation, incentives for lower list prices, lowering out-of-pocket costs.* For each of these four strategies, there are at least two consequences (immediate actions, on one side, and further opportunities, on the other).

Before specifying the features of these strategies, the Blueprint Program proposes a summary of the causes of high drug prices, like the expiration of patents of popular drugs (blockbuster drugs), the ACA taxes (on branded prescription drug sales to Medicare, Medicaid and other government healthcare programmes), the 340B growth (drug discount programme, created in 1992 and significantly expanded with Obamacare), the consequences of the financial crisis (with the austerity measures to contain government spending on prescription drugs) jointly with the lack of modern negotiation tools in government programmes.

Specifically, the measures for increasing the first strategy (*increasing competition*) concern the acceleration of the FDA process to approve generic drugs and speeding access to more affordable generics by spurring competition,[13] since greater competition is associated with lower prices. Since the beginning of the Trump Administration, a host of actions have been taken, such as the publication by the FDA of drug names that have no competitors "in order to spur new entrants and bring prices down". In 2017 over 1,000 generic drugs were approved, saving nearly $9 billion that year. Another important measure is the adoption of the *Drug Competition Action Plan,*[14] which enables patients to access more affordable medications, along with measures aimed at speeding access to more affordable generics and facilitating opportunities for information sharing between doctors, patients and manufacturers.

The measures aimed at the second strategy (*better negotiation*) are based on a range of actions intended to support better negotiation, which include changes to the *Medicare Prescription Drug Program* in Part C and Part D in order to allow a faster mid-year substitution of drugs into formularies, proposals to clarify the definition of brand drugs, analysing drug prices in the international market, especially in countries that are part of the OECD, or to increase the integrity of the *Medicaid Drug Rebate Program (MDRP).*[15] There were

12 The text is available at www.hhs.gov/sites/default/files/AmericanPatientsFirst.pdf.

13 The President proposed to review 180-day exclusivity for a generic manufacturer for being the first generic, preventing additional generic manufacturers from entering the market.

14 The Drug Competition Action Plan is based on three key areas: "improving the efficiency of the generic drug development, review, and approval process; maximizing scientific and regulatory clarity with respect to complex generic drugs; and closing loopholes that allow brand-name drug companies to 'game' FDA rules in ways that forestall the generic competition Congress intended".

15 The MDRP is a programme that includes Centers for Medicare & Medicaid Services (CMS), State Medicaid agencies and participating drug manufacturers aiming to offset the federal and state costs of most outpatient prescription drugs dispensed to Medicaid patients. Approximately 600 drug manufacturers currently participate in this programme.

also measures to establish an inflation limit for reimbursement of Medicare Part B drugs and to reduce the wholesale acquisition cost (WAC) when average sales price is not available and to analyse drug prices paid in member-countries of the OECD.

The third strategy of the Blueprint Program (*creating incentives to lower list prices*) includes measures – in the President's FY2019 Budget – to create incentives to lower list prices through actions that include the modernization of the Medicare Part D programme[16] and the reform of the *340B Program.*[17]

The fourth strategy (*Reducing Patient Out-of-pocket Spending*) is based on a range of measures to improve transparency and lower consumer out-of-pocket spending, in order to face the problem concerning the fact that many American patients do not know what their prescription drugs will cost before getting to the pharmacy and many of them are never informed of lower-cost options.

For each of these foregoing strategies, the HHS's blueprint proposes some specific actions.

In response to the measure to *improve competition*, the HHS will take steps to prevent gaming of regulatory processes, by issuing a guidance by FDA "to address some of the ways in which manufacturers may seek to use shared system REMS[18]" or policies to improve the availability, competitiveness and adoption of biosimilars, along with the education of patients, clinicians and payers to increase their awareness of biosimilar and interchangeable products.

With regard to the *better negotiation* strategy, the HHS may – among other measures – initiate the development of demonstration projects to lower drug prices through Centres for Medicare and Medicaid Services or improve and provide plans with full flexibility, since now Part D plans are unable to negotiate lower prices for high-cost drugs, and work with the Department of Commerce, the U.S. Trade Representative and the U.S. Intellectual Property Enforcement Coordinator to address unfair disparity between drug prices in America and other countries.

---

16 The aim of this measure is to reduce out-of-pocket spending for beneficiaries of the programme. According to the Trump Administration, these changes – by shifting more responsibility into plans – would create "incentives for plans to negotiate with manufacturers to lower prices for high-cost drug".

17 *340B Program* is a programme that "provides discounts on outpatient drugs to certain safety net health providers (…). The program's intent is to allow safety net providers to increase patient services with the savings realized from participation in the 340B program. Providers typically save 25-50% on outpatient drug costs through participation in the program. These savings can be used to reduce the price of pharmaceuticals for patients, expand services offered to patients, or provide services to more patients". *See* www.hhs.gov/opa/grants-and-funding/340b-drug-pricing-program/index.html.

18 A Risk Evaluation and Mitigation Strategy (REMS) is a drug safety programme that the U.S. FDA can require for certain medications with serious safety concerns to help ensure the benefits of the medication outweigh its risks. These strategies are designed to reinforce medication use behaviours and actions that support the safe use of that medication. So far only a few medications have required an REMS.

The possible actions pertaining to *lowering list prices* may include making Medicare and Medicaid prices more transparent[19] or calling on the FDA to evaluate the "inclusion of list prices in direct-to-consumer advertising", while measures to *reduce patient out-of-pocket spending* may include prohibiting pharmacists from being prevented from telling patients when they could pay less (so-called *pharmacy gag clauses*) and to require Part D Plan sponsors to provide more information about drug price increases.

In addition to the strategies already proposed, the U.S. Department of Health and Human Services considers bolder actions to lower drug prices and is also interested in public comments about how the department could improve competition or intervene in the general structure and function of the pharmaceutical market. The bolder actions aimed at solving problems include the limitation on distribution of certain prescription drugs, the facilitation of access to reference product samples by companies engaged in biosimilar or interchangeable product development, the improvement of the Purple Book,[20] the implementation of education – e.g. through programmes like the Biosimilar Education and Outreach Campaign, launched by the FDA in 2017[21] – among patients and healthcare professionals, the improvement of price transparency in Medicare and Medicaid. Further actions include the identification of long-term financing models "to help states, insurers and consumers to pay for high-cost treatments", the movement of some Medicare Part B drugs to Medicare Part D[22] and the review of the 340B Drug Pricing Program.[23]

About 100 days after the Trump Administration Blueprint was adopted, the HHS published a *report* showing the measures adopted and the related consequences.[24] It revealed that during the first 100 days of the Blueprint Program the HHS has taken various actions that have helped to focus on the need for a more competitive pharmaceutical marketplace. During this period, 15 companies have reduced list prices and rolled back planned price increases or committed to price freezes for the rest of 2018. Two main shifts in drug pricing behaviour are underlined in the report: there have been 60% fewer brand-drug price

19 According to the Administration, this measure will be able to provide patients with additional information "to make informed decision and predict their cost sharing".

20 The Purple Book is a document that lists information about biological products, including any biosimilar and interchangeable biological products, licensed by FDA under the Public Health Service Act.

21 The campaign was launched on 23 October 2017 by the FDA, and its main goals include increasing understanding of biologics, reference products; knowledge of the data and information FDA reviews/requires to determine biosimilarity and interchangeability; knowledge about the prescribing of biosimilar and interchangeable products.

22 This measure is requested to the authority by the President's Budget in order to help reduce out-of-pocket costs for 27% of beneficiaries without Medicare prescription drug coverage or Medicare supplemental benefits in Part B.

23 The programme was established by Congress in 1992 to lower the cost of pharmaceuticals reimbursed by state Medicaid agencies and requires drug manufacturers that participate in the Medicaid Drug Rebate Program to provide covered outpatients drugs to eligible healthcare providers at reduced prices.

24 The report is available at https://www.hhs.gov/sites/default/files/ReportOn100DaysofAction_AmericanPatientsFirstBlueprint.pdf

increases than during the same period in 2017 and 54% more generic and brand-drug price decreases than during the same period in 2017.

However, the actual situation is not so good, as reported by a recent article in the *Wall Street Journal*.[25] It mentioned that a recent letter addressed to Secretary Azar by Senator Collins (R-ME) talks about the increasing trend in drug prices: in fact, the article reported that more than three dozen pharmaceutical companies have started to rise prices for hundreds of medicines. The average price increase reported was 6.3%, although the prices of several products were increased by much higher percentages, in double digits, one such drug being insulin, most commonly in use among diabetic patients.

10.5 Fiscal Year 2020 Budget and the Pharmaceutical Policy

In Fiscal Year 2020 Budget – A Budget for a better America,[26] the US Administration reaffirms the four strategies of the Administration's American Patients First Blueprint; in particular, it is willing to modernize the Medicare Part D Prescription Drug Benefit (for example, by encouraging the utilization of higher-value drugs by eliminating cost sharing for generic drugs for beneficiaries who receive low-income subsidies) and to Reduce Costs for Part B Drugs by using free-market competition in this drug category. Another important target is increase access to more affordable generics through greater competition. The Budget would include many proposals to speed the development of generics and eliminate loopholes that have allowed drug companies to use the regulatory framework to hinder competition. Moreover, the FY2020 Budget includes 'lower costs and increases flexibility for Medicaid prescription drugs': the Budget proposes to remove the cap on Medicaid manufacturers' drug rebates, to ensure rebates reflect all price increases for a drug. These measures are part of the wider plan to overcome Obamacare (e.g. the Tax Cut and Jobs Act, which eliminated Obamacare's individual mandate penalty, and took swift administrative actions that empower individuals to purchase health coverage that best suits their needs). In other words, the reconfirmation of the Blueprint Program and of its four strategies lead – again – to the pursuit of two main goals: appealing to the popular argument (high drug price) and trying to create the conditions to weaken some elements of Obamacare, without proposing a strategy or a structural reform programme. The writer's own opinion, on this political line, which finds confirmation in FY2020 Budget, is that there is more shadow than light and that the Blueprint Program is likely to remain only a declaration of intent lacking effective consequences, except for the degrees of checks on drugs in the name of the free market. Similarly, the will to incentivize the liberalization has generated

25 *See* www.wsj.com/articles/drugmakers-raise-prices-on-hundreds-of-medicines-11546389293.

26 The FY2020 Budget is available at www.whitehouse.gov/omb/budget/.

side effects on drug quality, and the will to fight against Big Pharma is only in words, not indeed.[27]

10.6 THE EMERGENCE OF OPIOID CRISIS: THE TRUMP ADMINISTRATION'S MEASURES TO COMBAT THE EPIDEMIC

The first two years of the Trump Administration have been particularly marked by the opioid crisis issue, and the Trump Administration has applied an all-of-Government approach to this problem, considering that it needs a comprehensive approach.[28]

According to the National Institute on Drugs Abuse,[29] more than 130 people in the States die every day after overdosing on opioids.[30] The opioid crisis – related to the misuse of and addiction to opioids – is a serious national crisis, whose roots can be traced to the late 1990s, when pharmaceutical companies promised that the use of opioid pain relievers would not lead to patient addiction, sparking a trend of high prescription rates.

However, it became immediately clear that those medications were highly addictive. The opioid overdose rates began to increase, and in 2016 more than 64,000 Americans died after opioid overdose.

The fight against the US opioid crisis was one the features of Trump's electoral campaign, along with the promise that its defeat would be a priority of his Administration; and soon after his election, President Trump declared the country's increasing opioid overdose epidemic a public health emergency.

"We will work to strengthen vulnerable families and communities, and we will help to build and grow a stronger, healthier and drug-free society" President Trump vowed. To this end, on 29 March 2017 Trump signed an Executive Order establishing the President's Commission on Combating Drug Addiction and the Opioid Crisis, which published – in

27 The debate on Trump's actual will to strike Big-Pharma is interesting. I would like to remember that there are some people connected to Big Pharma (or agreeable to Big Pharma) sitting in US Federal Administration main offices, such as Dr. Scott Gottlieb (who was sworn in as the 23rd Commissioner of Food and Drugs Administration on 11 May 2017) or the Secretary of Health and Human Services, Alex M. Azar, who was sworn in as the Secretary, nominated on 13 November 2017 and confirmed by the United States Senate in January 2018 (Azar was preceded by T. Price, who resigned as head of HHS on 29 September 2017, following criticism of his use of private charters and military aircraft for travel. Azar was a manager of Eli Lilly, an important leader of the drug industry).

28 The all-of-Government approach is proved by the adoption by President Trump of a Presidential Memorandum for the Heads of Executive Departments and Agencies to use all lawful means to combat the opioid crisis. *See* whitehouse.gov/articles/will-win-war-opioids/.

29 The National Institute on Drug Abuse (NIDA) is a federal government research institute, whose mission is "to advance science on the causes and consequences of drug use and addiction and to apply that knowledge to improve individual and public health".

30 The term includes prescription pain relievers, heroin and synthetic opioids such as fentanyl.

November 2017 – a very wide-ranging final report[31] including many recommendations. At the same time, the Council of Economic Advisers (CEA) released a report on the economic costs of the opioid crisis.[32]

The *National Drug Control Strategy*[33] elaborated by the Trump Administration is focused on reversing the development of drug use and reducing the number of Americans dying from drugs. The strategy consists of three elements: *prevention, treatment and recovery and reducing the availability of drugs in America. Prevention* means an early intervention through media campaigns and a drive to reduce risk factors. It has been noticed that "substance abuse prevention is a process which requires a shift in the behaviour, culture and community norms", so it is useful to base prevention on three main elements, namely universal, selective and appropriate intervention. The first one aimed to reduce specific health problems across all people through reduction of a variety of risk factors; selective intervention is targeted at particular communities, families or children who are at increased risk of substance misuse; the last one concerns those who are involved in risky behaviours. Prevention is being conducted by using nationwide mass media campaigns aimed at educating the entire nation on the drug-related vulnerabilities. It is also based on measures like the diffusion of safe prescribing practices, the expansion of the use of prescription drug monitoring programmes[34] or the strengthening of the ONDCP's Drug-Free Communities (DFC) Support Program to prevent and reduce youth substance use. The *treatment and recovery* strategy is connected with the need to improve the availability of treatment and the response to overdose by using naloxone (the FDA is working towards facilitating the development of non-prescription naloxone). It is a key element in the effort to provide a pathway to evidence-based treatment for those who need it coupled with the elimination of barriers to treatment availability and the increase in recovery infrastructure. *Reducing the availability of drugs in America* requires the adoption of actions to prevent the further expansion of criminal enterprises and to attack criminal networks with foreign partners in order to stop the spread of illicit drugs and substances in the United States.

In the context of President Trump's *Initiative to Stop Abuse and Reduce Drug Supply and Demand,* several steps have already been taken.

31 The document is available at www.whitehouse.gov/sites/whitehouse.gov/files/images/Final_Report_Draft_11-1-2017.pdf.

32 *See* www.whitehouse.gov/sites/whitehouse.gov/files/images/The%20Underestimated%20Cost%20of%20the%20Opioid%20Crisis.pdf.

33 The document is available at www.whitehouse.gov/wp-content/uploads/2019/01/NDCS-Final.pdf.

34 A prescription drug monitoring programme is an important means of increasing accountability in opioid prescribing practices, preventing patients from receiving opioids and other controlled medications that may have adverse interactions with opioids from multiple providers.

The Administration secured $6 billion in two years to fight the opioid crisis by reducing drug demand through education, increased awareness and prevention, cutting the flow of illicit drugs and saving lives by expanding opportunities for treatments.

In 2018 more than $1 billion was awarded by the Administration to States and local entities to help them to combat the opioid emergency. In order to reduce demand and over-prescription, President Trump's Opioid Initiative sets out to educate Americans about the dangers of opioid misuse. Several measures have been adopted in this direction, such as supporting research for innovative therapies to prevent addiction by nearly doubling State funds for opioid and pain research from $600 million to $1.1 billion, and supporting research for a vaccine that can prevent addiction.[35] Moreover, a Safer Prescribing Plan[36] has been implemented in order to reduce the over-prescription of opioids, and important results have been achieved, such as a 16% fall in high-dose opioid prescription and a more than 50% fall in the number of first-users of heroin in 2017.

The Opioid Initiative also works by cutting off the supply of illicit drugs. Towards this end President Trump is working to secure land borders and waterways against illicit smuggling and fighting the prescription opioid crisis together with the Department of Justice Prescription (DOJ) Interdiction and Litigation Task Force, which is in charge of prosecuting corrupt or negligent doctors, pharmacies and distributors and of developing all available criminal and civil actions to hold opioid manufacturers accountable for any unlawful practices. These measures have already had positive results: the country's biggest Darknet distributors of drugs was shut down by the DOJ; the average federal sentence for drug trafficking has increased and more than 2,300 pounds of fentanyl was seized in FY 2017 by Immigration and Customs Enforcement.

To help those struggling with addiction, the Administration is working to ensure that the first responders are supplied with naloxone and to expand access to evidence-based addiction treatment in every State. These measures have been successful, as reflected by a more than 20% increase in young adults receiving outpatient treatment and an increase in the number of patients with illicit drug-use disorders treated at specialty facilities and private provider offices.

35 It seems appropriate to mention here – among the initiatives to make people aware of the opioid crisis and to remember its victims – the 'Prescribed to Death Memorial', created by the National Safety Council. It features a wall with 22,000 simulated pills, each with a face carved in it to represent the human toll that this crisis has on American communities. At the same time, the White House has launched a website, crisisnextdoor.gov, allowing Americans to share their stories about the opioid addiction.

36 The Plan's goals include cutting nationwide opioid prescription fills by one-third within three years, adopting best practices for opioid prescribing and helping States transition to a national network of prescription drug monitoring programmes.

It is notable that on 24 October 2018 President Trump signed the *Support Act*,[37] which is a bipartisan agreement born out of the House's work in June and the Senate's work in September.

The main points of the legislation are *new research*, since the act provides the National Institutes of Health with new authorities to conduct innovative research on new non-addictive pain medications; *Jessie's Law*, which ensures medical professionals have access to patients' health history before making treatment decisions; *safe disposal of unused medications*, aimed at reducing the number of unused controlled substances at risk of misuse; and *stopping fentanyl* by authorizing grants to State and local agencies to increase coordination between public health laboratories to improve the detection of fentanyl.

The Trump Administration's will to continue its fight against the opioid crisis is also reflected in the FY2020 Budget,[38] where significant investments have been proposed. In 2018 and 2019, $6 billion was secured in new resources to combat the epidemic, and the same line will be followed in 2020, since the FY2020 Budget sustains "investment in surveillance, prevention, treatment, access to overdose reversal drugs, recovery support services and research". In detail, the Budget includes $1.5 billion as State Opioid Response grants, more than $1 billion in the National Institutes of Health to support research, an investment of $221 million to expand the behavioural health workforce, maintaining $120 million "to support treatment and prevention of substance use disorder, including opioid abuse, in rural communities at the highest risk".

10.7 Some 'Mid-Term' Conclusions

It is not easy to make any definitive judgments on the first two years of Trump's term. If, on the one hand, the President has so far relied on statements that have a certain 'appeal' to public opinion (for instance, the decision to lower drug prices and the struggle to end the opioid crisis), on the other hand, the intent to dismantle Obamacare (the true goal of the Trump Administration) has not had the expected success. What is lacking is a strategic direction that is capable of giving rise to an alternative and structural reform, one that proves to be coherent with pharmaceutical policies aimed at drug price reduction and product liberalization. In this respect, the Blueprint Program – which summarizes the Trump Administration' strategic lines concerning healthcare, health and pharmaceutical policies and adopted after the failed attempt to repeal and replace Obamacare – does not seem to be incisive since it does not elaborate a complete structural reform. And considering that the FY2020 Budget confirms the Blueprint strategies, it is probable that no changes

37 The full text of the Act is available at www.congress.gov/bill/115th-congress/house-bill/6.

38 *See* FY2020 Budget, p. 39, available at www.whitehouse.gov/wp-content/uploads/2019/03/budget-fy2020.pdf.

will occur soon. The will itself to fight against Big Pharma is only in words but not in reality.

11 Environmental Policies

Roberto Louvin[*]

11.1 Commitments of Candidate Donald Trump

Donald Trump's environmental policy marked a clear turning point with respect to the strategies implemented by the Obama administration,[1] and the fruits of this turning point, in spite of the generally long times distinguishing these kinds of policies, have already begun to be seen since the first half of the presidential term.

Let's try to quickly reconstruct the premises of this policy starting from the commitments of the candidate Donald Trump during his election campaign. We can say it clearly: an explicit, even brutal and shocking electoral environmental programme.

A large part of the previous administration had been marked by pro-environmental interventionism, through restrictive regulations on emissions, abandonment of the most polluting energy sources (such as coal), industrial reconversion to reduce the impact of anthropical action on the climate. The highest point of this commitment was undoubtedly the decisive impulse of the United States to conclude the Paris Agreement (COP 21) in 2015.

The steering that Trump promised to give started from an opposite perspective. It was based on a sort of 'environmental denialism',[2] that is, an absolute denial of the direct relationship between human activities and climate change. The main goal of his new policy should have been, instead, the creation of new wealth and new jobs, whatever the ecological impact of these activities might have been.

---

* Trieste University.

1 Obama's strategy began by Executive Order 13514, *Federal Leadership in Environmental, Energy, and Economic Performance*, and was further summarized in the 2013 Climate Action Plan highlighting the steps that the executive branch would take to cut the carbon emission. This plan was based on three pillars: cutting carbon emission; preparing the United States to face the impacts of climate change; taking up the world leadership in efforts to combat global climate change and preparing to withstand its effects. The resulting actions were specified in Executive Order 13653, *Preparing the United States for the Impacts of Climate Change*, and in Executive Order 13677, *Climate-Resilient International Development*. A further concrete step was taken with the establishment of the State, Local, and Tribal Leaders Task Force on Climate Preparedness and Resilience.

2 Everybody remembers Trump's statements such as "no matter what science says, man is not a primary contributor to global warming" or "Global warming is a 'hoax', a plot of the Chinese government ...", with respect to which in the exercise of his mandate the President had to at least partially correct the shot.

Concretely, this should have resulted in the withdrawal of Obama's commitments (in particular from the Paris Agreement); restarting coal, oil and shale production (especially opening federal lands and offshore areas for the extraction of oil and gas); and a general environmental deregulation, as environmental protection regulations were consistently referred as barriers and obstacles to further development and job creation. Two specific commitments concerned the refocusing of the United States Environmental Protection Agency (EPA) on his primary mission and the overrun of the Obama Climate Action Plan.

11.2 The Patchwork of Environmental Law and Policy in the United States

The implementation of the promised goals, in the transition from electoral promise to administrative action, was to incorporate them in a very complex setting.

The United States has a 'naturally fragmented' approach to environmental policies. This is true, in general terms, for all the countries in the world, but it seems to be particularly the case of the United States. Environment involves solving complex issues and this is even more true for a federal state in which the constitutional framework divides the regulatory power in environmental matters between different levels, in particular between federal government on the one side and the states on the other side.

It's a complex and articulated game in which legislative, executive and judicial branches, as well as specific agencies (EPA, Food and Drug Administration, etc.), state powers, local powers and Indian tribes can interfere. Executive Order 13792,[3] for example, which contracted the boundaries of particularly sensitive areas such as the Bears Ears National Monument, has caused great alarm in many milieux, including environmental groups and Native American tribes. All this without forgetting the hidden player, a fundamental variable in the game: the ecosystem itself.

There is no level of power or branch of government holding exclusive power in this area: everything is subject to negotiations and long-term strategies, even if for some special issues a quick decision is essential.

In addition to the plurality of players in this matter, two other fundamental factors must be highlighted: the first one is the very close link between the environmental policies and the energy issues, since inevitably energy consumption increases stress on the environment and growing energy requirements are necessarily associated with environmental burdens (higher greenhouse gas (GHG) emissions, deforestation, desertification on rural societies, etc.).

3 Executive Order 13792, *Review of Designations under the Antiquities Act*, issued by President Donald Trump on 26 April 2017.

The second one is the international framework of multilateral commitments to prevent and counteract local and global deterioration of the environment,[4] which in its complex forms a vast patchwork.

The environment is a systemic matter in itself: it's impossible to give separate responses and to imagine exclusively sectorial solutions, since all issues are totally interlinked. The problems cannot just be faced and solved, in most cases, according to a purely domestic vision and without considering the effects produced beyond the borders: ecological issues always cross boundaries.

So, policies on these issues necessarily develop a complex dynamic and involve different actors in the pursuit of common aims: to reduce it to a purely top to bottom process is tantamount to triggering endless conflicts and introducing disorder in economic development and civil life.

Moreover, the consequences of these choices have a direct and heavy impact on the health and the quality of life, sometimes even on life itself, not only for animals and vegetables but also for humankind itself.

These complex issues have an impact on many areas: air pollution, water quality, hazardous lands, food safety, consumer product safety, fossil fuel scarcity and loss of biodiversity. In terms of administrative enforcement, it invests in industry, agriculture, commerce, transport, consumer goods, cultures and lifestyles. In short, it's a real cross-cutting theme with reflections often projected far beyond national borders.

On the other hand, it is not uncommon to face issues whose implications appear, at first glance, to be completely different – as social, cultural or religious – but which also produce, at the same time, heavy consequences on nature. The construction of the wall, for example, between the United States and Mexico is a problem which not only deals with security, socio-economic development and humanitarian law, but which also directly touches naturalistic profiles. This work, if fully realized, will block the movement of plenty of animals and seriously threaten the local wildlife. The problem of environmental sustainability of such a work, although properly pointed out by experts, is regularly overshadowed by more pressing interests.

11.3 From Candidate to President: First Moves

Donald Trump's inaugural speech as the 45th President of the United States does not contain any reference to environmental and climate issues: it even seems that these terms are deliberately banned from his vocabulary.

4 All of which are listed in detail on the website: www.ecolex.org.

Among the first initiatives taken and his more conspicuous actions there were those related to the restarting of the coal mining industry, accompanied by the pounding messages 'Jobs, jobs jobs' and 'Make America great again'. Unfortunately, nobody can escape from the equation 'more growth = more jobs = more consumption of resources' and in this operation, obviously, the environment is the predestined victim of the deal.

On the rhetorical level, this leap backwards was followed by the spread of the myth of clean coal. Clean coal does not exist in nature and there is no magical technique that allows this kind of processing: it's just a new narrative aimed at deluding public opinion that the use of fossil fuels has no heavy environmental impact: unfortunately, it always has.

On the normative level, the Trump administration has given a strong acceleration towards the announced deregulation: environmental regulations are considered just as impediments to business and some of the first Executive Orders have pointed straight in this direction.[5]

By the spring of 2017, it was announced that the Trump Administration would roll back the US government's fuel efficiency standards for cars and light-duty trucks to make these standards more openly advantageous to American producers.[6] In September 2018 new rollbacks were established, reducing requirements for oil and gas firms to monitor and mitigate releases of methane from wells and other operations.[7]

In June 2017 Donald Trump pledged to pull the United States out of the Paris Agreement,[8] reneging – as he rescinded almost all actions of its predecessor – on the US government's agreement to cut its emissions between 26% and 28% below 2005 levels by 2025. Shortly after, the trade war with China started on a ground which has undoubtedly a very heavy environmental impact: in early 2018 Trump, in fact, moved to safeguard domestic solar manufacturers by placing a 30% tariff on imported solar modules. In December 2018 the Trump administration rolled back another Obama policy, pledging to lift some restrictions on GHG emissions from coal power plants.[9]

5 In particular, Executive Order 13777, enforcing the Regulatory Reform Agenda, issued on 24 February 2017, aimed at implementation and enforcement of the President's deregulatory agenda.

6 Trump's decision was described by environmental health and public groups as a 'U-turn in the fight against climate change'. On their side, car manufacturers warmly welcomed the news as the 'right decision' and a move that would keep new vehicles affordable to more Americans.

7 Meanwhile, by the end of September 2018, a Washington Post story highlighted a shocking footnote in a US Government agency report which forecasted that global carbon emissions will nearly double by 2100.

8 Some scholars point out the "toothless outcome" of the Paris Agreement, signed by Barak Obama like a symbolic gesture, "more about public relations than about arriving at substantively effective solutions. Signing the Paris Agreement was as symbolic a gesture as President Clinton's signing of the Kyoto Protocol, knowing full well that there was no chance the Protocol would change anything in United States energy policy": J.D. Caytas, 'The COP21 Negotiations One Step Forward, Two Steps Back', *Consilience*, Vol. 19, 2018, p. 7.

9 This came during the COP24 negotiations in Poland. This change was intended to spur construction of new coal plants and was hailed by EPA's administrator Andrew Wheeler who said the move would "rescind excessive burdens on America's energy providers and level the playing field so that new energy technologies

A further front of action concerns the refocusing of EPA functions within the frame of the general 'freezing' of agencies. The primary mission of EPA, with respect to its original and very broad mission formulated since the Nixon Presidency, including a broad spectrum of activity and many powers, has been restricted only to the tasks of protecting air and water.

> If the Trump Administration's attack on EPA through its anti-environmental Administrator Scott Pruitt succeeds in deregulating the environment – and local air, water, and land become more toxic – the political opposition to Pruitt and Trump will be intense as the issue becomes more politically salient.[10]

A longer-term process then concerns the transformation of the Obama climate action plan[11] into an as yet undefined 'Clean Power Plan'.

11.4 Strategies and Legal Tools

Environmental policies are not only executed on the strictly normative ground by acts, a field in which Executive Orders play a hegemonic part as key tools of executive action, setting up a redrafting of the rules by Congress (in particular with regard to Clean water acts) or proceeding through shortcuts to achieve similar goals.[12]

In fact, they are also put in place in different ways that we must equally keep in mind.

First of all, we must consider the impact produced by increasing or reducing funding for economic activities (particularly by incentives for companies or taxes on production) and for supporting the action of many bodies that operate for the protection of the environment. This allocation of resources has already suffered a vertical collapse through the reduction of funds for environmental programmes by the new administration.

Another aspect relates to the appointments to key roles of the administration in the areas related to the environment. Here too, as in many other sectors, the choices have favoured people most known for their devotion and ideological loyalty, rather than for their specific skills.

---

can be part of America's future": J.A. Dlouhy, 'Trump Lifting Hurdle to Coal Plants No One Wants to Clear', *Bloomberg*, 6 December 2018.

10 S. Cohen, 'Democratic Grassroots Politics and Clean Economic Growth', *J. Int'l Aff.*, Vol. 71, No. 1, 2017, p. 105.

11 For an overview of this Plan, *see* N. Blake (Ed.), *President Obama's Climate Action Plan: Elements and Analyses*, Nova Science, 2013.

12 Strategies and tools used by US Presidents are well explained by D.M. Shafie, *Presidential Administration and the Environment: Executive Leadership in the Age of Gridlock*, Routledge, London, 2015.

Very few scientists, many less than those that were chosen by President Obama, have been appointed to these bodies, and the dynamics of the revolving door – that is, the movement of personnel between roles as legislators and regulators on one hand, and members of the industries affected by the legislation and regulation on the other – has marked the occupation of significant positions by managers or advisors generally very close to large industries. The President's constant preference for industry advisory circles and industrial law firms rather than for universities or specialized research centres seems to lead to an unhealthy relationship between the private sector and the American government.

The processes of deep state strengthening (or demolition) that can be developed over many years must also be taken into consideration: in this frame, the refocusing of the role of EPA certainly takes on very strong prominence.

Finally, in a country in which the jurisdictional bodies have always enjoyed great prestige and have contributed to determine fundamental orientations in many sectors, the importance of litigation triggered by the disruptive choices of the new administration is to be kept in mind. It is easy to prophesy that legal actions to the district courts and to the Supreme Court shall increase significantly and this obviously may slow down the processes planned by the administration.

11.5 Measures Announced and Actions Taken

The withdrawal from the Paris Agreement was certainly the most glaring occurrence, at least in the eyes of the international public opinion, of the first half of the mandate of Donald Trump, the most spectacular initiative taken and immediately made effective. In June 2017, President Trump announced the withdrawal of the United States from the Paris Agreement, making the United States the only nation that currently has not ratified the Paris Agreement.

In domestic politics, the return to traditional energy sources started with the Executive Order 13783 – Promoting Energy Independence and Economic Growth – which highlights the absence of environmental priorities.[13] It is, in essence, a real steering in the opposite direction to the guidelines expressed by Barak Obama's Clean Power Plan. It proposes a strong initiative for rolling back fuel economy standards, weakening environmental safeguards and lowering standards. Repealing the previous fuel economy standards, the orien-

13 The OMB Guidance Document on Implementation of Executive Order 13783 (8 May 2017) implemented Section 2 of Executive Order 13783, requiring agencies to review all existing regulations, orders, guidance documents, policies and any other similar agency actions that potentially burden the development or use of domestically produced energy resources, with particular attention to oil, natural gas, coal and nuclear energy resources.

tation of the new administration has been to restore less stringent guidelines. This is what Executive Order 13771 has worked towards since 2017.[14] New standards are now openly favourable to American producers: in short, many of these Executive Orders have been used not to strengthen, but rather to weaken the existing regulatory framework to protect the environment, in a systematic logic of deregulation.

A clear countermeasure, however, has been adopted by some states which have in fact voted in favour of measures in the opposite direction.

The momentum towards a new oil race has been strengthened by authorizing drilling in very sensitive areas and reviving plans that had previously been set aside, such as Keystone XL or the Dakota Access pipelines,[15] which provoked lively reactions and opposition from Indian tribes. Executive Order 13795,[16] which encouraged offshore energy exploration and production, as well as revoking decisions to withdraw certain areas of the Outer Continental Shelf from leasing and promoting fossil fuel development in federal waters, has also raised a lively concern, as well as ongoing initiatives in order to facilitate drilling in the Arctic.[17]

At the same time, the reduction of resources available for EFA programmes has led to a 31% reduction in its budget which means a partial dismantling and a substantial weakening of EPA.[18]

11.6 First Consequences

It is too early to attempt an assessment, even provisional, of Trump's environmental policy; perhaps it would be more correct to call it 'anti-environmental policy'. At most, we can make some general remarks, certainly influenced by our European sensitivity which is certainly different from the North American sensitivity on these issues.

We must first of all highlight the strength and the consistency of Trump policy: it is definitely a very clear, coherent policy, free of uncertainties or hesitations about the path he proposes to follow.

This policy is moving in the direction of a paradigm shift. What sounds somewhat suspect, beyond the aims of this new policy, is a kind of trivialization of public debate.

14 Executive Order 13771, Reducing Regulation and Controlling Regulatory Costs, 2017.

15 Indications contained in the *Presidential Memorandum Regarding Construction of the Dakota Access Pipeline* and in the *Presidential Memorandum Regarding Construction of the Keystone XL Pipeline*, both issued on 24 January 2017.

16 Executive Order 13795, Implementing an America-First Off-shore Energy Strategy, issued 28 April 2017.

17 Steven Mufson, 'Trump Administration Takes Another Step toward Oil Drilling in Arctic National Wildlife Refuge', *The Washington Post*, 20 December 2018.

18 Operated through the *Minibus funding bill*, also called the *Omnibus spending bill*, approved by the Senate on 12 September 2018.

There is a quick switching from scientific discussion (and pedagogical approach) of the Obama Presidency[19] to the radical, ideological and streamlined approach of the Trump era.[20]

Ecological thinking is challenging: it requires accepting and managing complexity. Donald Trump, for his part, is an extraordinary simplifier: ecology, in his vision and in his speeches, is just a colossal waste of time and the best way to kill the jobs. This approach has produced a deep break and a strong polarization of positions, with a strongly divisive impact on public opinion.

We must also bear in mind the consequences in international relationships of the international repositioning of the United States following the withdrawal from the Paris Agreements: it represents, in a way, the end of their world leadership in this field, with a temporary isolation which can, however, be followed by the creation of new alliances (such as the one with Brazilian President Bolsonaro). At the same time, the sceptre dropped by the United States was picked up by China and by the French President Macron, who guides the reaction of many other nations with the world initiative that repurposed Trump's slogan into 'Make Our Planet Great Again'.

In any case, the fact remains that the United States does not speak with a unanimous voice in this field. An internal front is in fact rapidly organizing itself and appears to be moving towards a very tough clash: the California leader of the coalition on the environment, Governor Jerry Brown, has stepped up as the global face of progressive climate policy in the United States. And after the Democrats won the House of Representatives in November 2018, it seems clear, according to the inaugural speech of the new House speaker Nancy Pelosi, that climate change actions will be a top priority for the Democrats in the Congress.

This is also a conflict that will certainly have vast judicial repercussions within the American society. The environmental associations – generally more effective and active in defending consumers than social rights – are quickly organizing themselves for the clash. Litigation will likely heat up more and more,[21] hindering at least in part the ambitions expressed by President Trump.

19 "President Obama ran a powerful 2008 campaign on the slogan of restoring science to its rightful place in US society (....) Obama's tactics worked because a significant majority of the public believed in 2008 in the virtue and value of science": C.A. Miller, 'It's Not a War on Science', *Issues Sci. Technol.*, Vol. XXXIII, No. 3, Spring, 2017.

20 B. Daniels, 'Come Hell and High Water: Climate Change Policy in the Age of Trump', *FIU L. Rev.*, Vol. 13, No. 65, 2018, consider that in terms of our political discourse, civility, partisanship and even our public aspirations, we sit at a low point of politics that we have not seen for decades.

21 The issue of climate change has increasingly arisen in litigation in many non-US countries. In general, the courts accept the scientific consensus about climate change and tend to treat climate change much like any other environmental issue: M. Wilensky, 'Climate Change in the Courts: An Assessment of Non-U.S. Climate Litigation', *Duke Environ. L. & Pol'y Forum*, Vol. 26, Fall, 2015, pp. 131-179.

12 IMMIGRATION: THE 'TRUMP EFFECT' FROM THE TRAVEL BAN TO THE SUBSTANTIAL WALL ON THE US-MEXICO BORDER

*Roberto Scarciglia**

As They Roared Into Battle, Only One Thing Was Missing...The Enemy!
1941, by Steven Spielberg

12.1 INTRODUCTION: THE 'TRUMP EFFECT'

This chapter aims to analyse legal immigration reforms during the first two years of President Trump's term, radically changing some policies of the former Obama administration. After the election in 2016, Donald Trump began to face global situations by adopting measures with impact at the international level. There are many fields in which the President intervened: from migration policies to the introduction of duties for commercial activities with China, from the withdrawal of American troops to climate agreements, as well as the Nuclear Non-Proliferation Treaty.

All those who study the global phenomena know the different forms of reaction that States interpose to favour or hinder these mechanisms, which, located outside the States, produce effects within them. What some scholars define as the 'Trump Effect'[1] provoked reactions from other States (like China, Russia, Iran, etc.) with consequences, also at the economic level, in Europe.

The restrictive changes made by the Trump Presidency on US immigration policy have been at the centre of a Presidential political agenda and constitutional debate, on which some Courts have intervened, including the Supreme Court. The impact on the nation's immigration policy has been profound. Before the Presidential election of 2016, during the electoral campaign, Trump argued that Muslims were more likely than members of other religions to pose a threat to American values and that the federal government should

---

* Full Professor of Comparative Public Law, University of Trieste.

1 The expression "Trump Effect" derives from: H. Pahm & V.H. Pahm, 'Subfederal Immigration Regulation and the Trump Effect', *New York University L. Rev.*, Vol. 84, No. 1, 2019, forthcoming, available at SSRN: https://ssrn.com/abstract=3171663.

adopt new measures that would restrict the ability of Muslims from other countries to enter the United States.[2]

In two years of administration, President Trump has implemented restrictive policies on every immigration front, through different legal instruments: executive orders, executive actions and agency memoranda.[3]

The structure of this chapter is simple. The first section explains the starting point and the meaning of the 'Trump Effect'. The second section deals with the saga of the 'travel ban' and analyses two Presidential Executive Orders (travel ban 1 and 2) and a Presidential Proclamation (travel ban 3). The third section explains the different orientation of the federal courts on the travel ban and the interpretation by the Supreme Court. The fourth section introduces some remarks on Trump's migration policies from a constitutional point of view. The last section deals with the problems arising from the construction of Trump's wall and a national emergency along the US-Mexico border.

12.2 THE SAGA OF THE TRAVEL BAN

The concept of 'saga' of the travel ban indicates a series of events – in this case, Presidential Executive Orders – to limit the ability of citizens of some Middle Eastern countries from entering the United States. We refer, firstly, to Executive Order No. 13,769, of 27 January 2017, titled *Protecting the Nation from Foreign Terrorist Entry into the United States* (or 'travel ban 1' or 'Muslim Ban').[4] This Order barred the people of seven Muslim countries (Iraq, Iran, Syria, Yemen, Libya, Sudan and Somalia) from entering the United States for 90 days, indefinitely suspending the resettlement of Syrian refugees. Moreover, it discriminates on religious grounds by giving preference to religious minorities (*i.e.* Christians from the Middle East) and reduces the cap on refugee admissions for the year 2017 from 110,000 to 50,000.

This Executive Order does not refer to the countries directly but has an indirect reference such as "217(a) (12) of the INA"[5] and "8 U.S.C. 1187(a) (12)".[6]

---

2 E.M. Malz, 'The Constitution and the Trump Travel Ban', *Lewis & Clark L. Rev.*, Vol. 22, No. 2, 2018, p. 392. *See also* N. Gass, 'Trump's Immigration Plan: Mass Deportation', *Politico*, 17 August 2015, available at https://www.politico.com/story/2015/08/donald-trump-immigration-plan-121420; D.J. Trump, 'Immigration Reform That Will Make America Great Again', available at https://assets.donaldjtrump.com/Immigration-Reform-Trump.pdf.

3 *See* D.C. Schmitt 'The Doctrine of Consular Nonreviewability in the Travel Ban Cases: *Kerry v. Din* Revised', *MPIL Research Paper Series*, No. 2018/03, available at https://papers.ssrn.com/sol3/papers.cfm?abstract_id=3122566.

4 Executive Order No. 13,769, of 27 January 2017, available at www.whitehouse.gov/presidential-actions/executive-order-protecting-nationforeign-terrorist-entry-united-states/.

5 Immigration and Nationality Act of 1952, Pub. L. 82-414, 66 Stat. 163, enacted June 27, as amended.

6 8 U.S.C. 1187 – Visa waiver programme for certain visitors.

As was foreseeable, Trump's Order provoked a massive and sudden revocation of visas, chaos at many international airports, a strong opposition from more than a dozen universities and a prompted emergency litigation in many districts. On 1 February 2017, the States of Washington and Minnesota sought a declaratory relief invalidating portions of Executive Order No. 13,769, of 27 January 2017, in the District Court for the Western District of Washington at Seattle.

The Federal District judge issued a restraining order temporarily barring the enforcement of the Executive Order.[7] Two days later, a three-judge panel of the US Court of Appeals for the Ninth Circuit affirmed the issuance of the restraining order, demonstrating that it adversely affects the States' residents in areas of employment, education, business, family relations and freedom to travel.[8]

Rather than appeal this decision in the Supreme Court, on 6 March the administration revoked the first version of the travel ban and issued a new Executive Order – No. 13,780 of 6 March 2017[9] – which was designed to address some of the problems that the Courts identified with the first order (travel ban 2). The new order was different in some critical respects.[10]

Firstly, it excluded Iraq from the list of the seven countries temporarily banned, and explicitly exempted legal permanent residents and those who already had a valid visa to come to the United States.

Secondly, the Order removed the indefinite restriction on the admission of Syrian refugees and the preference for religious minorities, introducing permissions on a case-by-case basis in the presence of specific conditions.

Thirdly, the second Executive Order refers to a *United States Department of State Country Report on Terrorism 2017*[11] and supports the claim that the protection of national security could justify the ban. Its purpose is to protect US citizens from terrorist attacks, including those committed by foreign nationals.

Anyhow, the Executive Order restricts, at Section 2, the entry of foreign nationals from six referred countries and suspends the US refugee programme for specified periods, providing, however, some exceptions. We can still observe that Section 6 of the Executive Order suspends the US *Refugee Admissions Program* for 120 days, both to travel into the United States and to decisions on applications for refugee status.

---

7 Temporary Restraining Order, *Washington v. Trump* (No. 2:17-cv-00141-JLR), available at www.clearinghouse.net/chDocs/public/IM-WA-0029-0005.pdf.

8 *Washington v. Trump* (No. 2:17-cv-00141-JLR), available at www.clearinghouse.net/chDocs/public/IM-WA-0029-0067.pdf.

9 Executive Order No. 13,780, 82, of 6 March 2017, available at www.federalregister.gov/documents/2017/03/09/2017-04837/protecting-the-nation-from-foreign-terrorist-entry-into-the-united-states.

10 *See* E.M. Maltz, 'The Constitution and the Trump Travel Ban', cit., 394.

11 *Washington v. Trump*, United States Court of Appeals, Ninth Circuit, No. 17-35105, 847 F.3d 1151, 17 March 2017. Available at https://caselaw.findlaw.com/us-9th-circuit/1863628.html.

In any case, it represents a response to the Ninth Circuit's *per curiam* decision in *Washington v. Trump*.[12] The District Court for the Western District of Washington entered a temporary restraining order blocking the entry restrictions, and the Courts of Appeals for the Ninth[13] and Fourth[14] Circuit denied the Government's request to stay that order.

Although some questions arose as to constitutional (Establishment Clause, Equal Protection Clause) and statutory violations (Immigration and Nationality Act (INA),[15] Religious Freedom Restoration Act, Refugee Act, Administrative Procedure Act[16]), the courts did not deal with the merits of the case, as the Fourth and the Ninth Circuit were only asked to decide on the granting of a preliminary injunction. While the Fourth Circuit Court answered the question by looking at the Establishment Clause, the Ninth Circuit focused on the (in-)consistency with the INA.

12.2.1 International Refugee Assistance Project v. Trump

On 15 March 2017, the District Court of Maryland issued a nationwide preliminary injunction stopping the implementation of the travel ban (§ 2 (c) Executive Order 2). On 25 May, the Fourth Circuit issued an opinion confirming the block of the travel ban.[17] The Court applied the *Lemon*-test[18] to determine a likely violation of the Establishment Clause of the US Constitution.[19] The Court decided that, because of legally relevant statements by President Trump and his representatives during the campaign and post-election, which seemingly influenced the issuance of Executive Order 1 and Executive Order 2, the primary purpose of Executive Order 2 was not secular, but 'anti-Muslim'.[20] This consideration implies the consequence that the *Lemon*-test was not fulfilled and the requirements of a preliminary injunction[21] – except for the District Court's inclusion of the President in the scope of the preliminary injunction – were undoubtedly satisfied.[22]

12 Available at: https://www.state.gov/documents/organization/283100.pdf.
13 *Hawaii v. Trump*, 859 F.3d 741 (9th Cir. 2017). Available at https://www.leagle.com/decision/infco20170612115
14 *International Refugee Assistance Project v. Trump*, 857 F.3d 554 (4th Cir. 2017). Available at http://coop.ca4.uscourts.gov/171351.P.pdf.
15 Immigration and Nationality Act of 1952, cit.
16 Pub. L. 79-404, 60 Stat. 237, June 11, 1946.
17 *IRAP v. Trump*, 857 F.3d 554 (4th Cir. 2017).
18 *Lemon v. Kurtzman*, 403 U.S. 602, 612-13 (1971).
19 *IRAP v. Trump*, 857 F.3d 554, 592-93 (4th Cir. 2017).
20 Id at 594-601.
21 *See Winter v. Nat. Res. Def. Council, Inc.*, 555 U.S. 7, 22 (2008).
22 *IRAP v. Trump*, 857 F.3d 554, 601-606 (4th Cir. 2017).

12.2.2 *Hawaii v. Trump*

Litigation was also happening at the same time in Hawaii.[23] The District Court of Hawaii also issued a preliminary injunction stopping the implementation of the entire Executive Order 2, affirmed by the Ninth Circuit Court in regard to stopping the implementation of § 2 ('travel ban') and § 6 Executive Order 2.[24] The Ninth Circuit Court dealt with two legal disputes: the breadth of the power granted to the President in 8 U.S.C. § 1182(f) and whether Executive Order 2 infringed upon the anti-discrimination provision in 8 U.S.C. § 1152(a) (1) (A).

8 U.S.C. § 1182(f) (Inadmissible Aliens) states that

> whenever the President finds that the entry of any aliens or of any class of aliens into the United States would be detrimental to the interests of the United States, he may by proclamation, and for such period as he shall deem necessary, suspend the entry of all aliens or any class of aliens as immigrants or nonimmigrants, or impose on the entry of aliens any restrictions he may deem to be appropriate.

The Court examined whether or not the President could show a "finding" that the entry of citizens of the six designated states for 90 days, the entry of every refugee for 120 days as well as every refugee that exceeded 50,000 would be "detrimental to the interests of the United States".[25] The Court concluded that the President could not sufficiently show this finding. Executive Order 2 argued among other things with national security concerns and state conditions, whereas the travel ban itself focused on citizenship.[26]

In other words, the government could not establish a connection between the security concerns arising from the state conditions and the potential threat by citizens of those states, and their relationship with terrorist organizations.

The Court concluded that Executive Order 2 infringed upon the anti-discrimination provision in 8 U.S.C. § 1152(a) (1) (A), which forbids, among other things, discrimination based on race or nationality. Although the provision itself only applies explicitly to the "issuance of an immigrant visa", the Court determined that it also applies here: while § 2 (c) Executive Order 2 only expressly targets the entry of non-immigrants and not the visa issuance for immigrants, the effect of the "travel ban" is that the affected persons will not receive a visa. We can consider that 8 U.S.C. § 1152(a) (1) (A) applies to 8 U.S.C. § 1182(f),

23 *Hawaii v. Trump*, 241 F. Supp. 3d 1119 (D. Haw. 2017).
24 *Hawaii v. Trump*, 859 F.3d 741 (9th Cir. 2017).
25 Id at 750-756 (9th Cir. 2017).
26 Id at 772.

so that the President cannot circumvent the anti-discrimination provision by restricting the scope of application to the entry of an alien.[27]

The Court ruled that the reduction of the refugee cap violated 8 U.S.C. § 1157.89, in accordance with "The statute requires the President to set the number of annual refugee admissions (1) before the start of the new fiscal year, and (2) after appropriate consultation with Congress."[28] Without these requirements, the President "ordered a midyear reduction in the level of refugee admissions [...] without consulting Congress".[29] The other *Winter* requirements of the preliminary injunction were met as well, except that the review procedures provided in §§ 2, 6 Executive Order 2 were allowed to take place, without including the President in the preliminary injunction.

12.3 The Saga Continues: A New Permanent Proclamation (Travel Ban 3)

Like every saga, the provisions on travel ban continue. On 24 September 2017, the administration issued a new Presidential Act, which once again changed the nature of the limitations that were being imposed by the first two versions of the travel ban. Unlike the two previous executive orders, the third version was adopted by a "Presidential Proclamation", "*Enhancing Vetting Capabilities and Processes for Detecting Attempted Entry Into the United States by Terrorists or Other Public-Safety Threats*" (travel ban 3).[30] President Trump exercised his President's authority under the INA.[31]

The Proclamation's objective was targeting travellers from nations that were either unwilling or unable to share sufficient information with the United States about their citizens, did not cooperate with the US government on immigration matters or were linked to terrorism.[32] The last version of the travel ban contains not only some general provisions but also some differences compared to previous orders. In particular, it includes some restrictions on Sudanese nationals and maintains the restrictions on citizens of Libya, Iran, Somalia, Syria and Yemen, adding further limitations on individuals traveling from Chad, North Korea and Venezuela. There are, however, some elements of differentiation from previous orders. The ban does not apply to lawful permanent residents, dual nationals and those holding a visa on 18 October 2017 – the date that the new travel ban went into effect – and does not exclude the admission of refugees to the United States.

27 *Hawaii v. Trump*, 859 F.3d 741, 777-78 (9th Cir. 2017).

28 Id. at 780.

29 *Hawaii v. Trump*, 859 F.3d 741, 780 (9th Cir. 2017).

30 Proclamation No. 9645, 82 Fed. Reg. 45161 (September 24, 2017).

31 Including Sections 212(f) and 215(a) of the Immigration and Nationality Act (INA), 8 U.S.C. 1182(f) and 1185(a), and Section 301 of title 3, United States Code.

32 Malz, 2018, p. 395.

From this point of view, we can see how the administration has extensive discretionary powers and, in essence, could possibly nullify the expectations of entry of refugees. The Proclamation provides that

> A waiver may be granted only if a foreign national demonstrates to the consular officer's or CBP official's satisfaction that: (A) denying entry would cause the foreign national undue hardship; (B) entry would not pose a threat to the national security or public safety of the United States; and (C) entry would be in the national interest.

The position of the opponents of the travel ban does not change, as also the orientation of the Courts of Hawaii and Maryland that had considered the first two Executive Orders to be illegal.[33]

12.4 US Supreme Court and the Travel Ban

The government, having lost in the lower courts, petitioned for a writ of certiorari and applied for a stay of the preliminary injunctions, and the US Supreme Court granted certiorari and stayed in part the preliminary injunctions by the lower courts. The Trump administration petitioned the Supreme Court to challenge that decision, and the *Trump v. Hawaii* case began hearing arguments before the high court in April 2018. The justices not only granted the petitions for certiorari but also held that, pending full consideration of the merits of the appeal, the order could be enforced against "foreign nationals who lack any bona fide relationship with a person or entity in the United States".[34]

This preliminary decision sparked further litigation, as the federal government argued that the concept of a "bona fide relationship with a person or entity in the United States" should be interpreted narrowly, while the opponents of the ban and the lower courts insisted on a broader interpretation of this concept.

In a split 5-4 decision, on 26 June 2018, the Supreme Court upheld the President's Proclamation No. 9645, and Chief Justice Roberts declared that President Trump had the authority to suspend the entry of noncitizens in the United States, according to the INA of 1952.

The Supreme Court rejected Hawaii's challenge to the Constitution's establishment clause which prohibits favouring one religion over another. Roberts pointed out that even

33 *Hawaii v. Trump*, 265 F. Supp. 3d 1140, 1145 (D. Haw. 2017); *Int'l Refugee Assistance Project v. Trump*, 265 F. Supp. 3d 570, 583 (D. Md. 2017).

34 82 U. S. (2017) Per Curiam, U.S. Supreme Court, Nos. 16-1436 (16A1190) and 16-1540 (16A1191). Available at https://www.supremecourt.gov/opinions/16pdf/16-1436_l6hc.pdf.

though five of the seven nations are Muslim majority, that fact alone "does not support an inference of religious hostility, given that the policy covers just 8% of the world's Muslim population and is limited to countries that were previously designated by Congress or prior administrations as posing national security risks".

Therefore, the Supreme Court does not rule out that President Trump had a "sufficient national security justification". This way, the Court decided in support of the Trump administration, declaring that "the terms of new proclamation could be enforced pending the ultimate resolutions of the legal challenges on their merits".[35]

12.5 Emergency Power and the Wall on the US-Mexico Border

The first Trump Executive Order relating to the border with Mexico was n. 13767, titled Border Security and Immigration Enforcement Improvements, issued on 25 January 2017. The problem of illegal immigration from Mexico had been one of the central themes of Trump's election campaign. He had announced his candidacy with "lurid images [of] Mexican drug dealers and rapists pouring into the country", asserting that this problem could only be solved by constructing a "great wall on the southern border".[36] The order also has an effect on the construction of that wall (the 'Trump wall'), along with the Mexico-US border.[37] According to some estimates, Congress needs to appropriate $20 billion to cover the costs for construction.

President Trump overlooked a political element that could have affected this project, namely the outcome of the midterm elections, which could have been unfavourable. In the weeks leading up to the election, President Trump drove fears of an 'invasion of foreigners' crossing the US-Mexico border – tweeting that the so-called caravan of migrants would bring a wave of criminals and terrorists to America's borders. On 22 December 2018, the federal government went into a shutdown due to Trump's demand for $5.6 billion in federal funds to begin work on the wall. By 12 January 2019, the shutdown became the longest budget shutdown in US history. The Democratic Party's conquest of the House of

35 Malz, 2018, p. 395.

36 Cfr. S. Gamboa, 'Donald Trump Announces Presidential Bid by Trashing Mexico, Mexicans', *Washington Post*, 16 June 2015, available at https://www.nbcnews.com/news/latino/donald-trump-announces-presidential-bid-trashing-mexico-mexicans-n376521. President Trump said: "When Mexico sends its people, they're not sending their best. They're not sending you […] They're sending people that have lots of problems, and they're bringing those problems with us. They're bringing drugs. They're bringing crime. They're rapists."

37 Executive Order No. 13,767 of 25 January 2017, at https://www.whitehouse.gov/presidential-actions/executive-order-border-security-immigration-enforcement-improvements/. In his address before Congress, President Trump stated, "[W]e will soon begin the construction of a great wall along our southern border": *see* A. Blake, 'President Trump's Surprisingly Presidential Speech to the Nation, annotated', *Washington Post*, 28 February 2017, available at https://www.washingtonpost.com/news/the-fix/wp/2017/02/28/president-trumps-first-big-address-to-the-nation-annotated/?utm_term=.af7dc0aa06af.

Representatives now represents for President Trump the main obstacle to the financing of the wall.

On 15 February 2019, to break the deadlock, President Trump declared a National Emergency Concerning the Southern Border of the United States, and this implied a plan to use emergency powers to spend billions of dollars on building the border wall. The House of Representatives approved – with 245 yes and 182 no – a resolution to block the Declaration of emergency by President Donald Trump to build the wall, and the text needed to be submitted to the Senate. To overcome the announced veto of Trump, Congress will need a two-thirds majority.

12.6 Some Reflections from a Constitutional Point of View

The restrictive measures of the right to immigrate in the United States have also raised some criticisms from a constitutional law point of view. There are many critical points, and I will address only a few of them here. One of the issues debated during the travel ban saga was the constitutionality of the three successive presidential acts. The attention of the public opinion has been focused primarily on the claim that the ban runs afoul of the fundamental constitutional norms embodied in the First Amendment.

12.6.1 The Plenary Power Doctrine

We point out how the Courts of Hawaii and Maryland invalidated the travel orders with what is generally known as the plenary power doctrine. Some cases decided in the late nineteenth and early 20th centuries traced the roots of this doctrine,[38] starting from the 1889 decision in *Chae Chan Ping v. the United States*. Nevertheless, another Supreme Court decision in *Kleindienst v. Mandel* (1972) was a premise in the debate on the travel ban.[39]

The Court rejected the constitutional challenge and concluded that the denial of the visa had been lawful. In the decision on this case, there were three dissenting judges in opposition to the prevailing opinion, summarized by Justice Harry A. Blackmun. According to him, we can say that the power to exclude aliens was "inherent in sovereignty, necessary for maintaining normal international relations and defending the country against foreign encroachments and dangers – [and was] a power to be exercised exclusively by the political branches of government".[40]

38 *See* for a list of the main cases: Malz, 2018, p. 397.

39 408 U.S. 753 (1972). In *Kleindienst*, the Court reviewed the decision to deny a visa to Ernest E. Mandel, a Belgian national, who described himself as a 'revolutionary Marxist'.

40 408 U.S. 753 (1972), at 765, *quoting* Brief for Appellants, *Kleindienst v. Mandel*, 408 U.S. 753 (1972), at 20.

A further consideration of Blackmun was to believe that

> when the Executive exercises [the power to exclude an alien] on the basis of a facially legitimate and bona fide reason, the courts will neither look behind the exercise of that discretion nor test it by balancing its justification against the First Amendment interests of those who seek personal communication with the applicant.[41]

Despite the majority decisions adopted by the Supreme Court, we, however, can highlight how the application of the *Mandel* standards does not preclude the judiciary from conducting a more searching inquiry into the factual purposes for the promulgation of the orders.

We can add, again, that the opponents to the travel ban referred to Justice Anthony Kennedy's concurring opinion in *Kerry v. Din.*[42] Following his opinion, we can point out that "an affirmative showing of bad faith" might provide judges with the justification necessary to "look behind" the expressed reason for the exclusion of an alien.[43] A specific element that would reinforce this opinion is in the language throughout President Trump's election campaign that left the assumption that the travel orders could be considered as enactments that penalized a group of people because of their religious beliefs.[44]

Another Supreme Court decision on immigration was *Fiallo v. Bell*, in which the Court considered the constitutionality of the distinctions drawn by the provisions of the *INA* that granted special immigration status to the noncitizen children of many American citizens.[45]

Both *Kleindienst* and *Fiallo* involved decisions based on criteria that called for enhanced scrutiny in other contexts. In this perspective, we can consider that the courts should not intervene in cases where the government asserts a "facially legitimate and *bona fide* reason" for its actions aptly reflect a general preference for judicial deference on immigration.[46]

12.6.2 The Travel Ban, the First Amendment and the Rights of Aliens

Leading critics of the travel ban challenged the infringement on the First Amendment of the Constitution. The challengers argued that the orders, designed to discriminate against

41 Id. at 770.
42 576 U.S. (2015).
43 Brief for Respondents, *Trump v. State of Hawaii*, No. 16-1540, at 47-60.
44 Id. at 48-49. *See* the corresponding reflections by Malz, 2018.
45 430 U.S. 787 (1977).
46 Malz, 2018, p. 395.

Muslims because of their religious beliefs, were in opposition to core values of religious freedom that the First Amendment protects.

As a preliminary, it is essential to point out that the US Supreme Court decision in *United States ex. rel. Turner v. Williams* established the principles governing the constitutional status of aliens.[47] John Turner was an English labour organizer who came to the United States in October 1903 to visit family and give a series of lectures. He was arrested in New York and brought before a board of exceptional inquiry appointed by the local immigration commissioner. The commission ordered him deported according to a 1903 statute that prohibited anarchists from entering the United States. Turner challenged the deportation order for the violation of both his due process rights and his right to free speech under the First Amendment.

12.6.3 The Travel Ban and the Establishment Clause

Firstly, I consider introducing some brief observations from a diachronic point of view concerning the origins of the Establishment Clause as useful for this debate. The concept of 'establishment of religion' – developed during the debate for the introduction of the First Amendment into the US Constitution – describes a special relationship between the government and one or more religious organizations. The specifics of the relationship is different from state to state, and, in any case, all of the relevant parties understood that the concept of the establishment is based on the theory that one or more religious organizations were entitled to special treatment from the proper state government.

In the 1971 decision in *Lemon v. Kurtzman* Chief Justice Warren E. Burger noted the "three main evils against which the Establishment Clause was intended to afford protection as sponsorship, financial support, and active involvement of the sovereign in religious activity".[48] *Lemon*'s case involved situations in which the government was providing financial support to religious institutions.

However, the Supreme Court pointed out that the government had in effect given its endorsement to the doctrines of certain religious groups (*McCreary County v. American Civil Liberties Union*[49] and *Santa Fe Independent School District v. Doe*).[50] In the case of the travel ban, there is a *different* set of *presuppositions, and these orders do not make explicit reference to any religious belief or group. From another point of view, it is not easy to demonstrate that the ban runs afoul of the* Establishment Clause.

47 194 U.S. 279 (1903).
48 403 U.S. 602, 612 (1971) *quoting Walz v. Tax Commission*, 397 U.S. 664, 668 (1970).
49 545 U.S. 844 (2005).
50 530 U.S. 290 (2000).

The reasons for this critical position are on the public declaration of President Trump during his 2016 electoral campaign. We can still observe that the 1982 decision in *Larson v. Valente* is the only case in which the Court has relied on the Establishment Clause to strike down a state law that singled out a small number of religious organizations for unfavourable treatment.

As Malz noted,

> [the] state law that the Court invalidated in Larson case, the government action at issue established a classification that left the interests of the vast majority of mainstream religious groups untouched but created significant difficulties for a small number of other religions.[51]

Nevertheless, it is difficult to demonstrate that the decision of the Supreme Court does not respect the scope of the First Amendment and also if a different conclusion could be possible if the Court, in another case, analyses the merits of the challenges to the actions of the Trump administration.

12.7 Concluding Remarks

Donald Trump ascended to the presidency mostly on the promise to protect the American people against an invading alien menace.[52] It is a central thought in the utterances of the American President, whose implementation, entrusted *with* a wide variety of legal instruments, has not always met the favour of the American public and the American courts. For the past two years, Donald Trump, first as a candidate and then as President, "has offered spectacular proof that the invasion metaphor continues to resonate with many Americans".[53]

Trump's original idea was that of a "total and complete shutdown of Muslims entering the United States".[54] We can say that his election promise has been kept by his issuance of the first of three orders barring migrants from several predominantly Muslim countries

51 Malz, 2018, p. 392. *See also* Gass, 2015; Trump, 'Immigration Reform That Will Make America Great Again'.

52 From this point of view, *see* M. Fisher & A. Taub, "How Donald Trump Hacked the Politics of Foreign Policy', *New York Times*, 19 October 2016, available at https://www.nytimes.com/2016/10/20/world/americas/donald-trump-foreignpolicy.html.

53 M.J. Lindsay, 'The Perpetual "Invasion": Past as Prologue in Constitutional Immigration Law', *University of Baltimore Legal Studies Research Paper*, No. 2018-10, available at https://ssrn.com/abstract=3178230.

54 J. Johnson, 'Trump Calls for Total and Complete Shutdown of Muslims Entering the United States', *Washington Post*, 7 December 2015, available at https://washingtonpost.com/news/post-politics/wp/2015/12/07/donald-trump-calls-for-total-and-complete-shutdown-of-muslims-entering-the-united-states/?utm_terms=.bfbf614a81fb.

from entering the United States. That order was soon replaced by a second and then, nearly six months later, by the third and current iteration, which indefinitely prohibits travel to the United States by citizens of six Muslim-majority countries (Chad, Iran, Libya, Somalia, Syria and Yemen) and North Korea.

The decisions of the federal courts were not favourable to the American administration because of the strong suspicion that the provisions of President Trump violated the Constitution and, in particular, the First Amendment and the Establishment Clause. On that point, quoting *Clark v. Jeter*,[55] we might argue that the travel bans were unconstitutional because they discriminated between prospective entrants on the basis of national origin – a type of classification that is generally subject to strict scrutiny in cases arising in a purely domestic context. We do not doubt that a ban on national origin discrimination can destabilize the entire structure of immigration law. If the Supreme Court saved the Trump Administration, the political project of President Trump has come to a standstill after the midterm elections, in which the Democratic Party got the majority of the House of Representatives, stopping the loan for constructing the wall on the US-Mexico border.

President Trump initiated a political tug of war with Democratic parliamentarians, provoking the most extended shutdown in US history without any funding for his proposed border wall. The 35-day shutdown produced the effect of sending home 800,000 government workers without pay since before Christmas 2018. To overcome the deadlock, President Trump declared a national emergency at the border to access billions of dollars to build a border wall that Congress refused to give him, transforming a highly charged policy dispute into a first confrontation over the separation of powers.

The House of Representatives approved with 245 votes in favour and 182 against a resolution to block the Declaration of Emergency by Donald Trump to build the wall. After the submission to Senate, which did not approve his border national emergency, the President issued the first veto of his presidency on 15 March 2019.

We cannot know what the fate of the wall on the US-Mexico border will be in concrete terms, as well as the American immigration policy in the coming years. Inspired by the novel by American writer Paul Auster, *The Music of the Chance*, we can say that all will depend on the "chance", on the results of the upcoming presidential elections: a "requiem for a (dystopic) dream"?[56]

55 486 U.S. 456, 461 (1988).

56 This expression derives from: N. Palazzo, 'Requiem for a Dream: The Switch of the Trump Administration on Transgender Rights', *DPCE Online*, 2018, available at http://www.dpceonline.it/index.php/dpceonline/requiemforadream.

13 Religious Freedom under the Trump Administration

Davide Bacis[*]

13.1 Introduction: The Impact of Religious Vote on Presidential Elections

In order to properly understand the reasons behind President Trump's electoral promises and the policies adopted by his administration concerning the protection of religious freedom, one ought to take into account the significant impact of religiously influenced votes in US presidential elections. Indeed, post-New Deal elections showed the strong influence exercised by religion over individuals' party affiliation: voters belonging to proactive religious communities tend to hardly ever move away from the party embodying the values shared by their own confession.[1] This is especially true with regard to certain faiths, whose members have been strong supporters of the Republican party for over 40 years.

Catholics, Evangelicals and Mormons alike began to be politically involved following the 1973 *Roe v. Wade* Supreme Court ruling on the right to abortion;[2] however, it was only with the election of President Reagan in 1980 that commentators started to refer to these religious groups as the Religious Right. On that occasion, religious communities belonging to those three confessions abandoned the Evangelical candidate – *i.e.* President Carter – seeking re-election to support soon-to-be President Reagan, whose views were much more conservative than those of his predecessor.[3] From that moment, the so-called Religious Right, especially its Evangelical component, has been playing a relevant role in American politics.[4] As a matter of fact, according to a 2015 survey, members of the Evangelical

* PhD student at Università degli Studi di Pavia, Italy.

1 C. Brooks & J. Manza, 'The Religious Factor in U.S. Presidential Election 1960-1992', *Am. J. Soc.*, Vol. 103, 1997, p. 38.

2 *Roe v. Wade*, 410 U.S. 113 (1973). *See* R. Wuthnow, 'Mobilizing Civic Engagement: The Changing Impact of Religious Involvement', *in* T. Skocpol & M.P. Fiorina (Eds.), *Civic Engagement in American Democracy*, Washington, DC, The Booking Institution Press, 1999, p. 331, spec. p. 338.

3 *See* J.L. Brudney & G.W. Copeland, 'Evangelicals as a Political Force: Reagan and the 1980 Religious Vote', *Soc. Sci. Q.*, Vol. 65, 1984, p. 1072; C. Smidt & P. Kellestedt, 'Reagan Era: An Analysis of Evangelical Voters in the Presidential Election', *J. Sci. Study Relig.*, Vol. 31, 1992, p. 330.

4 One specifically refers to the example represented by the election of President G.W. Bush, who gained 68% of the Evangelical vote in 2000 and 78% of the Evangelical vote in 2004. *See* G.A. Smith & J. Martinez, 'How

community (which comprises around 73% of white people) constitute up to almost 26% of American Christians.[5] Not only are Evangelicals high in number, but when it comes to public involvement they also behave differently from the majority of other social groups. Specifically, in spite of the high rate of abstentionism at presidential elections, which even increases when mid-term elections are held, Evangelicals do not partake in the general trend, and they do vote, to the point where they generally constitute up to 26% of the electorate.[6] Needless to say, these numbers might not be decisive in ensuring a victory of the Republican candidate; what is certain is that the votes of the Religious Right, especially those of its Evangelical component, might effectively impact on the electoral results.

Eventually, and contrary to what was expected owing to some controversial episodes of his personal life, Donald J. Trump managed to benefit from the votes of the aforementioned religious communities. Indeed, 52% of Catholics and 62% of Mormons voted for the unusual Republican candidate, but, even more significantly, up to 82% of Evangelicals favoured the Trump-Pence ticket over their opponent, Hillary Clinton.[7]

Despite the lack of moral and religious stature that Evangelicals usually expect from a presidential candidate, President Trump gained support from conservative religious groups, especially from 'born-again' Evangelical Christians, thanks to his strong stance, during his electoral campaign, on the protection of religious freedom.[8] However, as this work will try to assess through the analysis of relevant policies and practices put in place during the first two years of the Trump administration, the protection of religious liberties appears to be merely instrumental to the achievement of a different purpose. This analysis will attempt to demonstrate how, by allegedly protecting religious freedom, the presidency seems to seek the repeal of all anti-discrimination policies implemented to protect women and Lesbian, Gay, Bisexual, Transgender, Queer and Intersex (LGBTQI) rights, while President Obama was in office.

---

the Faithful Voted: A Preliminary 2016 Analysis', *Pew Research Center*, 9 November 2016, available at www.pewresearch.org/fact-tank/2016/11/09/how-the-faithful-voted-a-preliminary-2016-analysis/.

5 Pew Research Center, 'Religious Landscape Study', available at www.pewforum.org/religious-landscape-study/.

6 *See* Smith & Martinez, 2016.

7 *See* N.J. Young, 'Catholics and Evangelicals: Does Donald Trump Mean the End of the Religious Right?', *in* M. Gayte, B. Chelini-Pont & M.J. Rozell (Eds.), *Catholics and U.S. Politics after the 2016 Elections. Understanding the 'Swing Vote'*, Palgrave Macmillan, Cham, 2018, p. 63.

8 *See* A.L. Whitehead, S.L. Perry & J.O. Baker, 'Make America Christian Again: Christian Nationalism and Voting for Donald Trump in the 2016 Presidential Election', *Soc. Relig.*, Vol. 79, 2018, p. 147; *see also* P. Gorski, 'Why Evangelicals Voted for Trump: A Critical Cultural Sociology', *in* J.L. Mast & J.C. Alexander (Eds.), *Politics of Meaning/Meaning of Politics. Cultural Sociology of the 2016 U.S. Presidential Election*, Palgrave Macmillan, Cham, 2019, p. 165.

13.2 Religious Liberties within the Constitutional Framework

Before engaging in a detailed analysis of the acts adopted by the administration, aimed at enhancing the protection of religious liberties, it behoves us to briefly recall the relevant constitutional framework, with specific reference to the jurisprudence of the Supreme Court. On the one hand, the Supreme Court case law on religion has been extensively taken into account by the presidency. Nevertheless, as will be clarified in the following paragraphs, the administration has apparently relied on a self-serving interpretation of the jurisprudence of the highest court in the land. On the other hand, a concise outline of the relevant case law could provide helpful insights on whether the policies implemented by the Trump administration might be either upheld or invalidated by the judiciary.

The First Amendment to the Constitution seems to design the United States as a non-denominational state. Yet the secular principle appears to be less rooted within the constitutional text.[9] Even if the Founding Fathers recognized the importance of faith and state being two separate entities, the degree of this separation has ever since been subject to debate among constitutional scholars, and within the Supreme Court as well. In fact, the provisions of the First Amendment protecting religion can be interpreted in accordance with two different theories: separatism and non-preferentialism (also referred to as accommodationism). The former has traditionally constituted the dominant view both among legal scholars and within the Supreme Court;[10] the latter, on the contrary, used to be relegated to a minoritarian position, although recent developments seem to be producing a shift in the balance between the two doctrines.[11] According to the separatist understanding of the First Amendment, and to use the words of Thomas Jefferson, there should be "a wall of separation between church and State".[12] As a consequence, all interferences of the

9 *See* M.W. McConnell, 'Accommodation of Religion', *The Supreme Court Rev.*, Vol. 1985, 1985, p. 1; Id., 'Accommodation of Religion: An Update and a Response to the Critics', *George Washington Law Rev.*, Vol. 60, 1992, p. 685. *See also* I.C. Lupu, 'Reconstructing the Establishment Clause Decisions: The Case against Discretionary Accommodation of Religion', *Univ. PA. Law Rev.*, Vol. 140, 1991, p. 555. For a comprehensive discussion on the history of the First Amendment protection of religion, *see* P.B. Kurland, 'The Origins of the Religion Clauses of the Constitution', *William and Mary Law Rev.*, Vol. 27, 1986, p. 839; M.W. McConnell, 'The Origins and Historical Understanding of Free Exercise of Religion', *Harv Law Rev*, Vol. 103, 1990, p. 1409.

10 *See* K.M. Sullivan & N. Feldman, *Constitutional Law*, 19th edn, Foundation Press, St. Paul, 2016, p. 1555. *See also* W.W. Van Alstyne, 'Trends in the Supreme Court: Mr. Jefferson's Crumbling Wall – A Comment on *Lynch v. Donnelly*', *Duke Law J.*, Vol. 33, 1984, p. 770.

11 C. Joppke, 'Beyond the Wall of Separation: Religion and the American State in Comparative Perspective', *Int'l J. Constitut'l Law*, Vol. 14, 2016, p. 984. A preference for the accommodationist approach might be identified in the most recent decisions of the Supreme Court, P. Annicchino (Ed.), *La Corte Roberts e La Tutela della Libertà Religiosa negli Stati Uniti d'America*, European University Institute, Florence, 2017.

12 Letter from Thomas Jefferson to a Committee of the Danbury Baptist Association, 1 January 1820, *The Writings of Thomas Jefferson*, Vol. 16, Thomas Jefferson Memorial Association of the United States, Washington, DC, 1903, p. 282.

one within the sphere of influence of the other should be regarded as highly unadvisable, if not forbidden at all. The non-preferentialist theory, however, offers a less strict reading of the separation between the two institutions at stake. Namely, what is prohibited is the establishment of a national church or the conferring of a preferential status on a specific religion. Therefore, the state can act to support religious activities, as long as no particular confession is preferred over another.[13]

Within this framework of constant debate, the Supreme Court case law on religious freedom developed at a steady pace and was highly influenced by the contraposition between the two theories mentioned in the preceding paragraph.[14] By this point, it should be highlighted that in protecting religious liberties, the First Amendment establishes two distinct religious clauses, deeply intertwined yet autonomous from each other: the Free Exercise Clause and the Establishment Clause. The two religious clauses gave rise to separate bodies of case law, in which the Court adopted a case-by-case approach.[15] As a consequence, identifying neutral standards applicable to a vast majority of scenarios has proved rather challenging. Nonetheless, a minimum content on which consensus has been reached can be acknowledged. Specifically, the Free Exercise Clause safeguards freedom *of* religion.[16] Hence, the mentioned religious clause prevents the government from intruding on the private dimensions of one's own religious beliefs.[17] As the Supreme Court stated in *Reynolds*

13 *See* Sullivan & Feldman, 2016, p. 1556.

14 Both doctrines can be traced in the Supreme Court case law, especially with regard to the Establishment Clause. On this topic, *see* R.H. Jones, 'Accommodationist and Separationist Ideals in Supreme Court Establishment Clause Decisions', *J. Church and State*, Vol. 28, 1986, p. 193. The author argues that Supreme Court justices are keener on deciding according to the theory they support, rather than resorting to the constitutional tests elaborated in previous decisions.

15 The case-by-case approach adopted by the Supreme Court has been favoured by the lack of a constitutional definition of religion within its jurisprudence; *see* J.H. Choper, 'Defining "Religion" in the First Amendment', *Univ. Ill. Law Rev.*, Vol. 1982, 1982, p. 579; Id., 'The Religion Clauses of the First Amendment: Reconciling the Conflict', *Univ. Pittsburgh Law Rev.*, Vol. 41, 1980, p. 673. *See also* M.W. McConnell, 'The Religion Clauses of the First Amendment: Where Is the Supreme Court Heading?', *Catholic Law.*, Vol. 32, 1989, p. 187, arguing for a unified interpretation of the constitutional clauses on religion.

16 B. Neuborne, 'An Overview of the Bill of Rights', *in* A.B. Morrison (Ed.), *Fundamentals of American Law*, 1 edn, Oxford University Press, New York, 1996, p. 83, spec. p. 87.

17 More in details, the State is forbidden from outlawing of forcing belief in a particular faith. On this matter, *see Torcaso v. Watkins*, 367 U.S. 488 (1961). The Court unanimously found that Maryland's requirement for public officials to declare their belief in the existence of God was unconstitutional. On this *see* 'Freedom of Religion, the Atheist, and the Torcaso Case', *VA. Law Rev.*, Vol. 47, 1961, p. 315.

v. United States[18] and confirmed in *Cantwell v. Connecticut,*[19] freedom of belief is absolute, whereas the freedom to act according to one's belief can be limited whenever the conduct is in violation of "social duties or subversive of good order".[20] Therefore, the state has the authority to interfere in the religious practices of the individual. This particular issue allowed the Court to develop its jurisprudence on religious exemptions[21] and to elaborate the so-called *Sherbert* test.[22] Correspondingly, whenever the state interferes in the religious sphere of the individual a burden is placed. That burden can be legitimate only if the government proves a compelling interest and such interest could not have been pursued by a less intrusive means.[23] The *Sherbert* test was further developed in 1972 with the *Wisconsin v. Yoder* decision.[24] There, the Court held that generally applicable laws could potentially violate the Free Exercise Clause if the law, despite being neutral, placed "undu[e] burdens on the practice of religion".[25] The application of this burdensome test was subsequently restricted by the majority opinion, written by Justice Scalia, in the 1990 *Employment Division v. Smith* case.[26] There the Court held that no test should be applied when generally applicable laws that do not directly target religion are concerned, thus spurring some controversies among scholars.[27]

---

18 *Reynolds v. United States*, 98 U.S. 145 (1878). The case dealt with the application of a federal law, making bigamy illegal. A member of the Mormon faith argued that polygamy was his religious duty. Chief Justice Waite upheld the legitimacy of the federal law, on the idea that the Legislature could "reach actions which were in violation of social duties or subversive of good order". The impact of this ruling on the compelling interest doctrine created by the Supreme Court is well described by R.J. Davis, 'Plural Marriage and Religious Freedom: The Impact of *Reynolds v. United States*', *Arizona Law Rev.*, Vol. 15, 1973, p. 287.

19 *Cantwell v. Connecticut*, 310 U.S. 296 (1940). The case represents a landmark decision as it incorporated the Free Exercise Clause, thereby applying the First Amendment protection against State actions and not only against the federal government.

20 *See Reynolds v. United States*, p. 164.

21 For some useful insights on the sensitive issue of religious exemptions, *see* P.A. Hamburger, 'A Constitutional Right of Religious Exemption: An Historical Perspective', *George Washington Law Rev.*, Vol. 60, 1992, p. 915. *See also* W.P. Marshall, 'The Case against the Constitutionally Compelled Free Exercise Exemption', *Case Western Res. Law Rev.*, Vol. 40, 1989-1990, p. 357, arguing against the right to religious exemptions.

22 *Sherbert v. Verner*, 374 U.S. 398 (1963). The case revolved around the refusal to grant unemployment benefits to a woman who refused to work on Saturdays because of her religion, being a member of the Seventh-day Adventist Church.

23 *See* I.C. Lupu, 'Where Rights Begin: The Problem of Burdens on the Free Exercise of Religion', *Harv. Law Rev.*, Vol. 102, 1988, p. 933.

24 *Wisconsin v. Yoder*, 406 U.S. 205 (1972). *See* S.F. Peters, *The Yoder Case: Religious Freedom, Education and Parental Rights*, University Press of Kansas, Lawrence, 2003.

25 *See Wisconsin v. Yoder*, p. 221.

26 Employment Division, Department of Human Resources of *Oregon v. Smith*, 494 U.S. 872 (1990). The case concerned the use of peyote for ritual purposes within the Native American Church and the Oregon criminal ban on the use and possession of the mentioned drug.

27 *See* W.P. Marshall, 'In Defense of Smith and Free Exercise Revisionism', *Univ. Chic. Law Rev.*, Vol. 58, 1991, p. 308; *see also*, R.J. Krotoszynski, 'If Judges Were Angels: Religious Equality, Free Exercise, and the (Unappreciated) Merits of Smith', *Northwestern Univ. Law Rev.* Vol. 102, 2008, p. 1189. For a critical comment of the decision, *see* M.W. McConnell, 'Free Exercise Revisionism and the Smith Decision', *Univ.*

Proceeding with the analysis, it is important to emphasize that the Establishment Clause, generally referred to as freedom *from* religion,[28] prevents confessions from being established as the official religion of the state and, moreover, it bans state actors from showing preference for one religion over another. In this regard, it is important to underline that the case-by-case approach adopted in this context showed that religion still amounts to a controversial issue within the American society: through the Establishment Clause, the Court ruled on significant cases that went on to strongly shape the role of religion in public life.[29]

As it happened with the Free Exercise Clause, the Supreme Court formulated a test for the solution of Establishment Clause cases. The so-called Lemon test[30] is based on the idea that government should be concerned with civil matters, leaving religion to the private dimension of individuals' lives. Thereby, the Court argued that state action should always have a bona fide secular purpose. Moreover, that very action should not have the primary effect of advantaging or disadvantaging any religion. Finally, the third element of the test requires the justices of the Court to consider whether there is an excessive entanglement between religion and government.[31]

The Court hardly ever resorted to the Lemon test[32] and, in 1997, went on to modify its core with the *Agostini v. Felton* decision, where the entanglement element was removed.[33] However, some Supreme Court justices had already moved away from the Lemon test, even before its modification in 1997, devising different standards in their opinions. Notably, Justice Kennedy resorted to the coercion test in his 1989 partial concurrence in *Allegheny County v. ACLU*.[34] Accordingly, government is in breach of the Establishment Clause

---

Chic. Law Rev., Vol. 57, 1990, p. 1109. To prevent an excessively broad application of the Smith precedent, Congress overwhelmingly approved the Religious Freedom Restoration Act 1993, aimed at reviving the *Sherbert* test. *See* The Religious Freedom Restoration Act of 1993, Pub. L. 103-141. The statute was approved unanimously by the House and 97-3 by the Senate. *See* R.F. Drinan & J.I. Huffman, 'The Religious Freedom Restoration Act: A Legislative History', *J. Law Relig.*, Vol. 10, 1993-1994, p. 531. The relationship between the RFRA and the Smith precedent is thoroughly accounted for in W. Travis, 'The Religious Freedom Restoration Act and *Smith*: Dueling Levels of Constitutional Scrutiny', *Washington & Lee Law Rev.*, Vol. 64, 2007, p. 1701.

28 *See* Neuborne, 1996.

29 *See* D. Laycock, ''Nonpreferential' Aid to Religion: A False Claim about Original Intent', *William and Mary Law Rev*, Vol. 27, 1986, p. 875.

30 *Lemon v. Kurtzman*, 403 U.S. 602 (1971), dealing with Pennsylvania legislation allowing the Superintendent of Public Schools to reimburse private religious schools for the salaries paid to their teachers.

31 In the context of the Lemon test, the word 'entanglement' means that government-religion interactions might sometimes be required, though they shall never intertwine so that people are unable to differentiate between the two entities.

32 For an inquiry into the Court's use of the Lemon test and its lack of principled approach, *see* J. Blackman, 'This Lemon Comes as a Lemon. The Lemon Test and the Pursuit of a Statute's Secular Purpose', *George Mason Univ. Civ. Rights Law J.*, Vol. 20, 2010, p. 351.

33 *Agostini v. Felton*, 521 U.S. 203 (1997). *See* J.T. Bunnow, 'Reinventing the Lemon: *Agostini v. Felton* and the Changing Nature of Establishment Clause Jurisprudence', *Wis. Law Rev.*, Vol. 1998, 1998, p. 1133.

34 *County of Allegheny v. American Civil Liberties Union*, 492 U.S. 573 (1989), spec. pp. 629, 659. *See* E. Fitch, 'An Inconsistent Truth: The Various Establishment Clause Tests as Applied in the Context of Public Displays

whenever it either provides direct aid to religion in a way that would establish a state church or coerces people to sustain, promote or participate in religion and religious activities against their will. Similarly, Justice O'Connor drew up the so-called endorsement test in her 1984 concurring opinion in *Lynch v. Donnelly*.[35] The justice held that government action violates the Establishment Clause if it leads a reasonable observer to believe that its action is either endorsing or disapproving of religion. Finally, and specifically on the matter of government funds, the Supreme Court often tackled the case through the lenses of neutrality. In other words, since the 1947 decision in *Everson v. Board of Education*, the Court found that indirect funding to religious groups in the context of a neutrally applied programme is constitutional.[36]

Going back to the case-by-case approach adopted by the highest court of the land when dealing with the Establishment Clause, some important case law to be considered for the purpose of this work is represented by the school prayers jurisprudence that was inaugurated with the *Engel v. Vitale* decision of 1962.[37] The Court, in adopting the separatist understanding and considering the peculiar circumstances of children who are easily influenced, held that prayers in public schools were unconstitutional. On the contrary, the same conduct was held to be constitutional when performed at the opening session of legislative assemblies. In those cases,[38] the Court embraced the non-preferentialist approach and, for historical and cultural reasons, held that prayers do constitute a religious activity, but that in the context of legislative assemblies, they do not amount to a preference of a specific faith as they are the product of a long-standing tradition.

The prayers cases show to what extent the Court values each and every specific aspect of a case when faced with the troublesome responsibility of defining the boundaries of religious intrusion within the public domain. The double standard adopted by the Court in the face of the very same issue, though within two distinct contexts, is the incontrovertible evidence of how the constitutional dimension of religion has no defined perimeter. The

of (Allegedly) "Religious" Symbols and Their Applicability Today', *Northern Ill. Univ. Law Rev.*, Vol. 34, 2014, p. 431, p. 437.

35 *Lynch v. Donnelly*, 465 U.S. 668 (1984), spec. pp. 687-694. *See* Fitch, 2014, p. 436. *See also* J.M. Lewis, 'Controversial Twist of Lemon: The Endorsement Test as the New Establishment Clause Standard', *Notre Dame Law Rev.*, Vol. 65, 1999, p. 671.

36 *Everson v. Board of Education*, 330 U.S. 1 (1947). *See* J.T. Valauri, 'The Concept of Neutrality in Establishment Clause Doctrine', *Univ. Pittsburgh Law Rev.*, Vol. 48, 1986, p. 83. Arguing against the concept of neutrality, *see* D.N. Cinotti, 'The Incoherence of Neutrality: A Case for Eliminating Neutrality from Religion Clause Jurisprudence', *J Church and State*, Vol. 45, 2003, p. 499. *See also* G. Bognetti, *Lo spirito del costituzionalismo americano. Vol II. La Costituzione democratica*, Giappichelli, Turin, p. 69.

37 *Engel v. Vitale*, 370 U.S. 421 (1962). *See* P.G. Kauper, 'Prayer, Public Schools and the Supreme Court', *Mich. Law Rev.*, Vol. 61, 1963, p. 1031.

38 *E.g. Marsh v. Chambers*, 463 U.S. 783 (1983). For an interesting analysis of the Supreme Court's case law on religious symbols, public prayers and the Establishment Clause, *see* L.P. Vanoni, *Pluralismo Religioso e Stato (Post) Secolare. Una sfida per la modernità*, Giappichelli, Turin, 2016, pp. 17-59.

ever-changing social and cultural context, the specific circumstances of the cases, the lack of a proper definition of religion, as well as the composition of the Court do effectively influence its understanding of the religious clauses. Therefore, the Court often finds itself with a flexible margin of manoeuvre when dealing with the constitutionality (or unconstitutionality) of state policies and legislation either directly concerning or at least interfering with the religious rights of Americans. For this very reason, the Trump administration effortlessly managed to reinterpret some of the Supreme Court's case law about religion to allow an instrumental enhancement of the safeguard granted by the First Amendment. Moreover, as finding a *file rouge* has proved to be an arduous task, no prediction on the outcome of potential constitutional challenges brought against the policies that will be discussed later can be made.

13.3 Christian Values on Trump's Presidential Agenda

Loyal to its own electoral base, President Trump did not hesitate and delivered on the promises he had made during the presidential campaign. Since the Inauguration, the presidency has been implementing a variety of initiatives, apparently aimed at the enhancement of the protection of religious freedom.

The following analysis will focus on Executive Order 13798 of 4 May 2017,[39] entitled 'Promoting Free Speech and Religious Liberty', whose contents present a number of troublesome issues. Then, attention will be paid to the 'Guidance on Federal Law Protections for Religious Liberty', adopted pursuant to Sec. 4 of the aforementioned Executive Order by Attorney General Jeff Sessions on 6 October 2017.[40] The purpose of the guidelines written by the attorney general is to direct the action of all federal agencies and departments with regard to religious freedom.[41]

To begin, one of the main points that deserves to be addressed is Sec. 2 of the said Executive Order.[42] The provision mandates all federal agencies to protect the right of

39 Executive Order 13798 of 4 May 2017, 82 F.R. 21675.

40 Office of the Attorney General, Memorandum for All Executive Departments and Agencies. Subject: Federal Law Protections for Religious Liberty, 6 October 2017.

41 On 3 May 2018, President Trump signed Executive Order 13831 'Executive Order on the Establishment of a White House Faith and Opportunity Initiative'. The act further expands the scope of application of both the previous Executive Order and of the Guidelines adopted by the Attorney General. Specifically, it formally declares that all faith-based organizations shall be able to compete for federal funding opportunities. Moreover, the Executive Order reorganizes the already existing White House Faith and Opportunity Initiative, which will now consult with religious leaders in order to advise the attorney general on government's compliance with federal law protections of religious liberties. *See* Executive Order 13831 of 3 May 2018, 83 F.R. 20715.

42 Sec. 1 of EO 13798 is a general provision, demanding that all agencies of the federal government fully apply the robust protection of religion granted by federal law.

individuals and organizations to engage in religious and political speech. As such, the Department of the Treasury will abstain from taking adverse actions against individuals, houses of worship and religious organizations that have participated in the political debate on religious and moral matters. In the context of this provision, adverse action refers to the enforcement of the so-called Johnson Amendment (hereinafter 'JA'),[43] which establishes a tax exemption for houses of worship, religious and non-profit organizations, as long as they do not either endorse or oppose political candidates. Since its approval in 1954, the JA has been the subject of many repeal attempts, the last one being the Tax Cuts and Jobs Act of 2017.[44] Despite the Republican majority in both Houses, the JA remained untouched.[45]

Provided that the presidential act cannot repeal the JA, as it is established by a higher source of law, the Executive Order can only go so far as to offer an alternative interpretation of that very piece of legislation. Sec. 2 aims to protect political speech on religious and moral issues when expressed within religious congregations or non-profit organizations. This has never been questioned; the JA exclusively bans political endorsements, de facto allowing for all political opinions to be voiced within religious circles as long as they do not amount to statements on a specific political candidate or to endorsement of one party over the other.[46] Moreover, religious leaders are still able to support candidates in their private capacity. Therefore, Sec. 2 allows for something that was already possible. One could say, then, that the provision at stake halts all actions by the Department of Treasury even when candidates have been endorsed. Even if this were to be the case, it would still prove to be ineffective, given that the JA has not been thoroughly enforced by the IRS ever since its approval. Given that Sec. 2 might not produce any actual effect, it appears to be nothing but a symbolic stipulation for electoral purposes only.[47]

43 *See* Sec. 501, subsection (c), par. (3), 26 U.S. Code. The provision is named after its proponent, the then Senator from Texas Lyndon B. Johnson.

44 An Act to provide for reconciliation pursuant to titles II and V of the concurrent resolution on the budget for fiscal year 2018, Pub. L. 115-97.

45 *See* K. Shellnutt, 'Johnson Amendment Repeal Removed from Final GOP Tax Bill', *Christianity Today*, 15 December 2017, available at www.christianitytoday.com/news/2017/december/johnson-amendment-repeal-blocked-final-gop-tax-bill-byrd.html.

46 For a comprehensive analysis of the mentioned provision and a discussion on whether to repeal it or not, *see* M.A. Goldfeder & M.K. Terry, 'To Repeal or Not Repeal: The Johnson Amendment', *Univ. Memphis Law Rev.*, Vol. 48, 2017, p. 209. For a critical comment on the ambiguity of the wording of the Johnson Amendment and its arduous enforcement, *see* A. Elacqua, 'Eyes Wide Shut: The Ambiguous "Political Activity" Prohibition and its Effects on 501 (c)(3) Organizations', *Hous. Bus. Tax Law J.*, Vol. 8, 2008, p. 113. Finally, for a discussion on the unconstitutionality of the provision, *see* E.W. Stanley, 'LBJ, the IRS, and Churches: The Unconstitutionality of the Johnson Amendment in Light of the Recent Supreme Court Precedent', *Regent Univ. Law Rev.*, Vol. 24, 2011, p. 237.

47 *See* P.J. Reilly, 'President's Religious Liberty Order Might Not Change IRS At All', *Forbes*, 4 May 2017, available at www.forbes.com/sites/peterjreilly/2017/05/04/presidents-religious-liberty-order-might-not-change-irs-at-all/#2eb1838241f2.

Moving forward with the analysis of the Executive Order, one might stumble upon what is likely to be the second criticality. In fact, Sec. 3 requires the Secretaries of Treasury, Labor and Health and Human Services to issue regulations to address the conscience-based objections to pay for health insurance plans that include birth control and contraceptive services, as mandated by the Affordable Care Act[48] passed under the Obama administration. The so-called Obamacare requires preventive-care services to be included in health insurance plans paid for by employers. The Obama administration carved out an exemption, allowing houses of worships and religious organizations connected thereto to object to these exact services. On this exemption, the Supreme Court intervened with the ruling in *Burwell v. Hobby Lobby Stores, Inc.*[49] Justice Alito, writing for the Court, extended the exemption to closely held corporations, whose owners' beliefs are sincere and constitute a significant dimension of their lives. Reinterpreting this precedent, the Trump administration further extended the exemption, allowing all employers, including large, publicly traded companies, to object to the contraceptive mandate established by the Affordable Care Act. Moreover, the Trump regulations on the matter allow for objections to be based not only on religious considerations but also on moral grounds, though only for small businesses and non-profit organizations.[50] These rules have been challenged in court and, in January 2019, both a District Court in California and a District Court in Pennsylvania granted a preliminary injunction, preventing their entry into force.[51]

The final controversial issue arising from the 2017 Executive Order has to do with the Memorandum issued by the attorney general to guide all federal agencies in granting the highest level of protection to religious freedom.[52] Among other things (the document is

48 The Patient Protection and Affordable Care Act, Pub. L. 111-148. *See* K.G. Holmes & J.C. Garand, 'The Clash of Rights: Explaining Attitudes toward a Religious Exemption to the HHS Contraception Mandate', *Political Science and Politics*, Vol. 51, 2018, p. 358.

49 *Burwell v. Hobby Lobby Stores, Inc.*, 573 U.S. _ (2014). *See* A. Madera, 'Nuove forme di obiezione di coscienza fra oneri a carico della libertà religiosa e *third-party burdens.* Un'analisi comparativa della giurisprudenza della Corte Suprema U.S.A. e della Corte di Strasburgo', *Stato, Chiese e pluralismo confessionale*, Vol. 16, 2017, p. 1.

50 *See* the Religious Exemptions and Accommodations for Coverage of Certain Preventive Services Under the Affordable Care Act. A Rule by the Internal Revenue Services, the Employee Benefits Security Administration, and the Health and Human Services Department on 15 November 2018, 83 F.R. 57536. *See also* the Moral Exemptions and Accommodations for Coverage of Certain Preventive Services Under the Affordable Care Act. A Rule by the Internal Revenue Services, the Employee Benefits Security Administration, and the Health and Human Services Department on 15 November 2018, 83 F.R. 57592.

51 R. Pear, 'Court Block Trump Administration Restrictions on Birth Control', *New York Times*, 14 January 2019, available at www.nytimes.com/2019/01/14/us/politics/court-trump-birth-control.html.

52 *See* S. Cahill, T. Wang & S. Geffen, *Executive Branch Actions Promoting Religious Refusal Threaten LGBT Health Care Access*, The Fenway Institute, Boston, 2017, available at https://fenwayhealth.org/wp-content/uploads/The-Fenway-Institute-Religious-Refusal-Laws-Policy-Brief.pdf. *See also* S. Gruberg, F.J. Bewkes, E. Platt, K. Franke & C. Markham, *Religious Liberty for a Select Few. The Justice Department Is Promoting Discrimination Across the Federal Government*, Center for American Progress, Washington, DC, 2018, available at www.americanprogress.org/issues/lgbt/reports/2018/04/03/448773/religious-liberty-select/.

made of twenty propositions), the Memorandum extends the scope of application of religious protection to organizations and businesses; it establishes that the government can never second-guess the authenticity of a religious belief, thus preventing government officials from effectively scrutinizing allegedly discriminatory conducts arguably based on religious claims. Furthermore, the guidelines unduly extend the already existing religious exemption set forth by Title VII of the Civil Rights Act of 1964,[53] allowing employers to prefer individuals belonging to their same confession. While the Civil Rights Act permits the hiring of employees who share the employer's belief, the Memorandum allows preference to be given to individuals whose conduct is consistent with their faith. According to the new understanding of the exemption established by Title VII of the Civil Rights Act, employers will be able to fire all employees who, notwithstanding the shared religious faith, do not strictly follow the scriptures in their day-to-day life.[54] Finally, the guidelines state that the government cannot exclude religious organizations from federal funds, as long as the financial aid is not used for proselytism. Nonetheless, proselytism is not an activity in itself, severable from all other activities carried out by houses of worship and organizations connected thereto. Ultimately, the guidelines seem to do away with the balancing of rights, favouring religious liberties over other constitutional rights. This has been achieved by reinterpreting – and at times misinterpreting – the Supreme Court's case law, specifically on the Establishment Clause.[55]

All these standards are elaborated, albeit not explicitly, to intervene on the anti-discriminatory policies put in place by the Obama administration, to safeguard minorities such as women and the LGBTQI community. Up to 87 regulations, 16 agency guidance documents and 55 federal programmes will be impacted by the new course undertaken by the Trump administration.[56]

13.3.1 Practical Effects of Religious Protection

The effects of religion guiding government activities can be better appreciated in some recent cases, dealing with the granting of funds to religious organizations or businesses, although their conducts disfavoured protected minorities.

The first example has to do with the foster care system. Specifically, Miracle Hill Ministries is an Evangelical foster agency that receives federal funds to operate. Being a 'born-again' Christian agency, they refused to let non-Evangelical couples foster the children

53 The Civil Rights Act, Pub. L. 88-352.

54 *See* Gruberg *et al.*, 2018, p. 6. For example, firing a woman for exercising her constitutional right to terminate her pregnancy would be possible.

55 *See* Gruberg *et al.*, 2018, p. 4.

56 Id., p. 9.

they had in custody. In so doing, the agency contravened regulations implemented by the Obama administration, according to which the enforcement of biased practices would have prevented those implementing such practices from receiving federal funds.

The governor of South Carolina – the state where the foster agency operates – reached out to President Trump to ask for an exemption based exactly on religious reasons.[57] Pursuant to the guidelines set out by the attorney general, the administration granted this exemption; as such, the agency would be able to exclude non-Evangelical couples from the fostering service. As briefly mentioned (*supra*, par. 2), the Establishment Clause prevents the government from favouring one religion over the others. The provision applies directly to the government as it does to all religious organizations, funded by US taxpayers, who provide services on behalf of the administration. By granting the exemption to Miracle Hill Ministries, the presidency allowed a religious organization performing government functions to show favour to one religion over the others.

The same path has been thoroughly followed by the Department of Labor. As a matter of fact, the other example of this new religion-oriented course is a Directive adopted by the Office of Federal Contract Compliance Programs.[58] Previous regulations implemented during the 'Obama era' established sanctions against federal contractors who put in place discriminatory policies against their employees. The new directive of the mentioned Office now requires that public inspectors of the Department of Labor will have to take into account religious factors when assessing contractors' compliance with the ban on discrimination. Therefore, whenever discrimination has its basis in religiously mandated conducts, the employer will hardly suffer any consequences. Even this case could amount to a violation of the Establishment Clause, as employees might plausibly be forced to accommodate certain religious beliefs or practices to their detriment.

Setting aside the topic of religious organizations and federal funding, one should consider another recent example of how religion has intruded into all policy considerations made by the administration. Indeed, the Secretary of Education has recently notified to Congress that her department will no longer enforce portions of the Elementary and Secondary Education Act (hereinafter 'ESEA').[59] Under the ESEA, both federal and state educational agencies are required to provide services and benefits to low-income private schools' students equitably comparable to those offered to their counterparts attending public schools. The service provider must be independent of the private school as well as of any religious organization. Following the 2017 decision in *Trinity Lutheran Church of*

57 *See* C. Kuruvilla, 'Evangelical Foster Agency Gets Federal Waiver to Reject LGBTQ or Non-Christian Parents', *Huffpost*, 24 January 2019, available at www.huffpost.com/entry/miracle-hill-south-carolina-foster-care_n_5c49d498e4b0287e5b88b91d.

58 Directive (DIR) 2018-03, U.S. Department of Labor, Office of Federal Contract Compliance Programs.

59 The Elementary and Second Education Act, Pub. L. 89-10.

Columbia, Inc. v. Comer,[60] read together with the Memorandum of the attorney general, the Secretary of Education felt that the mentioned provisions were unconstitutional. The *Trinity Lutheran Church* case, however, is understood to be expressly limited to religious organizations providing materials for playground renovations.[61] On the contrary, the activities required by the ESEA are much more connected to children's education.[62] In this regard, the *Engel v. Vitale* case law should be recalled. When dealing with religious influence in schools, the Court recognized that children are highly impressionable and thereby need stronger protection. For this very reason, the Court has always been extremely scrupulous in deciding cases regarding the relationship between religion and the education of young students.[63] Therefore, the *Trinity Church* case should be interpreted with great care, in order to avoid any chance of proselytism under such delicate circumstances.

Finally, it is worth mentioning that the Health and Human Services Department created a task force for the safeguard of conscience-based objections concerning medical care. The task force will make sure that medical personnel will be granted unlimited conscience rights, even if that would result in patients unable to have their right to medical care granted.[64]

Although at first glance, the apparent purpose of the current administration is to guarantee religious liberties to American citizens, a more in-depth analysis shows that the presidency might be after something quite different, especially the establishment of Christian values as the law of the land. This trend can be traced back up to at least the Bush jr. presidency, as President Bush – a 'born-again' Evangelical Christian – strongly favoured restrictions on abortion and contraception, contrasted stem cells research and proposed a constitutional amendment to define marriage as the union between a man and a woman.[65] These policies have now been embraced by the Trump administration as well, yet with one major difference: what used to constitute a mere petition for LGBTQI and women's

---

60 *Trinity Lutheran Church of Columbia, Inc. v. Comer*, 582 U.S. _ (2017). *See* A. Madera, '*More than a playground dispute:* il caso *Trinity Lutheran Church c. Pauley* e le nuove traiettorie interpretative dell'Establishment Clause', *Stato, Chiese e pluralismo confessionale*, Vol. 23, 2017, p. 1.

61 Footnote 3 of the Opinion of the Court expressly limits the decision to the specific issue of funds for playground renovations. However, the footnote was not joined by Justices Gorsuch and Thomas, thus casting doubts on it constituting an expression of the will of the majority. On this issue, *see* T.A. Mattei, '*Trinity Lutheran v. Comer*: Footnote 3, Gorsuch's Opinion and Scalia's Legacy of a Law of Rules', *Penn State Law Rev. Penn Statim*, Vol. 122, 2018, p. 14.

62 According to Sec. 1003, third parties' funds can cover professional development, tutoring and family engagement activities.

63 *See* L.P. Vanoni, 2016, pp. 29-31.

64 Protecting Statutory Conscience Right in Health Care; Delegations of Authority. A Proposed Rule by the Health and Human Services Department on 26 January 2018, 83 F.R. 3880. The final version of this regulation has yet to be approved.

65 *See* B.P. Volochinsky, 'The Bush Presidency: Undermining the Separation Between Church and State', *Inquiries J./Student Pulse*, Vol. 2, 2010, available at www.inquiriesjournal.com/articles/266/the-bush-presidency-undermining-the-separation-between-church-and-state.

rights or for general protection of worthy demands during the Bush era was turned by the Obama administration into either an effective right or a guaranteed stance, especially fighting discriminatory practices through federal funds and federal regulations. In other words, the sociocultural context seems to have changed profoundly. The minorities opposed by previous Republican administrations have now been acknowledged and their rights have been recognized and protected by the Obama presidency.

What the Trump administration, following the precedent set by his Republican predecessor, seems determined to do is to narrow – or even eliminate – the protections granted to those minorities. The path seems to be moving backwards through the discard of all those policies put in place by the previous President, by means of functional use of religious freedom. Religious freedom, in fact, is used as a tool to advance values dear to Christianity, allowing conducts that are religiously mandated or inspired, even when such behaviours might result in unfair and unequal treatment of individuals.

13.3.2 Further Arguments on the Instrumental Use of Religion

Both Executive Order 13798 and the Memorandum adopted by the attorney general, whose proclaimed purpose is the protection of religious freedom, seem to use freedom of religion as a tool to advance a specific agenda. Christian values gained a preferential position not only within several administrative acts adopted either by the President himself or by federal departments, but also thanks to a variety of other policies that, even if not directly adopted in the context of religious protection, are strongly influenced by Christian values.

In this respect, the tendency to promote Christian values over the newly acquired rights of certain minorities is eloquently revealed by the *amicus* brief filed by the Department of Justice in favour of the owner of Masterpiece Cakeshop.[66] What deserves to be underlined in this case is not the Supreme Court's decision in itself,[67] but rather the strong stance taken by the Trump administration against same-sex marriages. Indeed, the presidency argued in favour of the position of the baker who refused his services to a same-sex couple. The *amicus* brief made its case focusing on the right to free speech in connection with freedom of religion, rather than on freedom of religion by itself. It argued that making a wedding cake constitutes expressive conduct, and, as such, that it is protected by the free

66 Brief for the United States as Amicus Curiae Supporting Petitioners, filed on 7 September 2017, available at www.scotusblog.com/wp-content/uploads/2017/09/16-111-tsac-USA.pdf.

67 *Masterpiece Cakeshop v. Colorado Civil Rights Commission*, 584 U.S. _ (2018). The Court ruled 7-2 in favour of the baker, reversing the decision made by the Colorado Civil Rights Commission. Justice Kennedy, writing for the Court, argued that even if the baker's right to free exercise could have been limited by generally applicable laws, the State showed hostility against the belief of the petitioner, thus violating the State's obligation of neutrality. *See* D. NeJaime & R. Siegel, 'Religious Exemptions and Antidiscrimination Law in *Masterpiece Cakeshop*', *Yale Law J. Forum*, Vol. 128, 2018, p. 201.

speech clause of the First Amendment. Religion was considered only as the reason underlying the baker's refusal to express an idea on which he disagreed. Using free speech was perceived to be much more effective, rather than resorting to the burden theory elaborated by the Court in respect of the Free Exercise Clause. It is safe to argue that states have a compelling interest in fighting discrimination (as the Colorado legislation intended to do) through generally applicable laws, and thereby, if one recalls the standard set out in the *Sherbert* case, the burden on religion might have been considered to be legitimate, and no religious exemption might have been admissible.

Here, the discontinuity with the Obama approach as well as the intent to discard the safeguard of LGBTQI rights is self-evident. Indeed, the Obama administration strongly took the side of same-sex couples, defending the constitutionality of their right to marry, when the Court was about to decide the *Obergefell v. Hodges* case,[68] which eventually granted the said constitutional right.

Moving forward, one additional example of this Christian-oriented government action can be found in the long-standing attempts undertaken by conservative Republicans to restrict the scope of application of the right to abortion.[69] In this respect, President Trump very recently implemented financial and structural constraints on services like Planned Parenthood, burdening access to pregnancy termination.[70] Moreover, constraints on abortion are the paramount rationale of another policy that needs to be considered. In his 2019 State of the Union address, the President strongly voiced anti-abortion opinions, saying, "All children, born and unborn, are made in the holy image of God."[71] This statement summarizes the idea, widespread within high-ranking members of the administration, that life must be protected from the moment of conception. Thus, since the beginning of Trump's term, this notion has been guiding the administration, which is currently forcibly preventing undocumented illegal teenage immigrants in its custody from getting abortions.[72] A notable case is that of a seventeen-year-old girl who petitioned the Court, as required by Texas law when parents cannot be found, for the permission to get the procedure. The Court allowed. The administration denied her the possibility to have a legal guardian to accompany her outside the detention facility in order to exercise her right. Eventually,

68 *Obergefell v. Hodges*, 576 U.S. _ (2015).

69 The Republican Party moved from a pro-choice stance to a pro-life position on abortion around the end of the 1970s. For a discussion on this matter, and specifically for a discussion on the role of religion, *see* D.K. Williams, 'The GOP's Abortion Strategy: Why Pro-Choice Republicans Became Pro-Life in the 1970s', *J. Pol'y His.*, Vol. 23, 2011, p. 513.

70 Compliance with Statutory Program Integrity Requirements. A Rule by the Health and Human Services Department on 4 March 2019, 84 F.R. 7714.

71 Remarks by President Trump in State of the Union Address, 6 February 2019, available at www.whitehouse.gov/briefings-statements/remarks-president-trump-state-union-address-2/.

72 B. Amiri, 'Access to Abortion for Young Immigrants in Government Custody', *ACLU*, 3 April 2018, available at www.aclu.org/blog/reproductive-freedom/abortion/access-abortion-young-immigrants-government-custody.

following more litigation in courts, the procedure was allowed.[73] This shows how the administration is behaving following religious teachings, regardless of the fact that abortion has been recognized as a constitutional right for over 40 years.

Finally, one last policy that needs to be addressed concerns the admission to the United States of citizens coming from Muslim countries. Indeed, the Trump administration adopted the so-called *travel ban*[74] with the intention of foreclosing entry into the United States to citizens of seven selected Muslim countries,[75] though allowing an exemption for prosecuted religious minorities – *i.e.* their Christian citizens.[76] This first edition of the travel ban blatantly disfavoured individuals belonging to the Islamic confession, essentially proving how freedom of religion is not the real prominent interest of the administration. First of all, the presidency discriminates against individuals coming from the same country exactly on the basis of religion (effectively doing the opposite of what 'ensuring religious freedom' means).

Following a restraining order from the District Judge, then upheld by the Ninth Circuit Court of Appeals, the administration attempted to mitigate the discriminatory effects of the first ban and adopted its second[77] and third editions,[78] in which differential treatment against Muslims was less blatant (the last version of the ban included Chad, Iran, Libya, Somalia, Syria, Yemen and two non-Muslim countries, namely North Korea and Venezuela).

The final edition of the ban made its way to the Supreme Court, which put a momentary stop to the controversies with its 5 to 4 ruling in *Trump v. Hawaii.*[79] Chief Justice Roberts, writing for the majority of the Court, argued that the ban did not violate the Establishment Clause as it did not favour or disfavour any religion, being facially neutral. Despite President Trump's declarations against Muslims, highlighted by the dissenting opinion of Justices Sotomayor and Ginsburg, the final version does not express animus against the Islamic faith itself. Moreover, the chief justice resorted to the rational basis test. In order to pass this test, government's actions should pursue a legitimate state interest, and there must be a rational connection between the contested policy and the goals to be achieved. According

73 *Garza v. Hargan*, 584 U.S. _ (2018).

74 Executive Order 13769 of 27 January 2017, 82 F.R. 8977. For a complete recollection of all events of the travel ban saga, *see supra* Ch. 12, R. Scarciglia, 'Immigration: The 'Trump Effect' from Travel Ban to the substantial Wall on the United States-Mexico Border'.

75 The selected countries were Iran, Iraq, Libya, Somalia, Sudan, Syria and Yemen.

76 Sec. 5 of Executive Order 13769 vested the Secretary of State with the power to prioritize refugee claims on the basis of religious-based persecutions, as long as the individual seeking asylum belongs to a confession representing a minority in his or her country of nationality.

77 Executive Order 13780 of 6 March 2017, 82 F.R. 13209.

78 Presidential Proclamation 9645 of 24 September 2017, 82 F.R. 45161.

79 *Trump v. Hawaii*, 585 U.S. _ (2018). *See* J.L. Barrow, 'Trump's Travel Ban: Lawful but Ill-Advised', *Harv. J. Law Public Pol'y*, Vol. 41, 2018, p. 691. *See also* S. Penasa, '*Mr. President and Dr. Trump:* La Corte Suprema Americana tra "facial neutrality" e "reasonable observer" standard. Ultima puntata della saga *Travel Ban*?', *DPCE Online*, Vol. 36, 2018, p. 679.

to the Court, the travel ban met such requirements, being facially neutral and providing bona fide arguments connected to national security interests. Provided that the government managed to give neutral explanations, and considered the context of national security, the travel ban had to be regarded as constitutional; otherwise the executive branch would have been prevented from facing the ever-changing challenges of our contemporary society. The majority of the Court, once again, resorted to the formalist scrutiny, which had been deferentially used in cases concerning national security and, connected thereto, immigration policies.

Justice Sotomayor, joined in her dissent by Justice Ginsburg, strongly criticized the deference showed by the majority of the Court to the national security arguments raised by the government. The two justices argued that all the declarations of President Trump and senior government officials constitute evidence of "an impermissible discriminatory animus against Islam".[80] For this very reason, the Court should have resorted to a heightened standard and, instead of accepting a formally neutral justification, it should have required the government to prove that its actions did not amount to a discriminatory policy. However, the unconstitutionality of the third and final edition was such that no strict scrutiny would have been required for its adjudication. As a matter of fact, a reasonable observer would have detected the biased intent of what was defined as "a total and complete shutdown of Muslims entering the U.S."[81]

13.4 Concluding Remarks

Freedom of religion, a fundamental right, can be regarded through the lenses of human rights culture, and as such it should be protected from abuses and be balanced with other fundamental rights. Alternatively, if one adopts the conservative Christian interpretation as its own, freedom of religion might become a way to supersede other constitutional rights in order to advance the values and traditions of that specific confession. In light of the above, this second approach is the one adopted by Republican presidents, especially by the Trump administration for political reasons – *i.e.* keeping the votes of the Christian (and especially the Evangelical) electoral base.

The policies adopted during the first two years of the Trump presidency actually show a change in perception regarding religions within the United States. The majoritarian confession has been and still is represented by Christianism. Therefore, the First Amendment was drafted to protect religious minorities from any kind of persecution – even if

80 *Trump v. Hawaii*, Justice Sotomayor dissenting, p. 13.
81 Statement published on the website of President Trump electoral campaign on 7 December 2015 and subsequently removed.

only remotely comparable to those suffered by the Pilgrims and the Puritans before they left England – that the Christian majority could potentially put in place. Nowadays, American Christians are perceiving themselves as the new minority to be protected against discriminations. According to this view, the First Amendment should be a shield, behind which members of the Christian faiths can find shelter against, to use the words of Justice Alito, the 'new orthodoxy',[82] which seems to stand for a liberal and progressive development of culture, society and fundamental rights. To face what is read as an imposition of immoralities, absolutely incompatible with Christian values, that was strongly enhanced by the Obama administration, the Trump presidency is expanding the scope of application of religious protections. Nevertheless, instead of allowing wider pluralism, Trump's attitude towards religion is de facto granting a getaway car for prejudiced conducts against minorities. The development of a human rights culture that is democratically achieved is being battled by religious conservatives through the facade offered by a self-serving interpretation of religious liberties. As a result, both new and consolidated constitutional rights risk being either overturned or strongly restricted, and, not least, one among the fundamental rights pertaining to the so-called first generation of rights is being diminished by resorting to an instrumental use thereof.

82 *Obergefell v. Hodges*, Justice Alito dissenting, p. 6.

14 Developments in US Development Aid

Mark E. Wojcik[*]

14.1 Introduction

Foreign development aid helps individuals in some of the world's poorest countries. Foreign aid promotes economic prosperity and progress towards global development goals.[1] Foreign aid can also help serve political goals of the donor countries. US policymakers and political leaders have long viewed foreign aid as an "essential instrument of U.S. foreign policy" that has also "increasingly been associated with national security policy."[2] But although US foreign aid "has never been totally divorced from political considerations, ... tying it directly to loyalty remains controversial even among conservative scholars."[3]

The Trump administration does not necessarily see providing foreign aid as an 'essential instrument of US foreign policy' but rather as a possible target to cut or even eliminate from the federal budget. Under a policy of 'America First', money was seen as being better spent on a border wall than on promoting economic development in other countries.[4] The Overseas Private Investment Corporation was also a foreign aid target

* Professor of Law, The John Marshall Law School, Chicago. Fulbright Professor (Spring 2019), Università degli Studi di Bari "Aldo Moro" Facoltà di Giurisprudenza, Bari, Italy, and former Fulbright Specialist (2017 and 2018), Jigme Singye Wangchuck School of Law, Thimphu, Bhutan. This article was written for presentation at a conference at Bocconi University in Milan, Italy, on the subject of 'The American Presidency after the First Two Years of President Trump'. The author thanks David Austin for comments on an earlier draft of this article and Jacob Nabat for research assistance. Views expressed in the article are the author's own.

1 D. Selby & J. Sepehr, 'Trump Says Countries That Receive Foreign Aid Do 'Nothing for Us' – We Crunched the Numbers', *Global Citizen*, 4 January 2019, available at www.globalcitizen.org/en/content/trump-cabinet-meeting-foreign-aid.

2 C. Apodaca, 'Foreign Aid as Foreign Policy Tool', *Oxford Research Encyclopedia of Politics*, 2017. The United States gives most of its aid for strategic reasons; the largest US aid recipients are Israel, Egypt, Afghanistan, Pakistan and Iraq. E. Voeten, 'Did Trump Try to Lose Today's United Nations Vote on Israel?', *Washington Post*, 21 December 2017, available at www.washingtonpost.com/news/monkey-cage/wp/2017/12/21/did-trump-try-to-lose-todays-united-nations-vote-on-israel/?utm_term=.68d302c0704c.

3 J. Hudson & J. Dawsey, 'Trump Vowed to Slash Foreign Aid. Here's Why It Hasn't Happened', *Mercury News*, 26 September 2018, available at www.mercurynews.com/2018/09/25/trump-vowed-to-slash-foreign-aid-heres-why-it-hasnt-happened.

4 Haaretz, 'Trump 2020 Budget Slashes Foreign Aid, Hikes Defense Spending', 12 March 2019, available at www.haaretz.com/us-news/trump-s-2020-budget-raises-defense-spending-by-4-percent-cuts-foreign-aid-1.7016363 ("President Donald Trump ... told Congress to slash funding for foreign aid and the State Department and increase spending for the military and the wall he wants to build on the U.S.-Mexico border in his 2020 budget, the opening move in his next funding fight with Congress.").

until the Trump administration observed the benefits that the People's Republic of China was reaping from its Bridge and Road Initiative (BRI) foreign aid programme.[5] Seeing those benefits, the Trump administration reversed course and quietly created an international development agency with twice the budget of its predecessor agency.[6] Foreign aid remains a continuing target for budget cuts, however, because administration officials and political leaders either see little benefit in spending on foreign development or see the threat of cutting off foreign aid as the only foreign policy tool.[7]

14.2 DEVELOPMENT AID

"Academic researchers have studied foreign aid since the establishment of aid giving," but these researchers "are perplexed as to why and under what circumstances the leaders of one state would provide valuable resources to another state".[8] Some countries may give development aid to less-developed countries for humanitarian reasons. It is seen as the right thing to do for responsible global citizens, particularly in response to humanitarian crises.[9] Countries may give aid for strategic and political reasons[10] or to reduce the threat of terrorism.[11] Foreign aid may also be given to avert public health and environmental

5 As discussed in Part IV, the Belt and Road Initiative ('BRI') of the People's Republic of China is also known as 'One Belt One Road' ('OBOR'), the 'Silk Road Economic Belt', and the '21st-century Maritime Silk Road'.

6 The United States International Development Finance Corporation (USIDFC) is discussed in Part VI.

7 *See, e.g.*, P. Beaumont, 'Trump Has Turned Foreign Aid into Shabby Political Theatre', *The Guardian*, 20 February 2019, available at www.theguardian.com/global-development/2019/feb/20/trump-has-turned-foreign-aid-into-shabby-political-theatre ("how the US does aid in the Trump era" is a period characterized "by a transactional world view and a foreign policy that seems often more in service of the US president's personal standing than America's position as a global player. While US aid policy has been politicised since the post-war Marshall Plan, no US president has been so obvious and crude as Trump in their approach to using assistance for global leverage.").

8 Apodaca, 2017.

9 *But see* Beaumont, 2019 ("If the Trump administration's method can actually be called doctrine – as opposed to a series of attention-seeking and ego-driven impulses – it has revealed itself in the past two years to be unconcerned with much pretence of generally accepted humanitarian principles, instead often favouring gesture politics even at the expense of wider US foreign policy interests.").

10 Apodaca, 2017 ("Foreign aid is used predominantly to promote geostrategic interests, for the right to build and maintain foreign bases, to strengthen alliances, or to keep allied regimes in power. Foreign aid is also used to maintain friendly relations with foreign governments. Foreign aid facilitates cooperation, and it builds strong alliances.").

11 Id. ("There is a general belief that foreign aid could reduce the likelihood of terrorist attacks by averting the causes of terrorism – namely, hopelessness and resentment as the result of extreme poverty, illiteracy, and hunger. Foreign aid would also be used to reduce poverty and inequality in the recipient state, thought to be a source of terrorist activity.")

catastrophes that might later affect the donor country if the problems are left unchecked.[12] Foreign aid can also be used to promote the economic interests of the donor state.[13]

Recipient countries, for their part, accept financial support from these donor countries, recognizing that development aid may be 'earmarked' for particular purposes. The donor countries may expect that the recipient countries will enact certain laws or follow certain laws and policies favoured by the donor countries. Some aid may also be 'tied' to requirements that the aid recipients

> purchase the equipment, arms, materials, supplies, parts and services, or other commodities made in the donor country or from the donor's corporations; use contractors or consultants from the donor country; or that the equipment be shipped via ships or airplanes flagged in the donor country.[14]

In addition to the categories of donor and recipient countries, a country may also find itself on both sides of the foreign aid equation: both receiving financial support from donor countries while giving some financial support to even less-developed countries.

Although foreign aid can be provided for purely humanitarian reasons, it is an undisputed foreign policy tool that provides recipient countries with either a reward for some behaviour or an inducement to change its behaviour.[15] Foreign aid may also follow military action to help ensure that a country's foreign policy goals are met and secured.[16]

In various speeches at his campaign rallies, President Trump promised to end or at least sharply curtail foreign aid.[17] His administration and some members of Congress apparently saw the expenditures for development as wasteful and not supportive of the United States or of American values.[18] Some argued that money spent on foreign aid should

12 Id. ("Foreign aid is given to a recipient country to facilitate economic development, alleviate poverty, and improve human welfare. Aid contributes to global security by tackling threats to human security, such as human rights violations, disease, population growth, environmental degradation, peacemaking, and the growing gap between the rich and the poor. Poverty and extreme inequalities are often causes of social instability and civil unrest, which, in turn, can produce flows of refugees and acts of terrorism. Thus, aid helps build a safer, more peaceful, and more secure world.")

13 Id. ("For instance, [foreign aid] can be used to open foreign markets to multinational corporations headquartered in donor countries, to subsidize the donor's domestic firms, or to provide employment for the donor's domestic workers.")

14 Id. ("[H]istorically, the United States has tied approximately 75% of its aid.")

15 Id.

16 Id. A famous example of US foreign aid after military conflict would include the Marshall Plan to assist in the reconstruction of Europe.

17 *See, e.g.*, Hudson & Dawsey, 2018 ("The populist ultimatum [of ending foreign development aid] has been a frequent applause line at Trump rallies and speeches since the early days of his presidential campaign.").

18 *See, e.g.*, J. Campbell, 'President Trump Embraces Foreign Aid After Trying to Gut It', *Council on Foreign Relations*, 26 October 2018, available at www.cfr.org/blog/president-trump-embraces-foreign-aid-after-

instead be diverted to help pay the construction costs of a wall along the southern border of the United States, fulfilling one of Mr. Trump's main campaign promises.[19]

14.3 Threats to Cut Off Development Aid

Donald Trump has viewed foreign aid as 'entirely transactional',[20] something given for something in return. And while not extolling the benefits of foreign aid, his administration has used threats to cut off foreign aid as a somewhat clumsy tool of foreign policy. Three situations illustrate various threats to cut off foreign aid.

First, at the end of 2017, Mr. Trump threatened to cut off foreign aid to countries that were going to vote in support of a U.N. General Assembly Resolution opposing the recognition of Jerusalem as the capital of Israel.[21] Mr. Trump told a press conference that those countries "take hundreds of millions of dollars and even billions of dollars, and then they vote against us. Let them vote against us. We'll save a lot. We don't care".[22] The General Assembly Resolution was in response to Mr. Trump's decision to recognize Jerusalem as the capital of Israel. The United States had vetoed a similar resolution before the U.N. Security Council,[23] where the vote was 14-1. The General Assembly Resolution,[24]

trying-gut-it ("In its early days, the Trump administration's rhetoric was hostile to the United States funding overseas economic development and skeptical of the benefits of soft power.").

19 J. Rogin, 'Will Trump Go after Foreign Aid to Pay for His Border Wall?', *Washington Post*, 10 January 2019, available at www.washingtonpost.com/opinions/global-opinions/will-trump-go-after-foreign-aid-to-pay-for-his-border-wall/2019/01/10/22b2673a-14fd-11e9-803c-4ef28312c8b9_story.html?noredirect=on&utm_term=.1d8818367797; Haaretz, 2019 ("Trump's budget asked for $8.6 billion to build a wall on the southern border with Mexico, more than six times what Congress gave him for border projects in each of the past two fiscal years, and 6 percent more than he has corralled by invoking emergency powers this year after he failed to get the money he wanted.").

20 Beaumont, 2019.

21 *See* 'Jerusalem UN Vote: Trump Threatens US Aid Recipients', *BBC*, 20 December 2017, available at www.bbc.com/news/world-middle-east-42431095.

22 Id.

23 *See* 'Jerusalem: US Vetoes UN Resolution Rejecting Trump's Declaration', *BBC*, 16 December 2017, available at www.bbc.com/news/world-middle-east-42394264 ("The text put forward by Egypt affirmed that any decisions on the status of Jerusalem had 'no legal effect, are null and void[,] and must be rescinded.'").

24 U.N. General Assembly Res. ES-10/L.22, 19 December 201), available at https://undocs.org/A/ES-10/L.22. The nine states voting against the resolution were Guatemala, Honduras, Israel, Marshall Islands, Micronesia, Nauru, Palau, Togo and the United States. The 35 states abstaining from the vote were Antigua and Barbuda, Argentina, Australia, Bahamas, Benin, Bhutan, Bosnia and Herzegovina, Cameroon, Canada, Colombia, Croatia, Czech Republic, Dominican Republic, Equatorial Guinea, Fiji, Haiti, Hungary, Jamaica, Kiribati, Latvia, Lesotho, Malawi, Mexico, Panama, Paraguay, Philippines, Poland, Romania, Rwanda, Solomon Islands, South Sudan, Trinidad and Tobago, Tuvalu, Uganda and Vanuatu. And the 21 states not present for the voting were the Central African Republic, the Democratic Republic of the Congo, East Timor (Timor Leste), El Salvador, Georgia, Guinea-Bissau, Kenya, Mongolia, Myanmar, Moldova, Saint Kitts and Nevis, Saint Lucia, Samoa, San Marino, São Tomé and Príncipe, Sierra Leone, Swaziland, Tonga, Turkmenistan, Ukraine and Zambia.

drafted by Turkey and Yemen, passed by 128 votes to nine against with 21 absentees and 35 abstentions. The General Assembly Resolution on Jerusalem was non-binding.

The Trump administration was condemned for trying to bully countries to support the United States in that vote of the U.N. General Assembly.[25] One analyst suggested that the United States did so because it wanted to appear 'isolated' in the United Nations.[26] And although the United States "has a long and at least partially successful history of buying U.N. votes with foreign aid", the United States has typically done so privately rather than with public threats.[27] "Buying votes is frowned upon," and "[i]ssuing public threats may make it harder for some governments to vote with the United States."[28]

Second, in September 2018, during his second speech at the annual opening of a new session of the U.N. General Assembly, President Trump announced that he would stop giving foreign aid to countries that 'disrespected' or 'were disloyal to' the United States.[29] Expressing a transactional view of foreign aid, President Trump told the U.N. General Assembly that:

> The United States is the world's largest giver in the world by far of foreign aid, but few give anything to us. That is why we are taking a hard look at U.S. foreign assistance .... We will examine what is working, what is not working, and whether the countries that receive our dollars and our protection also have our interests at heart. Moving forward, we are only going to give foreign aid to those who respect us and, frankly, are our friends.

And as a third example of threatening to cut off foreign aid, in October 2018, Mr. Trump announced that he would cut off or substantially reduce aid to El Salvador, Guatemala and Honduras because those countries were unable to stop migrants from leaving their countries and 'coming illegally' to the United States.[30] The timing of this threat may have had something to do with US mid-term elections, giving Mr. Trump another opportunity to rally his base by condemning 'caravans' of asylum seekers who were fleeing gang violence and targeted persecution in Central America. Individuals and families coming to the United States to claim asylum are not 'coming illegally' to the United States, however, but are coming to exercise a lawful right to claim asylum under US law. Nonetheless, in March

25 *See, e.g.,* Voeten, 2017.
26 Id.
27 Id.
28 Id.
29 *See, e.g.,* Hudson & Dawsey, 2018.
30 *See, e.g.,* S. Herman, 'Trump: US to Cut Aid to Guatemala, Honduras, El Salvador', *Voice of America*, 22 October 2018, available at www.voanews.com/a/trump-us-begin-cutting-aid-guatemala-honduras-el-salvador/4624760.html.

2019, Mr. Trump instructed the U.S. State Department to cut off foreign aid to El Salvador, Guatemala and Honduras because of these 'caravans' of migrants.[31] Among other things, the cut-off of aid will end financial support for security forces and police forces who are battling drug-trafficking to the United States.[32] And by cutting support for security and police forces, the cancellation of aid is likely to make the situation more dangerous for persons in those countries and thus increase migration to other countries.[33]

These three examples illustrate how the Trump administration has used threats of cutting off foreign aid as a tool of foreign policy. It may be fairly questioned whether using public threats is a productive strategy or one that inadvertently backfires.

14.4 Recognizing a Competitive 'Threat' from China: The Belt and Road Initiative

In addition to using public threats against countries that received US aid, the Trump administration saw that China was succeeding in its global strategy of infrastructure investment. While the United States was trying to threaten to cancel foreign aid, China seemed to be increasing its foreign influence by using investment and trade strategies.

The Belt and Road Initiative (BRI) of the People's Republic of China is also variously known as 'One Belt One Road' (OBOR), the 'Silk Road Economic Belt' and the '21st-century Maritime Silk Road'.[34] Chinese President Xi Jinping originally announced the BRI strategy during official visits to Indonesia and Kazakhstan in 2013. As of February 2019, China had reportedly signed 'Belt and Road' agreements with 152 countries and international organizations in Europe, Asia, Middle East, Latin America and Africa,[35] spending billions

31 *See, e.g.*, K. Rogers, Z. Kanno-Youngs & M.D. Shear, 'President Renews Threat to Close Mexican Border', *New York Times*, 29 March 2019, at A21, available at www.nytimes.com/2019/03/29/us/politics/trump-mexico-illegal-immigration.html (online version titled as 'Trump Directs State [Department] to End Aid to 3 Central American Countries); Go Home, and Don't Come Back', *The Economist*, 6 April 2019, at 27.

32 The Economist, 'Go Home, and Don't Come Back', 6 April 2019, at 27.

33 "Currently, the United States spends about $620 million a year for gang prevention programmes and other initiatives aimed at helping support civil society in [El Salvador, Guatemala and Honduras]. Advocates say that cutting the funds will only accelerate the migrant flows into the United States." Rogers *et al.*, 2019, at A21.

34 *See, e.g.*, U.W. Chohan, 'What Is One Belt One Road? A Surplus Recycling Mechanism Approach', at 1, 13 June 2017, available at SSRN: https://ssrn.com/abstract=2997650 or http://dx.doi.org/10.2139/ssrn.2997650.

35 Xinhua, '152 Countries, [International] Organisations Sign Belt and Road Deals with China', *Financial Express*, 4 March 2019, available at http://thefinancialexpress.com.bd/economy/global/152-countries-intl-organisations-sign-belt-and-road-deals-with-china-1551686061.

of dollars in developing countries around the world. The scale of the BRI has been correctly described as 'staggering'.[36]

Of course, the BRI did not appear just suddenly. It had been Chinese policy for more than five years. But when China and the United States entered into a trade skirmish, if not a trade war, greater attention fell on the benefits that China was seeing from its investment strategy.

The fear of 'losing out' to Chinese assistance forced the Trump administration to reconsider its plan to reduce foreign aid payments under an 'America First' strategy.[37] As one newspaper noted,

> President Trump, seeking to counter China's growing geopolitical influence, is embracing a major expansion of foreign aid that will bankroll infrastructure projects in Africa, Asia[,] and the Americas – throwing his support behind an initiative he once sought to scuttle.[38]

14.5 REVERSING ITS POSITION – FOREIGN AID IS GOOD AFTER ALL: THE BUILD ACT

In response to the BRI, the U.S. Congress passed the Better Utilization of Investment Leading to Development Act (the 'BUILD' Act) of 2018. With 'little fanfare'[39] because it represented a dramatic shift in the policy of foreign aid, President Trump signed the Build Act into law in October 2018 as part of H.R. 302, a non-controversial five-year renewal of the legislation establishing the Federal Aviation Authority.[40]

As part of the FAA Reauthorization Act of 2018, however, the BUILD Act was 'a major policy reversal' for a US administration previously set on drastically reducing expenditures on foreign development aid.[41]

---

36 S. Brown, 'Knowledge is the Key to BRI Financing: Closing the Data Gap Will Attract More Investors, Consultants to Belt and Road Projects', *China Daily*, 1-7 March 2019, at 22.

37 *See, e.g.*, C. Guensburg & P. Widakuswara, 'Trump Administration Rethinks Foreign Aid With Eye Toward China', *Voice of America*, 19 October 2019, available at www.voanews.com/a/trump-administration-rethinks-foreign-aid-with-eye-toward-china/4620187.html; Hudson & Dawsey, 2018 (Trump's "America First" mantra and adjusting foreign aid priorities in the budget "has faced stiff resistance from officials at the Pentagon, State Department[,] and U.S. Agency for International Development who said [the] proposals were counterproductive, contradictory[,] and could cede influence to China ....").

38 G. Thrush, 'China's Weight Fuels Reversal by Trump on Foreign Aid', *New York Times*, 15 October 2018, at B1, available at www.nytimes.com/2018/10/14/world/asia/donald-trump-foreign-aid-bill.html?emc=edit_nn_20181015&nl=morning-briefing&nlid=1418504420181015&te=1.

39 Id.

40 Pub. L. No. 115-254 (2018).

41 Id. ("President Trump, seeking to counter China's growing geopolitical influence, is embracing a major expansion of foreign aid that will bankroll infrastructure projects in Africa, Asia and the Americas —

14.6 A New US Government Aid Agency Doubles the Previous Budget for OPIC: The U.S. International Development Finance Corporation (USIDFC)

The BUILD Act, part of H.R. 302, the FAA Reauthorization Act of 2018, will create a new agency, called the United States International Development Finance Corporation (USIDFC).[42] It will be "a wholly owned Government corporation … under the foreign policy guidance of the Secretary of State".[43] The purpose of the USIDFC will be

> to mobilize and facilitate the participation of private sector capital and skills in the economic development of less developed countries … and countries in transition from nonmarket to market economies, in order to complement the development assistance objectives, and advance the foreign policy interests, of the United States.[44]

The USIDFC consolidates the Overseas Private Investment Corporation (OPIC) and the Development Credit Authority (DCA) of the U.S. Agency for International Development (USAID), and its mandate to promote international development. The USIDFC will have an annual budget of US$60 billion, more than double OPIC's annual budget of $29 billion.[45] And unlike OPIC, the USIDFC will have the ability to make equity investments and to make loans in local currency, reducing investor currency exchange risk.[46]

The creation of the USIDFC was expected to accomplish three goals: (1) it would align the US government's development finance tools with broader foreign policy and development goals and thereby enhance their competitiveness; (2) it would minimize risk to American taxpayers by establishing appropriate risk-management protocols, including

---

throwing his support behind an initiative he once sought to scuttle."). *See also* Guensburg & Widakuswara, 2019. The non-partisan Center for Strategic and International Studies (CSIS) in Washington D.C. described the BUILD Act as 'the most important piece of U.S. soft power legislation in more than a decade'. Id.

42 Legislation creating the USIDFC was quietly included in the 'FAA Reauthorization Act of 2018', which also reauthorized the Federal Aviation Administration and related revenue authorities through 30 September 2023; modified the Federal Emergency Management Agency's disaster assistance authorities; provided $1.68 billion in emergency supplemental appropriations for the Department of Housing and Urban Development's Community Development Fund for long-term disaster recovery; and further integrated unmanned aircraft systems into the nation's airspace systems. *See* www.whitehouse.gov/briefings-statements/president-donald-j-trump-signs-h-r-302-law/.

43 Pub. L. No. 115-254, § 1412(a) (2018).

44 § 1412(b). "In carrying out its purpose, the [USIDFC,] utilizing broad criteria, shall take into account in its financing operations the economic and financial soundness and development objectives of projects for which it provides support …." Id.

45 Guensburg & Widakuswara, 2019.

46 Campbell, 2018.

for co-investment with the private sector; and (3) it would increase efficiency by reducing duplicate efforts in the US government's development finance programmes.[47]

Although the USIDFC will be more competitive than OPIC and will operate with twice the budget, some observers note that the USIDFC is merely an 'improvement and rebranding of OPIC' instead of a radically different foreign aid agency.[48] "In that sense, it is reminiscent of the rebranding with improvements of the North American Free Trade Agreement (NAFTA) that resulted in the United States-Mexico-Canada-Agreement (USMCA)."[49] What is significant about USIDFC is that it represents a complete turnaround for an administration that was previously focused on reducing expenditures for foreign aid. The administration recognized that there are hard and soft benefits to foreign aid. It appears that "concern about China's growing influence in developing countries has been the driver of the administration's new embrace of development assistance and soft power".[50]

14.7 CONTINUED CHALLENGES

The creation of a single new development agency does not completely solve foreign development needs, nor does it eliminate hostility to foreign aid programmes. In the budget agreement reached in February 2019, the U.S. House of Representatives rejected Mr. Trump's proposals to eliminate the Asia Foundation, the United States-African Development Foundation, the Inter-American Foundation and the United States Trade and Development Agency.[51] The February budget agreement instead added hundreds of

47 Statement of U.S. Agency for International Development Administrator Mark Green on the creation of the U.S. International Development Finance Corporation (USIDFC) (3 October 2018), available at www.usaid.gov/news-information/press-releases/oct-3-2018-administrator-green-statement-creation-usidfc. Mr. Green also stated that the creation of the USIDFC "creates a unique opportunity for USAID to scale up its use of financing tools for development significantly" and that USAID missions would "be able to take advantage of an expanded toolbox of financing options beyond guarantees (including loans, political-risk insurance and equity) and a broader range of private-sector expertise to support and reorient ongoing programs towards enterprise-led development." Id. He also added that "[t]he USIDFC will catalyze market-based, private-sector development, spur economic growth in less-developed countries, and advance the foreign-policy interests of the United States." Id. Not included in his statement was any evidence that USAID lacked appropriate risk-management protocols for its lending programmes that required new protocols to be put into place for the USIDFC. His statement also did not elaborate on how the co-investments would be sought from the private sector or whether that private sector would be from the United States, the target country or a third country. One might imagine a system where only those who are well connected with the agency would receive timely notice of investment opportunities rather than information being provided at the same time to all interested persons.

48 *See, e.g.*, Campbell, 2018.

49 Campbell, 2018.

50 Id.

51 E. Cochrane & C. Edmondson, 'Raises and Rebukes: What's in Those 7 Spending Bills', *New York Times*, 15 February 2019, at A17, available at www.nytimes.com/2019/02/14/us/politics/congress-trump-border-deal-wall.html?login=email&auth=login-email.

millions of dollars for international disaster assistance and foreign aid, including an additional $1 billion towards peacekeeping activities, an additional $96 million to support U.N. peacekeeping missions (including those in Afghanistan, Iraq and Libya) and an additional $1.4 billion to respond to refugee crises overseas.[52] Global nutrition programmes will also receive enough money to exceed the President's budget request by $1.2 billion.[53]

But that was in February 2019. The proposed Trump Budget submitted in March 2019 asked for even more money to construct a southern border wall and again sought cuts to foreign aid.[54]

14.8 Conclusion

Foreign development aid will remain a target for US politicians who claim that it is wasted on countries that vote against the United States at the United Nations or who believe that money spent on foreign aid would be better spent building a southern border wall. Although the United States International Development Finance Corporation created a stronger version of OPIC funded at twice the level of its predecessor, the USIDFC came about only when the Trump administration feared that it would 'lose out' to China. Until the positive aspects of US foreign aid become better known to an administration that sees aid purely in a transactional setting ('do this for me and I'll do this for you'), foreign aid will remain a punching bag, if not a target for elimination.

52 Id.

53 Id.

54 Haaretz, 2019 ("Trump's budget asked for $8.6 billion to build a wall on the southern border with Mexico ...."). Observers note that Mr. Trump is unlikely to receive that amount because the Democrats oppose that expenditure and because they are in control of the U.S. House of Representatives.

15 Is There a 'Trump Doctrine'?

Mario Del Pero[*]

"Is there a Trump Doctrine?" is the highly rhetorical question that provides the title for this chapter. It is rhetorical because over time – and particularly after World War II – each US administration has been bestowed with (or has claimed to possess) its own foreign policy doctrine. Sometimes, presidential doctrines were created and named as such ex post, as in the case of the famous Truman (1947) or Reagan (1985) doctrines. More often, they were deliberately outlined in the attempt to impart to a given foreign policy outlook, and to its basic discourse, the gravitas that only the label 'doctrine' seemed capable of providing. Doctrines can be thus better understood as discursive artefacts, outlined primarily in carefully crafted presidential speeches and in paradigmatic public documents, which in the case of foreign policy are now primarily the quadrennial *National Security Strategy* and the various Defense Strategy papers.[1] Being (and being meant to be) public, these speeches and documents rarely offer in-depth, detailed, articulated and realistic sets of strategic assumptions bound to define priorities, inform policy choices and address unplanned contingencies. Foreign policy doctrines, to put it bluntly, provide at best a very broad compass to navigate the turbulent, and invariably unpredictable, waters of international relations. At worst, and much more frequently, they are rhetorical tools used (and designed) to build consensus, within and outside the United States, around specific foreign goals and means: instruments to convince (and gain the support of) the two publics – domestic and global – the United States is invariably called to address in its role of global hegemon and main pillar of the contemporary international system.[2]

The Trump administration is certainly no exception. It has – or, better, it pretends to have – its own, peculiar 'doctrine,' which in many ways looks less opaque and more clearly defined than many of those of his predecessors; so much so that the President and his main security and foreign policy advisors have made a major effort to delineate the precise contours of this doctrine and pitch them to the domestic and world public, first and foremost through the 2017 National Security Strategy (NSS) and 2018 National Defense Strategy (NDS). As with every foreign policy doctrine, even Trump's contains a mix of

---

* SciencesPo, Paris.

1 *See, e.g.*, H.W. Brands, 'Presidential Doctrines: An Introduction', *Pres. Stud. Q.*, Vol. 36, No. 1, March 2016, pp. 1-4; R. Sjöstedt, 'The Discursive Origins of a Doctrine: Norms, Identity, and Securitization under Harry S. Truman and George W. Bush', *Foreign Pol'y Analy.*, Vol. 3, March 2007, pp. 233-254

2 I have tried to examine this aspect in M. Del Pero, 'Dollars, Arms, Words: Barack Obama and the Dilemmas of American Hegemony', *Europ. Rev. Int'l Stud.*, Vol. 2, 2018, pp. 24-40.

innovation and tradition, consolidated refrains and not irrelevant (and sometimes even eccentric) novelties.

In a nutshell, we can identify five distinctive and strictly intertwined traits, which define and inform this 'Trump Doctrine': its hyperrealism; its non-exceptionalist nationalism; its anti-globalism/unilateralism; its often ostentatious nativism; and its militarism. Let us briefly examine each of them, before focusing on the inevitable, and sometimes radical, contradictions this combination of elements tends to produce.

The (hyper)realism, to begin with. In Trump's speeches and (in a less crude way) the 2017 NSS, the world is invariably presented as an anarchic, highly competitive and brutal arena, where each actor tries ruthlessly to maximize its own interest, in a sort of (highly state-centric) zero-sum-game, where the success of one side is proportionally offset by the defeat of its antagonist. Both the 2017 NSS and the 2018 NDS are very explicit on this point, particularly in their numerous sections dedicated to the two 'natural' current competitors and adversaries of the United States: China and Russia. According to this depiction, in terms of power – both capabilities and projection – Beijing and Moscow are, with Washington, in a league of their own. Theirs is a fairly conventional challenge, which the Trump Doctrine represents (and narrates) quite orthodoxly as a traditional, albeit updated, form of great power competition. For the 2017 NSS, Russia and China are "revisionist" subjects that aim at contesting both US global primacy and a world order centred on it. "China and Russia," the document maintains,

> want to shape a world antithetical to U.S. values and interests. China seeks to displace the United States in the Indo-Pacific region, expand the reaches of its state-driven economic model, and reorder the region in its favor. Russia seeks to restore its great power status and establish spheres of influence near its borders.

"For decades," the 2017 NSS continues,

> U.S. policy was rooted in the belief that support for China's rise and for its integration into the post-war international order would liberalize China. Contrary to our hopes, China expanded its power at the expense of the sovereignty of others.[3]

China – Trump stated in his own, inimitable way, before being elected President – is an

3 The National Security Strategy of the United States, December 2017 (hereinafter 2017 NSS), available at www.whitehouse.gov/wp-content/uploads/2017/12/NSS-Final-12-18-2017-0905.pdf, (accessed 1 September 2019).

> economic enemy, because they have taken advantage of us like nobody in history … it's the greatest theft in the history of the world what they've done to the United States.[4]

Russia, instead, "aims to weaken U.S. influence in the world and divide us from our allies and partners," the 2017 NSS claimed. If unchecked, the combination between its unique military capabilities ("including nuclear systems that remain the most significant existential threat to the United States") and "modernized forms of subversive tactics" used to interfere in the domestic affairs of other countries poses a major threat: it concurs to create an "unstable frontier in Eurasia, where the risk of conflict due to Russian miscalculation is growing".[5]

Such conviction is reiterated in the 2018 NDS, which postulates that "China and Russia" aim to confront "American power, influence, and interests, attempting to erode American security and prosperity". "They are determined," the document recaps,

> to make economies less free and less fair, to grow their militaries, and to control information and data to repress their societies and expand their influence. …China is a strategic competitor using predatory economics to intimidate its neighbors while militarizing features in the South China Sea. Russia has violated the borders of nearby nations and pursues veto power over the economic, diplomatic, and security decisions of its neighbors.[6]

The tone and substance of this narrative is markedly different from those of previous similar documents, which sometimes highlighted the incontestable competitive elements of the relationship with the two main global rivals of the United States, but invariably stressed the possibility, if not necessity, of collaborating with Russia and China, fostering their integration in the US-centred global order. George Bush's 2006 NSS, for example, emphasized the necessity to collaborate "with other nations that serve as regional and global engines of growth – such as India, China, the ROK, Brazil, and Russia – on reforms to open markets and ensure financial stability," and promised to continue "to work closely with China to ensure it honors its WTO commitments and protects intellectual property". "As China becomes a global player," the document stated, "it must act as a responsible

4 Donald Trump cited in M. Lander & A. Rappeport, 'Trump Plans Stiff Trade Tariffs and Other Penalties on China', *New York Times*, 21 March 2018.

5 2017 NSS.

6 Summary of the National Defense Strategy of the United States: Sharpening the American Military Competitive Edge, 2018 (hereinafter 2018 NDS), available at https://dod.defense.gov/Portals/1/Documents/pubs/2018-National-Defense-Strategy-Summary.pdf (accessed 1 September 2019). The integral version of this document is still classified.

stakeholder that fulfils its obligations and works with the United States and others to advance the international system that has enabled its success."[7]

Barack Obama's 2010 NSS was even more forthcoming in its opening to Beijing. The depth of Sino-US commercial and financial interdependence justified this kind of attitude. "We will continue to pursue a positive, constructive, and comprehensive relationship with China," and

> welcome a China that takes on a responsible leadership role in working with the United States and the international community to advance priorities like economic recovery, confronting climate change, and nonproliferation,

the document argued.

> More broadly, we will encourage China to make choices that contribute to peace, security, and prosperity as its influence rises. We will not agree on every issue, and we will be candid on our human rights concerns and areas where we differ. But disagreements should not prevent cooperation on issues of mutual interest, because a pragmatic and effective relationship between the United States and China is essential to address the major challenges of the 21st century.[8]

When it came to Russia the message of those two documents was somehow more ambivalent. "While actively seeking Russia's cooperation to act as a responsible partner in Europe and Asia, we will support the sovereignty and territorial integrity of Russia's neighbors," Obama's first NSS contended. Following the Ukrainian crisis and Moscow's annexation of Crimes, the second NSS of the Obama administration, issued in 2015, was understandably much blunter and stressed Washington's role in mobilizing and "leading global efforts to impose costs to counter Russian aggression"[9] And yet, particularly but not solely before 2014, the emphasis was not exclusively – or even primarily – on the antagonistic and conflictual dimension of the bilateral relationship with Moscow: the documents reiterated the importance of the US-Russian relationship, particularly when it came to arms control and the stabilization of key strategic regions, beginning, of course,

7 The National Security Strategy of the United States, March 2006 (hereinafter 2006 NSS), available at https://georgewbush-whitehouse.archives.gov/nsc/nss/2006/ (accessed 26 August 2019).

8 The National Security Strategy of the United States, May 2010 (hereinafter 2010 NSS), available at https://obamawhitehouse.archives.gov/sites/default/files/docs/2015_national_security_strategy_2.pdf. (accessed 27 August 2019).

9 The National Security Strategy of the United States, February 2015 (hereinafter 2015 NSS), available at https://obamawhitehouse.archives.gov/sites/default/files/docs/2015_national_security_strategy_2.pdf (accessed 1 September 2015).

with the Middle East. Even in the 2015 NSS, the stated goal of deterring 'Russian aggression' and "remain[ing] alert to its strategic capabilities" was matched by the reassertion of the willingness to "keep the door open to greater collaboration with Russia in areas of common interests, should it choose a different path".[10]

According to the Trump Doctrine, the intrinsically, and inescapably, competitive nature of the international system – one key section of the 2017 NSS is emblematically titled 'A Competitive World' – does not manifest itself only in the struggle for power primacy (or its preservation) vis-à-vis China and Russia. The revisionist challenge of these two 'great powers' is, for Washington, just one of the three fronts it has to address. The other two are represented by the 'rogue regimes' of Iran and North Korea and by transnational/non-state actors, 'particularly jihadist terrorist groups'. Here the analogies are particularly strong with the 2002 NSS, possibly the most radical document of that kind ever produced, which followed the shock of 9/11 and preceded, justifying it, the very ill-advised decision to launch a military intervention in Iraq. That document relied heavily on the notion that global stability and America's security are threatened by 'rogue states' – *i.e.* states that

> display no regard for international law … callously violate international treaties to which they are party …. are determined to acquire weapons of mass destruction …. sponsor terrorism around the globe …. and reject basic human values and hate the United States and everything for which it stands.[11]

And, just as in Trump's 2017 NSS, the 2002 NSS lumped together actors and threats – North Korea and Iran in this case, the two plus Iraq (the 'axis of evil' in Bush's dramatic rendering) in 2002 – that are and were very different in nature. "Both revisionist powers and rogue regimes are competing across all dimensions of power," the 2018 NSD confidently maintained. The symbolic dimension of the 'rogue regime's' danger is visible and paramount: whereas the 'revisionist' opponents are somehow normal, and even legitimate, actors in a state-centred context of ordinary great power competition, regimes that went 'rogue' are instead dangerous anomalies and therefore existential menaces that need to be eradicated, not just contained and defeated. They aim at

> destabilizing regions through their pursuit of nuclear weapons or sponsorship of terrorism …. North Korea seeks to guarantee regime survival and increased leverage by seeking a mixture of nuclear, biological, chemical, conventional,

10 Id.

11 The National Security Strategy of the United States, September 2002 (hereinafter 2002 NSS), available at https://georgewbush-whitehouse.archives.gov/nsc/nss/2002/ (accessed 1 September 2019).

> and unconventional weapons and a growing ballistic missile capability to gain coercive influence over South Korea, Japan, and the United States,

the 2018 NSD argues. "In the Middle East," the document continues,

> Iran is competing with its neighbors, asserting an arc of influence and instability while vying for regional hegemony, using state-sponsored terrorist activities, a growing network of proxies, and its missile program to achieve its objectives.

Iran and North Korea, the 2017 NSS adds, "are determined to destabilize regions, threaten Americans and our allies, and brutalize their own people". A 'layered missile defence system' – such as the one the US Right has long invoked – offers the best assurance against the Iranian and North Korean menace, along with the restoration of a traditional system of alliances and regional balances of power. This applies particularly to the Middle East, where after Obama's partial rupture and attempt to reinvolve Iran in the regional diplomatic game, the Trump administration has actively pursued a traditional policy based on the three key 'special relationships' with Israel, Saudi Arabia and Egypt.[12]

Non-state transnational threats are the third and last variable of this hyperrealist narrative of world politics and international relations. They are linked with the second (and therefore partially territorialized and 'state-ized') when the Trump Doctrine – again lumping together actors and issues that are very different – emphasizes the direct responsibility of a state actor. Iran, "the world's leading sponsor of terrorism," the 2017 NSS states, "has taken advantage of instability to expand its influence through partners and proxies, weapon proliferation, and funding". But transnational, non-state threats are multiple and range from jihadist groups and ISIS to criminal organizations. What binds them together is the common goal of "trying to harm America," exploiting its "open society," operating "in loose confederations" capable of "adapting rapidly," and relying on new technologies – the dark web overall – "to evade detection as they plot, recruit, finance, and execute their operations".[13]

In this threat-infested environment, all measures – beginning, of course, with a significant increase in military spending – are justified, and no concern is excessive or inflated. The narrative of the Trump Doctrine stresses, therefore, the inevitability of conflict, competition and antagonism; the world is a dangerous and unsafe place, where the main actors are involved in a mortal struggle for supremacy and survival and where lesser ones exploit ruthlessly the many interdependencies of the system. "I don't blame China," Trump said,

---

12 J.S. Krasna, 'It's Complicated: Geopolitical and Strategic Dynamics in the Contemporary Middle East', *Orbis*, Vol. 1, Winter 2019, pp. 64-79.

13 2017 NSS.

for example, during his friendly visit to Beijing in November 2017; "after all, who can blame a country for being able to take advantage of another country to the benefit of its citizens?"[14]

This hyperrealist (and very simplified) representation is, of course, light years distant from the language of ineluctable convergence, modernity and global integration many liberal internationalists, progressive and conservative, have long spoken.[15] Trump's is a Hobbesian world, where only the strongest, fittest and most unscrupulous survives and prospers. And this leads us to the second, and possibly most significant, pillar of the Trump Doctrine: its fairly eccentric (at least by modern US standards) combination of extreme nationalism and non-exceptionalism.

This non-exceptionalist nationalism is perhaps the most remarkable novelty of the Trump Doctrine, which seems to go against some traditional (and in theory deeply ingrained) tenets of modern US internationalism. A boasted, and again very crude, nationalism is a distinctive, if not the most distinctive, feature of Trump's political and foreign policy vision. It's on this raucous nationalism – encapsulated in the very popular slogan 'Make America Great Again' (MAGA) – that Trump has built his political and electoral fortunes. Trump's speeches are punctuated with references to the unique greatness of the United States, which alternate with constant denunciations of how his predecessors have guiltily sacrificed this greatness in their chimerical pursuit of amicable relations with devious adversaries, China overall. In his very populist inaugural address, the President promised to stop – 'right here' and 'right now' – what he called 'the carnage' of America.

> From this moment on, it's going to be America First. Every decision on trade, on taxes, on immigration, on foreign affairs, will be made to benefit American workers and American families,

he continued;

> We must protect our borders from the ravages of other countries making our products, stealing our companies, and destroying our jobs. Protection will lead to great prosperity and strength … America will start winning again, winning like never before.[16]

---

14 Trump cited in D. Nakamura & A. Parker, 'In Beijing Trump Declines to Hit President Xi Jinping on Trade: 'I Don't Blame China', *Washington Post*, 9 November 2017.

15 J.G. Ikenberry, *Liberal Leviathan. The Origins, Crisis and Transformation of the American World Order*, Princeton University Press, Princeton, 2011.

16 D.J. Trump, 'Inaugural Address', 20 January 2017, available at www.whitehouse.gov/briefings-statements/the-inaugural-address/ (accessed 22 August 2019).

Again, in a more moderate form these kinds of tropes are also present in official documents such as the NSS and the NDS. "The whole world is lifted by America's renewal and the re-emergence of American leadership," Trump wrote in his preface to the 2017 NSS. But this "great" (or "great again") America is not to be placed at the service of global redeeming missions or messianic and transformative projects as those advocated, for example, under Bush Jr. A great America is also, and foremost, an "America first," another historically very controversial slogan Trump has appropriated.[17] "This national security strategy puts America first," the 2017 NSS proudly proclaimed, because "putting America first is the duty of our government and the foundation for U.S. leadership in the world". Trump's strategy must therefore be an "America first foreign policy" and "national security strategy," to mention another recurrent slogan of this document. Foreign policy and US global power projection are presented as tools in a struggle for defeating the adversaries and reasserting America's primacy, not for co-opting the latter and in the process transforming the world.[18]

Such nationalism does not appear, in other words, to be matched by the traditional exceptionalism informing and shaping American nationalism, *i.e.* by the inner, almost constitutive, universalism of this nationalism and the ensuing belief that there is a natural, almost preordained, convergence between the interests of the United States and those of humankind at large: that it is up to the United States to promote an active and globally interventionist foreign policy aimed at shaping and redeeming such a world. In a brutal and anarchic system, the United States is no different from the other great powers in pursuing its interests, even if (and when) they clash with those of the others, allies included; in this zero-sum-game view of world politics, your gain is ipso facto a loss for your competitor. There is no common destiny; no civilizational bandwagon led by the United States, and driving inescapable forms of global integration; no paradisiacal end of history in sight. The basis of America's claim to be exceptional or, better, an exception – US historian Daniel Rodgers wrote two decades ago – is the preventive claim to enjoy an exemption: from history and its inexorable constraints. US exceptionalism, Rodgers wrote, posits "its identity in difference, and its difference in exemption from the rule. The American myth lies, in its own way elsewhere".[19] With Trump, this double, interdependent claim – to benefit from an exemption and be consequently an exception – is simply discharged. There is no 'elsewhere' anymore, but only the gloomy and very tangible 'where' of the here and now. In this harsh and cruel Trumpian world, the United States is placed back in a history

17 *See* the roundtable edited by M.P. Leffler & W. Hitchcock, 'America First: The Past and Future of an Idea', *Passport*, September 2018, pp. 33-52.

18 2017 NSS.

19 D.T. Rodgers, 'Exceptionalism', *in* A. Mohlo & G.S. Wood (Eds.), *Imagined Histories. American Historians Imagine Their Past*, Princeton University Press, Princeton, 1998, p. 24. *See also* Id., 'American Exceptionalism Revisited', *Raritan*, Vol. 2, 2004, pp. 21-47 and A. Stephanson, *Manifest Destiny. American Expansion and the Empire of Right*, Hill & Wang, New York, 1994.

(and in a very historical narrative) of conflict and competition, survival and decline, rise and decay. And, de facto, it is not different from other great powers in its objective to pursue its goals, guard the national interest, put its citizen first, reaffirm a national sovereignty threatened by multiple forms of 'global interdependence' and by unconstrained and, until Trump finally arrived, much smarter enemies.[20]

"We will promote a balance of power that favors the United States, our allies, and our partners," Trump argued relying on another, quintessential realist trope: the 'balance of power' and its beneficial effect on international relations and global stability. But the United States will do so, not by launching global messianic crusades or supporting the expansion of an already overextended set of norms and rules: by relying on its exceptional nature and/or by fostering and expanding a norms-based liberal world order. "We will pursue this beautiful vision – a world of strong, sovereign, and independent nations, each with its own cultures and dreams, thriving side-by-side in prosperity, freedom, and peace." Trump added: "We are not going to impose our values on others" and we "will lead by example." Both the 2018 NDS and a similar document, the Joint Chiefs of Staff's December 2018 National Military Strategy, are punctuated with references to the necessity of updating US 'lethal' military force not to coerce other actors – not to reshape the global landscape according to US interests but also 'mission'– but to "ensure favorable balances of power," "deter competitors," "defeat adversaries" and "prevent war." ("The surest way to prevent war is to be prepared to win one," the 2018 NSD summarized.)[21]

The language of sovereignty – its violations, its centrality, the ensuing necessity to re-create the conditions for its fulfilment – permeates the rhetoric of the President and those of the strategic documents of his administration. According to the 2017 NSS (where the terms 'sovereignty' and 'sovereign' appear more than 30 times), the key duties of a government are "to serve the interests of its own people" and "strengthening its sovereignty," defending it "without apology". The strategy outlined in the document, it is argued in the last section, is one of "principled realism": it "acknowledges the central role of power in international politics, affirms that sovereign states are the best hope for a peaceful world, and clearly defines our national interest".[22]

Again, Trump himself has often given vent to this normalization and 'de-exceptionalization' of the United States via his uniquely binary and sometimes caricature-prone sort of lexicon. During a televised interview, accused by his host, the famous conservative journalist Bill O'Reilly, of pandering to a "killer" like Putin, Trump emblematically retorted that "there are a lot of killers. We've got a lot of killers. What do you think: our country is

20 A. Iriye, *Global Interdependence. The World after 1945*, Harvard University Press, Cambridge, 2014.

21 2018 NSD. 'The National Military Strategy', (hereinafter 2018 NMS), December 2018, available at www.jcs.mil/Portals/36/Documents/Publications/UNCLASS_2018_National_Military_Strategy_Description.pdf (accessed 22 August 2019).

22 2017 NSS.

so innocent?"[23] The presumption of innocence gone; the full return to a dark history of competition and conflict; the necessity to resort to all the means necessary to pursue and defend the national interest, if necessary sacrificing, or subordinating, ethical imperatives and moral constraints. All these elements converge in shaping a discourse, that of Trump's foreign policy and of its representations of the United States in the world, that is simultaneously aggressively nationalist and surprisingly non-exceptionalist.[24]

If the world is an anarchic and ruthless arena, and the United States must wage a constant competition, learning – as Henry Kissinger once put it during the other, quintessential realist moment of US foreign policy, that of the Nixon administration (1969-1974) – "to conduct foreign policy as other nations had to conduct it for so many centuries – without escape and without respite,"[25] what are the instruments Washington must use? What is the toolbox at its disposal in responding to these threats and pursuing its interest? We get here to the third pillar of the Trump Doctrine: its unilateralism and anti-globalism.

The Trump Doctrine is founded on a categorical rejection – on cultural, ideological and pragmatic grounds – of those forms of regulated interdependence that the US has long supported, fostered and (but this goes unsaid under Trump) frequently exploited and benefited from. This is, of course, visible in the protectionist policies the Trump administration has promoted. And it is also visible in the rejection of the set of norms and rules that try to discipline the international system – providing a limited and yet crucial form of global governance – as well as in the distrust of the institutions that act as custodians and enforcers of such discipline. Examples, of course, abound, from the aforementioned references to state sovereignty as the foundational element of international politics to frequent attacks to the World Trade Organization (which a White House memo described as resting on "an outdated dichotomy," penalizing the United States and favouring China, "between developed and developing countries that has allowed some WTO members to gain unfair advantages in the international trade arena".)[26]

---

23 Cited in F. Slaveski, 'In the Outrage over the Trump-Putin Meeting, Important Questions Were Overlooked', *The Conversation*, 15 August 2008, available at https://theconversation.com/in-the-outrage-over-the-trump-putin-meeting-important-questions-were-overlooked-99930 (accessed 29 August 2019).

24 S. Wertheim, 'Donald Trump versus American Exceptionalism: Toward the Sources of Trumpian Conduct', *in* D.N. Labrosse, F.J. Gavin, J. Rovner, R. Jervis (Eds.), *Chaos in the Liberal Order: The Trump Presidency and International Politics in the 21st Century*. Columbia University Press, New York, 2018, pp. 125-135.

25 H.A. Kissinger, *American Foreign Policy*, 3rd edn, Norton, New York, 1977, p. 302 and 'Address by Secretary of State Kissinger', Boston World Affairs Council, 11 March 1976 *in Foreign Relations of the United States* (hereinafter FRUS), 1969-1976, Vol. XXXVIII: *Foundations of Foreign Policy, 1973-1976*, Washington, DC, United States Government Printing Office, 2012, available at https://history.state.gov/historicaldocuments/frus1969-76v38p1/d71 (accessed 30 August 2018).

26 The White House, 'Memorandum on Reforming Developing-Country Status in the World Trade Organization', 26 July 2019, available at www.whitehouse.gov/presidential-actions/memorandum-reforming-developing-country-status-world-trade-organization/ (accessed 28 August 2019). *See also* Y. Huang, 'U.S.-China Economic Tensions: Origins and Global Implications', *China Int'l Strat. Rev.*, Vol. 1, 2019, pp. 127-138. "The WTO is BROKEN when the world's RICHEST countries claim to be developing countries to

The global competition – the 2017 NSS stressed – requires now

> the United States to rethink the policies of the past two decades ... based on the assumption that engagement with rivals and their inclusion in international institutions and global commerce would turn them into benign actors and trustworthy partners.

For the most part, the document confidently maintains, "this premise turned out to be false."[27] In a nutshell, Trump rejects the idea that global integration – economic and cultural – is both benign and, for the United States, advantageous. This anti-globalism (and anti-cosmopolitanism) combines with the invocation – central already in the 2002 NSS and then greatly tempered down in Obama's NSSs – of the possibility and necessity to act alone and if necessary through a radical disengagement from all the institutions of global governance. The protectionist turn, symbolized by the various rounds of tariffs imposed against enemies (China) and allies (the EU), is just the peak of this unilateralism, which coherently complements the previously discussed realism of the Trump Doctrine.

The reference to the anti-globalism/cosmopolitanism of the Trump Doctrine leads us to its fourth pillar: nativism. Trump's nativism is linked to the aforementioned nationalism and to the brutal, zero-sum game view of international relations, but also – and more crucially – to domestic political dynamics and to the way through which Trump has been able to rally certain segments of the American population, obtaining a support that has been instrumental to his electoral successes. Trump's speeches have been, and still are, punctuated with quintessential US nativist tropes, being Europhobic or anti-Mexican.[28] The cultural relativism of realism therefore leaves a lot of room for playing the card of national and sometimes racial stereotypes. Politically and electorally, it is a sort of discourse that plays both on a widespread Islamophobia among conservative US voters and on an implicitly, and sometimes explicitly, racialized partition between the undeserving (and mostly African-American) poor and the deserving (and mostly white) middle class, the latter allegedly subsidizing the former via fiscally redistributive policies. The Tea Party

avoid WTO rules and get special treatment," Trump recently erupted in one of his usual, unfiltered tweets. "NO more!!! Today I directed the U.S. Trade Representative to take action so that countries stop CHEATING the system at the expense of the USA!," available at https://twitter.com/realdonaldtrump/status/1154821023197474817.

27 2017 NSS.

28 For a bizarre example of this Europhobia, *see* the report of Trump's Council of Economic Advisers comparing the US model with the socialist ones of Europe's Nordic countries. The Council of Economic Advisers, 'The Opportunity Costs of Socialism', October 2018, available at www.whitehouse.gov/wp-content/uploads/2018/10/The-Opportunity-Costs-of-Socialism.pdf (accessed 28 August 2019).

somehow popularized (and relied on) this kind of partition, which Trump has effectively exploited and exasperated.[29]

Fifth and last: militarism. Epitomized by the emphasis placed on the necessity to reverse the course of action undertaken in the previous years, increase military expenditures and regain a full-spectrum global dominance, Trump's foreign policy discourse has been highly militaristic. There is here a clear and coherent interdependence between the realist description of international relations, Trump's nationalism and his militaristic rhetoric: US' unique military might – it is argued – serves to protect the country and help it reacquire its sovereignty, via full-spectrum superiority and a defence system protecting the US from missile threats, old (Russia or China) and new (Iran and North Korea). "Our task is to ensure that American military superiority endures," the 2017 NSS proclaimed. "The United States will seek areas of cooperation with competitors from a position of strength, foremost by ensuring our military power is second to none." Even in this case, political and electoral considerations have played a major role in informing this militarism, given the unique popularity of the military, the armed forces being now the most revered and credible institution in the United States (according to Gallup, 74% of Americans have a "great deal/quite a lot" of confidence in the military, which in this ranking is followed by small business, at 67%, and the police at 54%; Congress gets 11%, television news 20% and newspapers 22%.)[30] But Trump's militarism has deeper, and one could say more structural, roots in the US political and even popular culture. On the one hand, it reflects a broader infatuation with the military: what it is and symbolizes. On the other, this "militaristic brand of foreign policy" shows well how a realist strategy of global interventionism is not at all "contingent upon support for the liberal international architecture".[31]

Unilateralist; Nativist; Militaristic; Nationalist; Non-Exceptionalist; allegedly Realist: those are, in a nutshell, the basic pillars of a foreign policy doctrine, Trump's, that is anything but isolationist, as it is instead often – and very superficially – labelled. Isolationism is, in fact, a mostly inadequate, and uselessly abused, category to examine the past and present of the foreign policy of a country that is structurally engaged in world affairs and capable of projecting its power globally as no other country does (or has ever been able to do). A country, the US, that dominates global finance and still enjoys the privilege of owning the indisputably and unrivalled hegemonic currency, in which commodities' prices

29 T. Skocpol & V. Williamson, *The Tea Party and the Remaking of American Conservatism*, Oxford University Press, Oxford, new edition, 2016.

30 L. Saad, 'Military, Small Business and Police Still Stir Most Confidence', *Gallup News*, 28 June 2018, available at https://news.gallup.com/poll/236243/military-small-business-police-stir-confidence.aspx (accessed 23 August 2019).

31 P. Harris, 'Why Trump Won't Retrench: The Militarist Redoubt in American Foreign Policy', *Polit. Sci. Q.*, Vol. 4, 2018, pp. 611-640 and A.J. Bacevich, *The New American Militarism. How Americans Are Seduced by War*, Oxford University Press, Oxford, 2005.

are denominated and that, more importantly, is by distance the most used foreign currency in global world reserves (according to the latest data, on the first quarter of 2019, the dollar still makes up for two-thirds of world allocated currency reserves).[32]

The Trump Doctrine appears, therefore, to be terse and coherent: perhaps less articulated and, in ambition, comprehensive than Obama's, but more clearly defined and outlined. And yet, multiple (and inevitable) short circuits and inconsistencies ensue. Given what we said at the beginning of this chapter, this is possibly true for all foreign policy doctrines. But it seems to be particularly the case for Trump's, whose foreign policy outlook – binary and simplistic as it certainly is – is also uniquely contradictory. In a nutshell, and in conclusion, we can identify four fundamental contradictions.

The first – the 'impossible dual consensus' – is in many ways the quintessential dilemma the hegemon (*i.e.* the United States) of the modern and contemporary international system has long faced. This hegemon is invariably called to address (and convince) two publics: to seek the approval of its foreign policy choices and discourse both within the United States and outside it, in the domestic as well as in the world public opinion. Particularly in the last 50 years, it has become extremely difficult to render complementary, if not even compatible, the two discourses necessary to convince these two publics: to build such a dual consensus. The nationalist/exceptionalist language increasingly used to arouse a reluctant domestic public, has often alienated the international one, as seen, for example, during the Reagan and the Bush Jr. administrations; on the contrary, a more cosmopolitan discourse, as the one deployed (and embodied) by Obama, tends to produce a backlash at least among some sectors of the domestic electorate. During his mandate, Obama retained remarkable (and unprecedented) levels of popularity outside the United States, particularly in Europe.[33] This sturdy global 'Obamania' was however matched by Obama's decreasing approval ratings within the United States, which plummeted from 67% on his inauguration day, in January 2009, to as low as 40% during the summer of 2011.[34] With Trump the dissonance is even more pronounced. Within the United States, the 45th President is extremely unpopular and highly polarizing. Compared with his predecessor, his approval ratings have, however, remained consistently stable: whereas Obama's have oscillated in a range of about 30% points (between 40% and 70%), Trump's have moved in a range of just ten points (between a maximum of 46% and a minimum – in late 2017 – of 35%).[35] Trump's

32 *See* International Monetary Fund, 'Currency Composition of Official Foreign Exchange Reserves', available at http://data.imf.org/?sk=E6A5F467-C14B-4AA8-9F6D-5A09EC4E62A4 (accessed 30 August 2019).

33 *See, e.g.*, the extremely rich polls of the German Marshall Fund, 'Transatlantic Trends', available at www.gmfus.org/initiatives/transatlantic-trends-%E2%80%93-public-opinion (accessed 1 September 2019).

34 Gallup, 'Presidential Approval Rating – Barack Obama' available at https://news.gallup.com/poll/116479/barack-obama-presidential-job-approval.aspx (accessed 30 August 2019).

35 Gallup, 'Presidential Approval Rating – Donald Trump', available at https://news.gallup.com/poll/203198/presidential-approval-ratings-donald-trump.aspx (accessed 30 August 2019).

unpopularity does not extend to the Republican voters, however, where record numbers (up to 90%) approve of his work. His nationalist/realist/unilateralist/anti-globalist/nativist argot evidently appeals to, and persuades, this portion of the general electorate that propelled him to the White House. But it also generates an extremely, and again unprecedented, negative reaction outside the United States. The polls we have at our disposal reveal the stunning global condemnation of Trump. Since such surveys have been introduced, no US leader has been as unpopular as the current President, not even George Bush Jr. in the midst of his Iraq fiasco. According to the most recent Pew Poll, taken in 25 countries and released in October 2018, the international confidence in the US President is at a historical low: just 27% versus the 70% who express no confidence in Trump. The data is even more dramatic in regard to some important and key allies of the United States: 10% in Germany (vs. the 86% of Obama in 2016); 9% in France (it was 84% for Obama in 2016); 6% in Mexico (vs. 49% in 2015). The 28% or 30% rate of approval the current President manages to get in the United Kingdom and Japan is almost considered a success, despite the net loss of 40 to 50 points vis-à-vis Obama.[36] Trump's consensus in the United States is low, but stable; but in order to produce (and preserve) it, also through the tenets of his foreign policy doctrine, he has to accept a dramatic plummeting of the global appreciation of his persona and policies.

The second contradiction has to do with the well-known resilience of international and multilateral institutions. This is a key assumption behind a lot of research on modern international relations: the pliability and sturdiness of global bureaucracies and their ability to absorb major political shocks and contain their effects. On the one hand, the difficulty and sometimes even crisis of some key international organizations predates, and even helps explain, the rise of Trump. The United Nations has long been plagued by its inefficiency, internal divisions and inherently obsolescent structure; in spite of the expectations produced by its creation, the WTO has often failed to deliver on its promise to foster more efficient and just forms of liberalization and trade integration; the International Criminal Court was born without the United States and has fulfilled its original goals only in a very limited way. The examples abound and extend also to non-institutionalized, and in theory more flexible, ad hoc structures such as the G-7/8. Trump has not provoked these problems and, in fact, has done relatively little to exacerbate them. On this, the mismatch between Trump's bombastic and crude rhetoric, and his actions and policies has been particularly acute. NATO provides a very banal and convenient example. Trump has attacked the organization on multiple occasions, accusing (correctly) the European allies

36 R. Wike, B. Stokes, J. Poushter, L. Silver, J. Fetterolf & K. Devlin, 'Trump's International Ratings Remain Low, Especially Among Key Allies', *Pew Research Center*, 1 October 2018, available at www.pewresearch.org/global/2018/10/01/trumps-international-ratings-remain-low-especially-among-key-allies/ (accessed 30 August 2019).

of free-riding and not contributing enough to the common Atlantic defence, threatening to further decouple U.S. defense defence strategies, and even refusing to mention the key Article 5 of the North Atlantic Treaty (according to which an attack against one member of the alliance should be considered an attack against them all). Observers, pundits and 'Atlanticists' were horrified, and many predicted a new, and this time terminal, crisis of the alliance.[37] And yet, NATO continues operating as if nothing had happened. It produces its anodyne and mostly useless 'Strategic Concepts,' expands its missions and activities,' tries to follow an agenda whose basic timetable was defined long before the US election of 2016 and has not been changed as a consequence of it.

Third, the protectionism and anti-globalism clash visibly with the key political (and electoral) goal of relaunching domestic consumption, if necessary re-granting easy access to credit and dismantling many pieces of the regulatory apparatus introduced under Obama. The tension between protectionism and in-debt consumption – tariffs and deregulation – is possibly one of the most visible contradictions of Trump's foreign policy doctrine. If there is one field of action where the Trump administration has been very effective, it is in reversing the course undertaken with Obama, *i.e.* eliminating a broad array of regulations, particularly when it comes to environmental and financial issues.[38] Tax cuts and cheap, deregulated credit also have the objective of stimulating economic growth via consumption, satisfying a key electoral constituency of Donald Trump: the (predominantly white) middle class, which has been badly hit by the 2008 recession and the drastic contraction of credit (and consumption) that has ensued.[39] All the data we have at our disposal shows how the deficit-stimulated economic growth of the Trump years has been driven not by some highly chimerical and unrealistic re-industrialization of the United States, but by a new (and accelerating) consumerist frenzy and the rebound of the traditional sectors now dominating the US economy, healthcare and finance overall.[40] Meanwhile, Trump's trade wars have contributed to a global economic slowdown, a contraction (of about 10%) in the Sino-American trade volumes, but not an improvement in the US trade balance, en route in 2019 to recording its highest deficit ever.[41] US consumers have yet to feel the pain of an unconstrained and all-out trade war with China and other countries

37 J. Goldgeier, 'NATO at 70: Is the USA Still in for the Long Haul?', *J. Transatl. Stud.*, Vol. 2, June 2019, pp. 255-257; J.P. Kaufman, 'The U.S. Perspective on NATO under Trump: Lessons of the Past and Prospects for the Future', *Int'l Aff.*, Vol. 1, March 2017, pp. 251-266.

38 The Brooking Institution, 'Tracking Deregulation in the Trump Era', 14 August 2019, available at www.brookings.edu/interactives/tracking-deregulation-in-the-trump-era/ (accessed 1 September 2019).

39 H.P. Kitschelt & P. Rehm, 'Secular Partisan Realignment in the United States: The Socioeconomic Reconfiguration of White Partisan Support Since the New Deal Era', *Politics Soc.*, Vol. 3, 2019, pp. 425-479.

40 *See, e.g.*, Bureau of Economic Analysis (BEA), U.S. Department of Commerce, 'GDP by Industry', available at www.bea.gov/data/gdp/gdp-industry (accessed 1 September 2019).

41 U.S. Census Bureau, 'Trade in Goods with the World, Seasonally Adjusted', available at www.census.gov/foreign-trade/balance/c0004.html (accessed 1 September 2019).

(such as Germany) that have long enjoyed a major trade surplus with the United States. Leaving aside other political and economic effects – including those on the many sectors of US manufacturing that are fully integrated into transnational supply chains and whose disruption would badly damage them – Trump's unilateral protectionism clearly clashes with his political and electoral interest in continuing stimulating consumption growth via financial deregulation and loose fiscal and monetary policies.

The fourth and last contradiction is that Trump's militarism collides with the widespread anti-interventionism of a domestic public opinion burned by the post 9/11 wars and opposed to new military adventures (a mood the President has effectively exploited during the 2016 campaign and that helps explain its meteoric political ascent). The infatuation with the military, and an often a-critical support for it as an institution, does not automatically translate into support for militarism, new wars or even the vastly increased military budget Trump has requested. It is true that in 2018 the United States finally reversed the course undertaken in 2010 and that for the first time in a decade its defence budget increased. This increase, however, has been much more limited than the one requested in Trump's first budget proposal (4.6% instead of 10%), and as a percentage of the GDP it is still well below what it was before 2008 (about 3.5% vs. 4.5%), not to mention the early Cold War, when it remained stably between 8% and 10%.[42] Meanwhile, poll after poll reveals very limited public support for both drastic increases in military spending and new American wars. Since 2005, when the full fiasco of the intervention in Iraq and the difficulties in Afghanistan became impossible to conceal, the percentage of Americans who believe the country is spending 'too little' on defence has remained stably under 25% to 30%; furthermore, a consistently high percentage of Americans (65-70% or more) seems to now support bipartisan legislation by Congress that would restrain executive authority in undertaking military action or providing military aid to unsavoury allies such as Saudi Arabia.[43]

In this climate, where a clear majority of Americans prefer a more restrained and less militaristic foreign policy, Trump's hawkish and bellicose stance appears to be a posture

42 Stockholm Institute for Peace Research (SIPRI), 'World Military Expenditure Grows by More To 1.8 Trillion in 2018', 29 April, available at www.sipri.org/media/press-release/2019/world-military-expenditure-grows-18-trillion-2018 (accessed 28 August 2019); Office of the Management and Budget, *America First. A Budget Blueprint to Make America Great Again*, U.S. Government Printing Office, Washington, DC, 2017, available at www.govinfo.gov/content/pkg/BUDGET-2018-BLUEPRINT/pdf/BUDGET-2018-BLUEPRINT.pdf (accessed 29 August 2019).

43 Gallup, 'Military and National Defense', available at https://news.gallup.com/poll/1666/military-national-defense.aspx (accessed 29 August 2019); Eurasia Group Foundation (EGF), 'Worlds Apart', July 2018, available at https://egfound.org/stories/independent-america/worlds-apart (accessed 29 August 2019); J. Wallin Opinion Research Center, 'Nationwide Voter Survey', 28 January 2018, available at http://responsibleforeignpolicy.org/wp-content/uploads/2018/02/J-Wallin_Nationwide-Voter-Survey_Gunster-Worldwide-Strategies_Committee-for-Responsible-Foreign%E2%80%93Policy_Presentation.pdf (accessed 29 August 2019).

used to score easy political and electoral points, more than a concrete blueprint for action. And this adds another, further inconsistency to Trump's contradictory and very distinctive foreign policy doctrine.

Printed by Libri Plureos GmbH in Hamburg,
Germany

9 789462 369764